THE BATTLE OF JUTLAND 1916

GEORGE BONNEY

SUTTON PUBLISHING

First published in the United Kingdom in 2002 by
Sutton Publishing Limited · Phoenix Mill
Thrupp · Stroud · Gloucestershire · GL5 2BU

This revised paperback edition first published in 2006

British Library Cataloguing in Publication Data
A catalogue record for this book is available from the British Library.

ISBN 0 7509 4178 2

Typeset in 10/14pt Sabon.
Typesetting and origination by
Sutton Publishing Limited.
Printed and bound in England by
J.H. Haynes & Co. Ltd, Sparkford.

CONTENTS

LIST OF ILLUSTRATIONS

Maps

PREFACE TO PAPERBACK EDITION

I am very grateful to Sutton Publishing for the opportunity to revise the text and illustrations of *The Battle of Jutland 1916* afforded by the production of the paperback edition. I received many letters about the first edition of the book: all were welcome, some, more welcome than others. One reviewer criticised the asides and the occasional discuvsiveness: I appreciate his concerns, but I hope that most readers will agree with me in thinking that many of these digressions add to our understanding of the people and events here described. After all, this is not and is not intended to be, simply a technical description of the battle. For me, the most useful comments were those in which error and omission were indicated. I am very grateful to all who took the trouble to write, and hope that I have at least reformed things indifferently, if not altogether. It is invidious to mention names, but I feel bound to record the particular contributions from the late Godfrey Carter CBE, formerly of Parliamentary Counsel and of the Rifle Brigade, Señor Fernando Garcia Llaneras of Modesto Lafoente, Spain; Professor Richard Johns PhD; David Dawson FRSA and Vicky Dawson, my younger daughter. I had help, too, from Robert White, of the Imperial War Museum and Michael Chambers, of the Humanities Reference Service of the British Library. I am much grieved to have to record the death of Dr Chris Howard-Bailey, formerly Keeper of Collections and Head of Publications at the Royal Naval Museum, Portsmouth, a prime mover in the genesis of this work. I only wish that the book might be thought worthy to stand as part of the memorial to her and her work.

INTRODUCTION TO THE FIRST EDITION

It is bold, perhaps even rash, to propose to add to the literature about the Battle of Jutland, which has over the last eighty-five years been examined in detail by naval historians expert in their subject and by serving or former naval officers with first-hand experience of battle. It is even bolder for one who has spent most of his working life in the study and practice of medicine to undertake such a task. A connection fifty-five years ago with the Royal Naval Volunteer Reserve and later with the Royal Naval Reserve offers little excuse. I only hope that my lifelong interest in the Royal Navy and my profound admiration for its officers, petty officers and ratings, combined with a belief that the lessons of the dreadful event and the origins of the conflict of which it was a part, are relevant to our present situation, will be seen to justify the present study. The work itself owes all to the real historians such as Correlli Barnett, Richard Hough, Arthur Marder, Stephen Roskill and others who have studied and written about the Royal Navy and the battle and its origins.

It was my good fortune that Sutton Publishing had the good sense to think of this book as a joint production with the Royal Naval Museum, Portsmouth. Reproduction of material from that source forms a principal justification for the publication, and I am deeply grateful to Dr Chris Howard-Bailey, Keeper of Collections and Head of Publications, and to Mr Stephen Courtney, Curator of Photographs, for their massive contribution.

I hope that this re-examination of the battle and surrounding events adds something to what has already been written. I have in particular drawn attention to certain unchanging features of governments and politicians and of the management of departments of state. Politicians have always been interested principally in the next election; 'spin doctors' are nothing new: the name alone is new; being right has always been the most certain route to unpopularity; it has always been difficult for institutions and professions to accept the need for change: it is clear that British soldiers have quite recently been sent into a combat zone with inadequate equipment; the ingenuity and resolve of enemies are constantly underestimated; the perversion of the 'honours system' to provide an instrument for ensuring conformity is nothing new.

Evidently, this book is not primarily intended for the professional historian; rather, it is intended for the reader interested in the recent past, the role of personalities in public affairs and the relevance of the past to the present. I hope that it will remind readers of the debt owed to the men of both nations who strove and suffered and died, and that it may encourage British readers in particular to widen their experience of the life and culture of our partners in Europe. Should anyone be encouraged by it to keep an eye on the doings of his or her representatives and to make known to them that failure in duty will lead to loss of office, that would indeed be a bonus.

I have throughout adopted the 24-hour clock and used Greenwich Mean Time (GMT). These usages are not, I think, strictly correct, but they seemed at the time to be a good idea. They helped me, and I hope that they may help readers too.

ACKNOWLEDGEMENTS

I wish to acknowledge first the kindness of Rose Knowles in permitting me to use an extract from the Diary of her late husband, Charles Ingram Knowles, which reflects the reaction in England to the news of the battle. I am grateful too, to her son and my son-in-law, Christopher Knowles, for reading the text and for penetrating comment, and to David Dawson, County Museums Officer for Somerset, my other son-in-law, who read the text, indicated mistakes and provided sources of information and the Wyllie drypoint reproduced in Figure 10.22. I was much helped in this work by the staff of the Caird Library at the National Maritime Museum, Greenwich, and of the British Library, London. My daughter, Vicky Dawson, gave invaluable help in the preparation of the text and figures. Thanks are also due to Bow Watkinson for drawing the maps that accompany the text, to my editors at Sutton Publishing, Jonathan Falconer and Paul Ingrams, and to Dr Frank Merrett for his invaluable work on the index.

I gratefully acknowledge the kindness of the following in permitting me to use material in the text and images in illustration: Judy Taylor-Hough MBE, for the use of an extract from the works of her late husband Richard Hough; Rodney Wilkinson MC, for help in identifying and use of work by his father Norman Wilkinson *(Fig 7.6)*; Guy Goodwin of Macmillan Publishers Ltd, for use of extracts from the work of A.G. Macdonnell; Peter Tummons of Methuen Publishers Ltd, for use of extracts from the work of Stephen King-Hill; and Will Francis, of PFD Ltd, for use of extracts from the works of Hilaire Belloc. Surgeon-Commodore N.E. Baldock RN, Editor of the *Journal of the Royal Naval Medical Service*, was kind enough to permit me to quote from early volumes of that Journal, and to correct some of my errors. John Lee, Publisher of the Conway Maritime Press, kindly gave permission to quote from John Campbell's *Jutland: an Analysis of the Fighting*. Extracts from *The Thirty Years' War* by C.V. Wedgwood, and from *Fear God and Dread Nought, the Correspondence of Admiral of the Fleet Lord Fisher of Kilverstone, Volume 1*, edited by Arthur J. Marder, both published by Jonathan Cape, are used by kind permission of the Random House Group Ltd. David Higham Associates kindly gave permission for the use of extracts from *The Navy and Defence*, the autobiography of Admiral of the Fleet Lord Chatfield. Extracts from H.A.L. Fisher's *History of Europe* (Edward Arnold, 1936) are reprinted by kind permission of the publisher. Extracts from Stephen Roskill's *Admiral of the Fleet Earl Beatty* (William Collins Son & Co. Ltd, 1980) are reprinted by kind permission of HarperCollins Publishers. The quotations from the works of Rudyard Kipling are used with the permission of A.P. Watt Ltd on behalf of the National Trust for Places of Historical Interest or Natural Beauty. The material from Geoffrey Bennett's *The Battle of Jutland* (Batsford, 1964) is used by permission of Salamander Books. The Raven Hill cartoon in *Punch*, 11 June 1916, is reproduced by courtesy of *Punch* Ltd.

PART ONE
PREPARATION

Now I am seven I mean to go
On the Iron Duke with Jellicoe;
I'll do my best to fire the guns
And sink the warships of the Huns.
When I'm grown up, perhaps I shall
Sail as a gold-laced admiral;
I'll wear a sword and cocked hat fine,
And never go to bed till nine.

The Royal Navy, An ABC for Little Britons (Thomas Nelson & Sons, London)

CHAPTER ONE

THE GROWTH OF ANGLO-GERMAN RIVALRY

On the afternoon of Wednesday 31 May and during the night of 31 May/1 June 1916 there took place the first and last engagement between the battlefleets of Germany and Great Britain. The carnage was fearful, though the scale of the battle hardly matched that of later naval engagements in the Pacific between the Japanese and American fleets. The battle remains in the public consciousness because of its continuing relevance to current events, the continuing dispute about its significance, the remarkable personalities of many of those directly or marginally concerned and their influence on the course of events, and the persistence of professional and amateur naval historians.

The battle took place in the confined waters of the North Sea (as the Germans called it) or German Ocean (as the English called it), in an area bounded by latitudes 55 deg. and 58 deg. N and longitudes 5 deg. and 6 deg. 30′ E, off the entrance to the Skagerrak and the Danish province of Jylland (Jutland, Jütland), in the area of the 'Jutland Bank'. The British array included nine Dreadnought battlecruisers and twenty-eight Dreadnought battleships, with scouting cruisers and protecting destroyers; the German, five Dreadnought battlecruisers and sixteen Dreadnought battleships, six pre-Dreadnought battleships, with scouting cruisers and torpedo-boats. By the time the fleets returned to port the British had lost three battlecruisers, three armoured cruisers and eight

The Battle of Jutland represented the culmination of . . . preparations that began in 1897

destroyers; the Germans, one Dreadnought battlecruiser, one pre-Dreadnought battleship, four light cruisers and five torpedo-boats. In all, 6,097 British seamen and 2,551 German seamen had lost their lives in the engagement. The Germans claimed and continue to claim the victory; the British public had early apprehensions of defeat, which were later modified by management of the news. The chief effect of the engagement on the progress of the war was to fix the thoughts of the German High Command on the destruction of supply lines by submarine warfare in preference to a challenge to the domination of the sea by surface forces. The Battle of Jutland, or Skagerrak-Schlacht, represented the culmination of the war on the surface of the sea between Britain and Germany, and of the preparations for naval combat that began in 1897.

The development of Anglo-German hostility

Until the latter part of the nineteenth century British, and before that English, sentiment was clearly favourable to the Germans. The two peoples shared a common ancestry; the languages were related; the interests of the Holy Roman Empire of the German Nation were only rarely in conflict with those of England, or later with those of the British Empire; no individual German state was powerful enough to interfere with the interests of either. Since the accession of George I Britain had been ruled by members of the House of Hanover, tracing their descent from King James I and VI through his daughter Elizabeth, wife of the Elector Palatine and, briefly, Queen of Bohemia. British monarchs sought their consorts from the princely houses of the German states. So profound were the destruction and disorganisation wrought by the Thirty Years' War of 1618–48 that the loose confederation of German states that existed for the next 150 years posed no threat to the nascent British Empire. Austria was busy in Italy and Hungary and constantly on the watch to the East. The rise of Prussia under the Great Elector and later Friedrich II caused no alarm; Hessian soldiers were hired to assist the British in the attempt to suppress the revolt in North America in 1776.

Napoleon I provided, perhaps, the stimulus for German unification: although his termination of the Holy Roman Empire and defeat of Prussia must at the time have seemed to do the opposite, they led to the substitution of Prussian for Austrian hegemony in the German lands and eventually to German unification under that hegemony. Certainly, Germans now look on the Battle of Leipzig in 1813 as the decisive event of the Napoleonic wars, transcending Trafalgar, Borodino and Waterloo as the principal factor in the destruction of the French Empire. Without the aid of the King's German Legion and contingents from the Netherlands and German states, and without the intervention of the

Prussians, Wellington would not in 1815 have emerged victorious. On the other hand, without the aid of Britain and allies, Prussia, Austria and Russia would not have overcome the French. The rise of Prussia led to Bismarck's unification of the German nation and to its supremacy in Europe after the foundation of the Second Empire in 1871. Defeated by the French and Piedmontese at Solferino and Magenta and by the Prussians at Königgrätz, Austria was obliged to take the second place. Bavaria, having allied itself with Austria, also suffered defeat and was obliged to ally itself with Prussia in the later war and to accept its eventual hegemony. In effect, Bismarck showed Europe by his three wars against, successively, Denmark, Austria and France, that this extension of politics into warfare, to paraphrase Clausewitz, could be made to pay. The keys to success were technological superiority and more efficient organisation. 'Watch out for that man,' said Disraeli, 'he means what he says.' The compliment was returned by Bismarck in 1879: 'Der alte Jude, dass ist der Mann.'*

The German Empire had become a force with which a reckoning might have to be made

The first stirring in Britain of apprehension about the rise of German power began, perhaps, with the defeat and humiliation of France in 1870–1. Queen Victoria, herself of German stock and married to a German, was naturally sympathetic at first to German aims, though distrustful of Bismarck and his policies. Her eldest child was married to the Crown Prince Friedrich, the heir apparent in the imperial succession. The Crown Prince himself was a soldier of distinction, who had won fame in the war against Austria and was to win more renown in the French conflict. It seems likely that the early and overwhelming success of German arms came as a surprise to Queen Victoria; the later humiliation of France and its Emperor and Empress seems to have roused in Victoria and her people a sense that the German Empire had become a force with which a reckoning might have to be made. Family feeling was in conflict with the friendly sentiments entertained by Victoria for Napoleon III and the Empress Eugénie. The mind of the Prince of Wales, later to succeed as King Edward VII, a lifelong lover of France and French culture, and probably of a number of French women, may have been influenced by the spectacle of German triumph and French humiliation. The triumph had been secured by superior organisation and technology and by the bravery and discipline of the German troops, but this lesson was not fully learnt by the British. They may have forgotten Disraeli's comment; may perhaps have failed to reflect that his warning might apply not only to Bismarck but to the whole German nation.

The rise of Germany

In the last years of the nineteenth century and the first of the twentieth the commercial and industrial development of Germany

* The old Jew, he's the one!

Fig. 1.1 One of the last three giant German trans-Atlantic passenger liners, two of which were awarded to Britain in reparation after the First World War. The *Imperator*, 52,000 tons, of the Hamburg-Amerika Line, renamed the *Berengaria* by the Cunard Line, at Southampton in the 1930s. (*Author's collection*)

at first rivalled and later in some fields surpassed that of Great Britain. In 1900 the *Daily Telegraph* could comment on the advance of Germany in education, war and industry and could compare German adaptability with British rigidity. By 1914 the German mercantile marine included about 2,000 steamships out of a total tonnage of almost 3 million. Britain's steamer tonnage was about 10 million. Giant German liners competed with their British counterparts for the passenger traffic across the Atlantic *(Fig 1.1)*. By 1903 the two largest passenger liner companies in the world were German. German steel production rose to equal and later surpass that of Britain. By the early part of the twentieth century Britain's industrial power began to decline as the sons of the original captains of industry turned away from their proper business and looked more to easy money and to the objects and people who could be bought by that money. In contrast, German industrial might and efficiency continually increased. Bismarck permitted little in the way of democratic process, but he did not trust the practitioners of private enterprise to look after those whose work provided their profits; his introduction of insurance against sickness (1883) and accidents (1884) and of old age pensions (1889) gave to German workers guarantees which were not enjoyed by their British counterparts until the early part of the twentieth century. The German workforce was not enfeebled by this solid evidence that the State cared for its welfare; rather, it exerted itself even more. As H.A.L. Fisher put it, 'The country which had been poor suddenly became rich.' Fisher points to the rapid rise in the production of coal and steel and to the development of the merchant fleet: between 1870 and 1890 its steam tonnage increased sevenfold. Electrical and chemical industries flourished alongside these basic developments. In 1882 began the colonial development that later did so much to embitter the relationship between Britain and Germany.

The theory and practice of conquest and colonisation are almost as old as the human race. The attachment to war and violence is an ineradicable component of human nature; indeed, many individuals, mostly men, actually enjoy war and take pleasure in killing human beings. The urge to subdue neighbouring peoples probably arose from an increase in population and shortage of food: families or tribes moved into new territories and drove out, subdued or killed the people they found there. Later, great movements of peoples took place, as in the periodic westward migrations of the Goths. With the establishment of states and empires, the idea of enrichment by invasion was developed: the Romans invaded Britain not only to subdue a recurrently troublesome neighbour but also to avail themselves of a rich supply of slaves and mineral resources. With the development of oceanic navigation the maritime states of Europe began that haphazard plundering of the Americas, Africa and Asia that has in so many cases left so dire a legacy. The Portuguese and Spanish were early in the field, at the end of the fifteenth century, destroying the advanced civilisations of central and south America and setting up their colonial rule. These states came to depend on the plunder of Brazil, Mexico and Peru to support their domestic economies and their struggles against rival European powers. The later justification for conquest and colonisation was the promotion of trade: raw materials were to be taken from the colony and exchanged for goods manufactured in the conquering country. A moral dimension was added by the supposed duty to spread the doctrines of Christianity; with the rise of Islam the thesis of the Holy War was advanced.

After 1815 the British came off best, with colonies scattered all over the world

Latecomers to the scenes of plunder and exploitation were the Dutch, the English or British, and the French. All did well, but after 1815 the British came off the best, with colonies scattered all over the world. The Germans, arriving on the scene in the 1880s, found the best and most productive areas already occupied. They secured in Africa the four colonies of Togoland, Cameroon, and South West and East Africa *(Fig 1.2)*. The possession of South West Africa was seriously marred by the fact that Walfisch Bay, its best port, and the one connected by railway to the interior, was in the hands of the British. It is doubtful if its African colonies were ever much of an advantage to the German state. The 'place in the sun' so earnestly desired by the German people and their leaders was in truth a place out of the sun, where a white race, accustomed to life in a temperate climate, could flourish. They would in fact, as was

Fig. 1.2 Tenniel's comment on German colonial aspirations in Africa (*Punch*, 26 April 1890). The great cartoonist's apprehensions were well-founded.

suggested by Tenniel in a *Punch* cartoon of 1885, have been better off in the Isle of Wight. The outlook for German colonial power and maritime strategy was, however, improved by the leasing in 1898 from the battered Chinese Empire of the Kiao-Chau enclave with its harbour of Tsingtao. That provided a base for the fleet necessary to protect the archipelago acquired by Germany in the West Pacific between 1885 and 1895, including the Carolines, the Bismarck Archipelago and the north-east part of New Guinea. Samoa too went to Germany. One of the remaining relics of the

Fig. 1.3 The Battle of Trafalgar, 21 October 1805. The British victory effectively ensured maritime supremacy for the next one hundred years. *(Painting by John Wilson RSA 1824, in the author's possession)*

German occupation of this area is the admirable beer still produced in Tsingtao.

All these overseas possessions were a hostage to fortune while the British Fleet commanded the seas. That command, established in the latter part of the eighteenth century, had survived contests with France, Spain, Portugal and even the United States, though a temporary loss of command in Chesapeake Bay in 1781 led to the final ruin of the British cause in the War of American Independence. Since 1805 the Royal Navy had had a tradition of victory, even of victory against the odds, which had survived the setbacks of the American War of 1812–14 *(Fig 1.3)*. Command of the seas was necessary for the protection of Britain's overseas trade and of the imports of food by which the increasing population was fed. It permitted the deployment of Britain's small army against the Russians, the insurgent Indians and Sudanese and a variety of colonial foes *(Fig 1.4)*. Finally, to the annoyance of many Europeans and Americans and some Britons, the Army was deployed in South Africa against the Boers, an enemy of tough European stock armed with modern weapons and led by men who knew the country and were not hampered by outdated ideas about tactics. Against this enemy it was necessary to mobilise the resources of the British Empire and to adopt some of the methods

Fig. 1.4 A reminder to the Portuguese of the supremacy of British sea-power at the time of an incident concerned with the railway from the interior of the Transvaal to Delagoa (Lourenço Marques) Bay. An irate Able Seaman John Bull prepares to teach the oldest ally a lesson. Cartoon by Tenniel in *Punch*, 18 January 1890.

of total war. It was fortunate for Britain that the Boer War taught the commanders of its armies so much about the power of the rifle when used by experts. Without that lesson the British Army might well have entered the war in 1914 quite unprepared to meet an enemy armed with modern weapons.

> Let us admit it fairly, as a business people should,
> We have had no end of a lesson: it will do us a world of good.
> (Rudyard Kipling: 'The Lesson')

It was fortunate too for the British that at the time of the Boer War the Americans were heavily engaged on the other side of the world, and that France, hobbled by the 'Dreyfus Affair', lived in fear of German aggression. Even so, the virtual guarantee of Britain's immunity in South Africa from interference by other powers largely because of the might of the Royal Navy was not lost on the Germans. Feelings ran high in Germany when German ships bringing supplies to the Boers were stopped and examined for war contraband by the Royal Navy. A particular cause for irritation was supplied by the interception of the *Bundesrath*, bound for Beira with a cargo intended for the Boers. The lesson was reinforced by the spectacle of the ease with which the Americans, the last imperialists, deprived Spain of her possessions in the Caribbean and Pacific by the vastly superior power of their Navy. Sadly for Europe, the greatest lesson provided by the United States was never learned. Between 1861 and 1865 the Americans shed their own blood in one of the most fearful wars of all time in order to preserve the Union and eventually to create a vast country whose inhabitants all owed allegiance to the same flag. Europe endured three destructive wars before that lesson even began to be learned.

By 1890 . . . Germany was the strongest military power in Europe

Bismarck

So far as it is possible for a State to be created and developed by the will and exertions of one man, the German Second Empire was the creation of Bismarck and its development was the result of his exertions. By 1890, when Bismarck's resignation was accepted by Kaiser Wilhelm II, Germany was the strongest military power in Europe and had the fastest-growing industrial base *(Fig 1.5)*. Its population was hard-working and generally obedient to its laws; its scientists led the world in many fields, and its achievements in the field of culture were widely admired. Bismarck had no particular animus against the 'English', but felt inhibited in his conversations with British politicians because of a feeling that the substance would probably be reported back to Parliament. Perhaps he was right: if he was, things have evidently changed. Bismarck was certainly as much an enemy of democracy as was Lord Salisbury: it was indeed that hostility that was foremost in creating the rift between him and the Crown Prince Friedrich and his English wife. Crown Princess Victoria's liberal sentiments had influenced her husband, and Bismarck feared, with some justification, that when he became Kaiser, Friedrich would begin the process of introducing constitutional government with an effective representative assembly.

Friedrich succeeded to the imperial throne in 1888. He was by then a sick man. It has until recently been perilous to be both royal and sick. A multitude of opinions have to be sought; few clinicians can be found to view matters dispassionately and to offer an opinion not influenced by the eminence of the patient. Charles II's death was hastened by his doctors; the diagnosis of typhoid fever

Fig. 1.5 'Dropping the Pilot', Tenniel's comment on the dismissal of Bismarck by the young Kaiser Wilhelm (*Punch*, 29 March 1890). This well-known picture has often been used since then to illustrate and comment on contemporaneous events. Tenniel has given the Kaiser a normal left upper limb.

was made only late in the last illness of the Prince Consort; in 1928 George V nearly died because of a delay in draining an empyema; it is widely believed that his end eight years later was deliberately hastened by his doctor. King George VI's 'sciatica' was in fact the pain of intermittent claudication from aorto-iliac disease. The admirable but unfortunate Kaiser Friedrich suffered from cancer of the larynx, a malady even then treatable by laryngectomy. Confusion about the diagnosis, in which the proceedings of the British surgeon Morell Mackenzie were unhelpful, led to the monarch's death in extremes of distress only ninety days after his accession to the throne. Friedrich's eldest son succeeded to the imperial throne as Kaiser Wilhelm II. He was later to be known and reviled throughout the English-speaking world as 'The Kaiser' or 'Kaiser Bill'. Certainly, he was one of the leading figures in the unfolding tragedy of the next twenty-five years.

Kaiser Wilhelm II

Wilhelm's early years were marred by the sequelae of complications attending his birth. His was a breech presentation; labour was prolonged and difficult; neonatal asphyxia and a serious lesion of the brachial plexus of the left arm were the result. Wilhelm endured prolonged and painful treatment, and was left with a virtually useless limb, whose growth failed to match that of the healthy one. With singular courage the young prince endured further pain and humiliation in learning to ride; later, he evidently took pains to conceal the fact of the disparity of his upper limbs *(Fig 1.6)*. It can hardly be doubted that the physical disability and marring of appearance affected Wilhelm's response to people and affairs; it could hardly have been otherwise in one whose life was so much to be spent in the public eye. The young prince's attitude to his English mother seems to have been ambivalent: although he was evidently affectionate, he came to resent her natural preference for things English, her liberal sentiments and her influence over his father. His feelings towards her clearly coloured his feelings about Great Britain: on the one hand, he revered his grandmother Queen Victoria, admired many aspects of the English aristocratic way of life and looked enviously on the history and achievements of the Royal Navy; on the other hand, he grudged Britain what he thought to be her place in the world – prosperous, secure, commanding the seas and having access through the Empire to an unlimited supply of raw materials. This estimate was, no doubt, flawed: Britain's empire was founded more on cheap labour and on cheap Welsh coal for export than on her overseas possessions; the Royal Navy was by no means the invincible force that the prince imagined.

He . . . looked enviously on the history and achievements of the Royal Navy

Kaiser Wilhelm II was undoubtedly a very able man, with a lofty vision of his responsibilities to the German people; perhaps with an even loftier one of the German people's responsibilities to him. It was certainly no joke to be the head of Europe's most formidable nation, much was going to be expected of such a person. On the other hand, the Kaiser had a mercurial, even unstable, temperament, and was prone to sudden changes of mood and even to violent rages. His injunction to German troops departing for China to behave 'like the Huns' cast a long shadow. Often enough, Wilhelm said and wrote what other people thought

but hesitated to express: that characteristic has never helped its possessors. He cannot have been a comfortable companion, for he did not hesitate to expose to ridicule those of lower rank, and he delighted in practical jokes. Those tendencies have, of course, long been detectable in members of the British aristocracy. '*Der hohe Herr*' seems to have been well liked by the more junior officers of the German armed services: von Hase, at the outset of war the First Gunnery Officer of one of the latest German battlecruisers, speaks of him with admiration and respect. Wilhelm's intervention in the strike by the miners of the Ruhr in 1889 indicates humanitarian feelings unusual in the European upper classes at that time or for that matter at any other time. A singular light is thrown on the Kaiser's personality by his protestations of friendship for 'England' in an interview given to the *Daily Telegraph* in 1908: 'You English are as mad, mad, mad as March hares. What has come over you that you are so completely given over to suspicions unworthy of a great nation?' Wilhelm went on to reproach the English for misinterpreting and distorting his actions, and concluded: 'How can I convince a nation against its will?' He may well have been sincere, but he was, at least, mistaken. We should recognise the symptoms: we have seen them in politicians of our own day whose judgement has been impaired and distorted through the exercise of power and the murmurings of sycophants.

'You English are as mad . . . as March hares'

The death of Queen Victoria substituted the despised though envied uncle for the revered grandmother. King Edward VII *(Fig 1.7)* was disliked because of his fondness for the good life and his familiarity with persons of inferior rank and for his effortless assumption of the hoarded riches of the Victorian age. The dislike seems to have been reciprocated: it may well be that King Edward's wife, the Danish Princess of Wales and later Queen Alexandra, influenced her husband's thinking here. She had loathed the Prussians since the invasion of Schleswig and the defeat of Denmark in 1864. Her disgust when her son George was obliged to assume the uniform of a German general was very forcibly expressed: 'So my Georgy-boy has become a real live filthy Prussian general.'

Von Tirpitz . . . at once began to put his plans for the creation of a High Sea Fleet into action

The Kaiser's enthusiasm for the sea and for its control that was to be an important factor in determining the breach between Britain and Germany was of long standing. Indeed, Wilhelm used a nautical metaphor in his message to his people on the occasion of the dropping of Bismarck: 'The position of officer of the watch on the ship of state has fallen to me . . .'. Tenniel's famous cartoon 'Dropping the Pilot' was, no doubt, derived from this remark *(Fig 1.5)*. Wilhelm's perusal of Captain Mahan's *The Influence of Sea Power on History* (1892) seems to have convinced him that sea power was the key to a nation's prosperity.

Opposite: Fig. 1.6 Two ill-fated Crown Princes. Kaiser Wilhelm II (1859–1941), then Crown Prince, in 1881, with Rudolf von Habsburg (1858–89), heir to the Austro-Hungarian imperial and royal crowns, who was to die at Mayerling with his mistress Marie Vetsera. The future Kaiser's left upper limb is held so as to disguise its shortness and deformity.

Fig. 1.7 King Edward VII (1841–1910) in later life. He waited sixty years to succeed to his Mother's throne. His support and friendship gave Admiral Fisher an important advantage in the latter's struggle to modernise the Royal Navy. *(By courtesy of the National Portrait Gallery, London)*

Another influence was at hand to put this feeling into practice: Alfred von Tirpitz *(Fig 1.8)* became navy secretary in 1897, and at once began to put his plans for the creation of a High Sea Fleet into action. 'For Germany', he stated, 'the most dangerous enemy at the present time is England.' The unit of strength was the battleship: at that time the true potential of the submarine had not been realised, and the days of naval aviation were far in the future. It followed that it was necessary to plan for a fleet in home waters of no fewer than nineteen battleships and twenty-four cruisers by 1905.

Successive Navy Laws (1898, 1900, 1906, 1908 and 1912) were introduced and duly approved by the Reichstag. As soon as the Dreadnought battleship became the 'ultimate deterrent' of the day, German energy and technology were directed to the production of these deadly and terrible weapons. By October 1914 Germany possessed sixteen Dreadnought battleships, five Dreadnought battlecruisers and thirty pre-Dreadnought battleships. The twenty

Fig. 1.8 Alfred von Tirpitz (1849–1930), German Navy Secretary from 1897, as a Rear-Admiral. The vigorous personality of this very able man is well conveyed by the photograph. (*Imperial War Museum HU 36313*)

battleships dating from the 1890s had been formidable vessels, but by 1914 were obsolete. Germany's North Sea outlets were at Wilhelmshaven, Bremerhaven, Cuxhaven and Hamburg; her outlets to the Baltic were at Flensburg, Kiel, Swinemünde and Danzig. There were naval dockyards at Kiel and Wilhelmshaven, and floating docks at Cuxhaven, Hamburg and Danzig. In the far east there was the fortified base at Tsingtao.

Tirpitz and Wilhelm were interdependent in achieving their ambitions for the German Fleet: from the former came the knowledge and the main part of the work; from the latter, the power and prestige necessary to secure the passage of the Navy Laws. The joint achievement was formidable, but the weapon forged by Tirpitz and launched by the Kaiser became in the end the cause of discord and of Tirpitz's resignation. From the outset of the war the Admiral advocated aggressive action by the battlefleet and unrestricted submarine warfare; Wilhelm's humanitarian instincts or perhaps his knowledge that war of the type that was urged on him would arouse the hostility of nations not as yet involved and in particular of the United States, led him to hesitate until it was too late. Tirpitz's resignation was accepted in 1915. Development of the German Navy was not dependent on any reduction of expenditure on the Imperial Army, which was steadily developed to be easily the most formidable in Europe in the quality of its officers and men, in its direction and in its armament. Alongside it, the German railways were developed and extended so that the rapid transport of large numbers of troops could be effected. Tarrant notes that, whereas in 1905 total German spending on defence was 35 per cent lower than the British, by 1914 it was 40 per cent higher.

CHAPTER TWO

THE GERMAN CHALLENGE TO BRITAIN

The British Empire

On the other side of the North Sea sat Great Britain astride Germany's maritime outlet to the oceans of the world, the centre of a worldwide Empire, professing pacific intentions, with a small professional army at home and a large professional navy distributed around the world. Then as now nominally a democracy, the country was at the end of the nineteenth century governed by a small clique of aristocrats and plutocrats depending on a professional and relatively uncorrupt civil service. The concept of democracy was as abhorrent to the Marquis of Salisbury as it would have been to his ancestor the 1st Earl. It was only just in jest that Hilaire Belloc wrote:

> We had intended you to be
> The next Prime Minister but three.
> (Hilaire Belloc: *Lord Lundy*, 2nd Canto)

The power of the House of Lords had not been curbed; the right to vote was by no means general: it had not been given to women, and was not fully to be accorded them until after the First World War. There were, however, fixed terms for Parliaments, so that every few years the limited electorate could cast an unpopular party out of office. This limited freedom still obtains. The Conservative Party was in the hands of the Cecil family; the Liberal Party was led by a Scottish aristocrat married to a Rothschild. There had never been a revolution in Britain or in England such as those which occurred in Europe in 1789 and 1848: the country was run by the heirs of the families enriched by Henry VIII from the spoils of the monasteries, by those who benefited from William III's distributions, and by the beneficiaries of *laisser-faire* capitalism. The situation is much the same today, though to the list of those in power must be added those enriched by Mrs (later Baroness) Thatcher's and Mr Major's distribution of the spoils of privatisation of the public services.

The British Army was often led by incompetent generals, but almost always the soldiers of all ranks behaved with unfaltering courage. Its officers were drawn from the aristocracy and moneyed classes, and many were ill-informed about their profession. A rigid, indeed cruel, discipline was enforced well into the middle of the nineteenth century; the conditions of the soldier's life were extremely severe and, until Florence Nightingale and Sidney Herbert undertook their great work, medical services were wholly inadequate, even by the standards of the times. When the system was put to the test in the Crimea and later in South Africa, the early results were disastrous. Fortunately for Great Britain, lessons were learned in the latter conflict and action was taken to improve the Army's fighting capability. However, the Army was never particularly popular with the British people: folk memories of Oliver Cromwell's Commonwealth and perhaps even of the 'Peterloo Massacre' were too strong to overcome hostility to a service which had from time to time been used as an instrument for civil repression. We have in our own time seen how the use of the police to suppress a strike by the mineworkers seriously impaired public confidence in that service. The Navy was always popular, the 'Senior' Service: the names of Drake, Frobisher, Hawkins and Grenville evoked thoughts of English resistance to the power of Spain; those of Duncan, Collingwood and Nelson recalled the struggle against republican and later imperial France; the role of the Navy in the suppression of the slave trade was recalled with admiration by all but the traders and their customers. The fashion for sailor suits for children of the middle class persisted well into the twentieth century and, at Eton on the Fourth of June, is still followed by the sons of the upper class *(Fig 2.1)*. With the reluctant abandonment of sail and sail training, the Navy had advanced into the mechanical age, though it was not until the twentieth century that naval officers of the executive branch came to accept engineers as equal colleagues. Officers were drawn from the middle and upper classes; promotion from the lower deck to commissioned rank was rare. There were, no doubt, some terrible captains and admirals, but the exigencies of life at sea enforced a degree of competence in all ranks. A large part of the burden of keeping the machine working fell, as no doubt it still falls, on the non-commissioned officers. *(Fig 2.4)*

The Army was never particularly popular with the British people

The late Victorian Navy was large and impressive and much loved by the British public; it was, unfortunately, out of date, having rested for too long on the laurels won at Trafalgar *(Fig 2.2)*. Its modernisation was to be foreshadowed in a curious manner. Up to the end of the nineteenth century marine steam engines were of the reciprocating type, in which a

Fig. 2.1 Jolly boating weather, before the mortal storm. Etonians in sailors' dress for the procession of boats commemorating King George III's birthday (4 June). Four of the ten in this photograph of the late 1930s were to die resisting the German onslaught of 1940. (*Author's collection*)

to-and-fro motion is converted into a rotatory motion by levers, pistons, connecting rods and cranks. The unsolicited appearance at the Naval Review of 1897 of the experimental vessel *Turbinia* initiated the change *(Fig 2.3)*. She was propelled by the marine version of the steam turbine invented in 1884 by the Hon. Charles Parsons, the youngest son of the 3rd Earl of Rosse. Whatever might be thought, brains and blue blood do from time to time co-exist in the same individual. In the steam turbine, the blades are rotated by the steam under pressure, so that a rotatory motion is produced without the intervention of pistons, connecting rods and cranks. The little vessel, capable of well over 30 knots, steamed in and out of the lines of ships, able by its speed to defy attempts to stop or capture it. Two years later the Admiralty gave orders for the construction of two turbine-driven destroyers. Over the course of time, turbine propulsion was introduced in all the major ships of the Navy. The Parsons Marine Steam Turbine Company provided most of these engines. The American Curtis turbine, produced in 1896 by Charles Curtis, was installed in some British vessels and in many American, German and Japanese ships. The Zoelly and Belluzzo types were in use in the Italian Navy.

The little vessel . . . steamed in and out of the lines of ships, able by its speed to defy attempts to capture it

The challenge offered by the development of the German Navy was perceived in Britain in the early part of the twentieth century. In the second year of that century Queen Victoria died, and in the next year the Boer War was brought to a conclusion. The end of the war was represented as a success for Britain, and the popularity accruing to the presiding Conservative Government secured the party a further term of office in 1902. It was, however, too late for a party which had been in office for so many years, just as the continuation of Conservative government in 1992 was too late for the same party. As Winston Churchill says, the new Prime Minister, Balfour, 'never

'Twas on a Sun-
day morning
In the first
month of the
year
That four great
German war-
ships
Were sighted,
sharp and
clear.
'Twas on a Sun-
day morn-
ing,
They were ten
miles away,
When Beatty,
in the LION,
Began the
deadly fray.
Our guns be-
gan a-roar-
ing,
Our shot fell
fast and
thick;

L is for the LION.

That's how we sank the Bluecher,
And drove the German ships
A-speeding to their homeland,
Like greyhounds from the slips.

With flame, and dead and dy
With bitter grief and wail,
They sped across the waters
To tell the dismal tale.

Fig. 2.3 The *Turbinia*, Parsons's revolutionary turbine-driven vessel which caused so much consternation at the Naval Review of 1897. (Imperial War Museum: RP 2583)

Soon two great ships were blazing,
And one was sinking quick.
We saw her heeling over,
We cheered; she sank, and then
The sea was black around her
With drowning sailor men.
We put out boats to save them,
For Britons, as you know,
Show mercy to the vanquished,
And spare the fallen foe.

That's how we keep you safely,
That's how we keep you free—
A-rolling on the billows,
A-fighting on the sea.

While Nelson's spirit lingers,
While British tars are true,
Be sure, my little children,
No harm can come to you.

Fig 2.2 From an early age, British children were brought up to believe in the invincibility of the country's Navy. The sinking of the *Blücher* in 1915 provided an opportunity to hail both the might and mercy of the 'Nelson spirit', and did not a little to inflate Beatty's reputation. From: *The Royal Navy, An ABC for Little Britons (Royal Naval Museum)*

had a fair chance. He succeeded only to an exhausted inheritance.' Balfour, a Cecil with all the ability and intelligence associated with that family, maintained his party in power until 1905 *(Fig 2.5)*. In the General Election of 1906 the parliamentary Conservative party was reduced to some one hundred and fifty seats, while the Liberals, under the leadership first of Campbell-Bannerman and later of Asquith, undertook the conduct of affairs. This administration was responsible for important changes in social legislation and in the balance of power between the Commons and the Lords, but found itself committed to the continuation of the struggle against Germany.

Some may see in these events a parallel with those of 1982 to 1997: a party gaining popularity by success in war; a long period in power; finally, an increasingly unpopular and incompetent government clinging to power and being dismissed by an incensed electorate. As this story unfolds, some may even see parallels between Prime Minister Blair's first and second New Labour administrations since 1997 adopting what had previously been perceived as the market-orientated principles of past Conservative governments, and the enforced adoption by the incoming Liberal administration of 1906 of the previous government's policies on defence. In both cases, external pressures were the cause of a necessary accommodation, in the first with the military and in the latter with global business.

Overleaf: Fig. 2.4 Stokers in training in the Fisher era. Probably not 'cleaning dynamos with brick-dust and oil'. *(Hulton-Deutsch Collection/Corbis: HU049362)*

KEY:

1 Cook
2 Bikaner (Maharajah)
3 Hughes
4 Lloyd George
5 Botha
6 Milner
7 Massey
8 Barnes
9 Churchill
10 Grey
11 Borden
12 Balfour
13 Asquith
14 Geddes (E)
15 Bonar Law
16 Morris
17 Kitchener

The rise of Anglo-German hostility

The first broad hint of German hostility to Britain came perhaps in 1896 with the message of congratulation sent by the Kaiser to Kruger, the President of the Transvaal Republic, on the defeat of the invasion led by Dr Jameson, administrator of Rhodesia. The Boer Republic of Transvaal had in 1881, after inflicting a serious reverse on the British Army, achieved independence. The grievances of the foreigners living in Johannesburg provided some sort of excuse for the Government of the Cape, led by Cecil Rhodes, to conspire with the great capitalists of the Witwatersrand ('The Rand') to restore the Transvaal to the Empire. The resulting raid was easily defeated by the Boer forces, but the suspicion remained that the British Government had had a hand in the endeavour. It had not in fact finished with the Boer republics: the finding of gold in the Transvaal made them too great a prize to be cast away. So there ensued the second Boer War and the demonstration that, with the Americans busy elsewhere and the French otherwise pre-occupied, the strength of the Royal Navy was sufficient to deter any European or American power from intervention. The Boers had had the foresight to arm themselves with French and German guns and with German Mauser rifles, so the struggle was long and bitter, and produced consequences which even now affect us all. It is interesting to note that two of the great South African capitalists, Beit and Wernher, were naturalised Britons of German origin, and that Milner, High Commissioner in Cape Town, whose father was half German, was a devoted admirer of Bismarck and Frederick the Great.

The strength of the Royal Navy was sufficient to deter any European or American power

Racial affinities with the Boers and revulsion against what was seen as – and almost certainly was – unprovoked British aggression against a peaceful nation of farmers caused great indignation in Germany. Germans were also angry at their impotence in the face of such aggression. There followed the German Navy Law of 1900. Britain had up to that time followed a policy of maintaining a navy strong enough to deal with a combination of the two navies next in power. It became clear that if to the strong navies of France and Russia a strong German fleet were added, Britain would have to find one or more allies and revise her notions about the extent of her maritime supremacy. So began the processes of reconciliation with France and Russia and of the formation of an alliance with Japan. The last step was, unfortunately, bound to sour relations between Britain and the United States of America.

Notable assertions of German power were made in 1905, 1909 and 1911. In 1905 the French Government appeared to intend to treat Morocco as a French Protectorate, in apparent breach of its obligations under the Treaty of Madrid. The Sultan appealed to the German Government, whose response was to send Kaiser Wilhelm to Tangier. Having disembarked from a cruiser in a very rough sea, at some personal risk and considerable inconvenience, the Kaiser delivered what amounted to a challenge to France. The French Government had chosen its time badly: the country was not prepared for war, and the

Opposite: Fig. 2.5 [Empire] Statesmen of the First World War, by Sir James Guthrie 1924–30. The subjects, 'in stately conclave met', are shown in the Paris Louvre, under the statue of the Winged Victory. Balfour (12) dominates the scene; Asquith (13) sits on his left. Churchill (9) faces the painter, with Grey (10) in profile on his left. On the left, Lloyd George (4) sits at the end of the table opposite Asquith. Standing behind him is Botha (5), the former Boer general. Kitchener (17), drowned in June 1916, stands, a brooding presence, in the shadows on the extreme right. *(By courtesy of the National Portrait Gallery, London)* army was not in a good state. The Foreign Minister, Delcassé, was jettisoned and the matter was later resolved at a conference of the Powers in Algeçiras. The support of Great Britain at that conference enabled France to agree to a compromise which was not humiliating. From this shock stemmed France's preparations for war, and the initiation of talks between the French and British General Staffs.

The crisis of 1909 stemmed from the annexation of Bosnia and Herzegovina by Austria in the previous year. The Government of newly independent Serbia voiced strong objections, and, aware of Russian support, mobilised its army. In April 1909 the German Government indicated to the Russians that it was prepared to join Austria in enforcing recognition of the annexation. As France had done four years previously, Russia submitted to *force majeure*. Another country was thus provoked into making preparations for a major war; Britain took further steps to strengthen the Navy.

In 1911 British interests were directly challenged: the occupation of Fez (Fès), the ancient and famous city in Morocco, by the French, led the German Government to lay claim to Agadir, a port on the Atlantic coast of Morocco situated just south of the 31st parallel. The gunboat *Panther*, a ship of 1,000 tons armed with two 4-inch (10.5-cm) guns, was sent to this port to represent the German interest. The firm possession of a harbour on the African Atlantic coast would of course have given Germany a great strategic advantage in any war against Britain, and a first-class crisis was thus produced. Much depended on the attitude of Britain: the view seems to have prevailed in Germany that the Liberal Government, committed to a programme of social reform and having only recently emerged from a confrontation in the House of Lords over radical budget proposals, would be inclined to seek settlement at any cost. The leader of the radical, or left-wing, section of the Cabinet was the Chancellor of the Exchequer, Lloyd George. To the surprise of the German Government and perhaps to that of some of his colleagues too, the Chancellor took the opportunity offered by a speech to the Bankers' Association to assert Britain's role as a major player in world affairs and to hint that German aggression against France would bring Britain into the struggle on the latter's side.

The firm possession of a harbour on the African coast would have given Germany a strategic advantage

The attitude of the German Government remained so threatening that the British Foreign Secretary, Edward Grey, feared a surprise attack on the Fleet and so warned his colleague McKenna, the First Lord of the Admiralty. It emerged that the Navy's plans for dealing with such an attack were far from perfect, and from this stemmed in part the replacement of McKenna by Winston Churchill. In the event, the crisis was resolved, the German Ambassador to Britain being sacrificed because of his perceived failure accurately to predict the attitude of the country to which he was accredited. So Europe entered the last years of peace, with France, Germany, Austro-Hungary, Russia, Italy and Britain arming and preparing plans for war.

CHAPTER THREE

THE MODERNISATION OF THE ROYAL NAVY

The activity on the other side of the North Sea obliged the British Government to think seriously about the readiness for war of the Army and the Royal Navy. It was R.B. Haldane, later Viscount Haldane, who as Secretary for War from 1906 to 1912 led the reorganisation of the Army in readiness for a European war. Two men of tremendous personality were chiefly responsible for the modernisation of the Royal Navy and for making it ready to confront German power. They were Sir John (later Lord) Fisher and Winston (later Sir Winston) Churchill. At this time the Navy cost a large proportion of the national income; the Admiralty was therefore an important department of government, and its political head, the First Lord, was a prominent figure in the government and a member of the Cabinet. We gain an indication of the importance of the post of First Lord from the fact that Winston Churchill was ready, indeed eager, to exchange his appointment as Home Secretary for it. Responsible to the First Lord were the Sea Lords, the senior naval officers who were the professional heads of the Navy, with the First Sea Lord at their head. The array was completed by the Civil Lord and the Secretary to the Admiralty.

Admiral Fisher

John Fisher, the son of Captain William Fisher of the 98th Highlanders and his wife, the former Sophie Lambe, was born in 1841 in Ceylon, where his father had been ADC to the Governor,

Fig. 3.1 Rear Admiral Sir John Fisher, Controller of the Navy, 1892. (*Royal Naval Museum*)

and was later to be a coffee planter and, later still, Inspector-General of Police. The curiously Asiatic cast of Fisher's features gave rise to rumours that his mother was a Cingalese princess, and formed the basis for various insults later hurled at him by Kaiser Wilhelm II and others, including the designation as a 'treacherous half-Asiatic' *(Fig 3.1)*. Fisher entered the Royal Navy in 1854 at the age of thirteen, obtaining a cadetship through the influence of Admiral Sir William Parker, a neighbour of Fisher's godmother, Lady Horton. Fisher entered the Navy 'penniless, friendless and forlorn', and indeed at that time the Service was a very rough one. Marder records that 'the day Fisher entered his first ship, he saw eight men flogged, and fainted'. Fisher was evidently lucky with the captains of his first ships; he was also hard-working and attentive, and after service in the Far East and in the Gunnery School HMS *Excellent* was in 1874 promoted to captain at the age of thirty-three. He married in 1866 Frances Katharine Delves Broughton, 'the most beautiful woman in mind and body that ever lived': the happy marriage lasted fifty-two years, until the death of the then Lady Fisher. The Delves Broughtons were and are one of the oldest families of England, and in the last century one of them achieved fame of a sort in East Africa, the playground of expatriate members of the British upper class, murdering Lord Erroll in a subsequently notorious *crime passionel*. These events were later portrayed in the film *White Mischief*.

Fisher entered the Navy 'penniless, friendless and forlorn'

Fisher's energy, enthusiasm, professional knowledge and restless quest for advance led to his appointment in 1881 as captain of the *Inflexible*, then the Navy's most advanced battleship. He never looked back. Today we can only marvel that it was possible for a man who was hard-working, competent in all branches of his field, forward-looking, dedicated to the improvement of the Royal Navy, perhaps a genius, to have got so far even with influential patrons. We are nowadays all too well accustomed to the award of the prime position to the second worst candidate, to the candidate who seems least likely to constitute a challenge to present incumbents, or to the mediocrity, over competing high-flyers, in order to avoid conflict. Above all, the palm must never be awarded to the man or woman who has been proved right by the event. It is too late now to go back to the idea of advancement through merit alone. Yet that is how Fisher obtained advancement and how he was able over the course of a few years to propel the Royal Navy into the twentieth century. He was, indeed, a success socially and at Court, and was particularly friendly with King Edward VII. But so, earlier, had been Lord Charles Beresford, the man who later became Fisher's greatest opponent. It is, of course, recognised that many of the British upper classes like a bit of rough trade, both socially and sexually. Jesters were allowed considerable freedom of speech in the courts of the medieval kings; Queen Victoria's attachment to the blunt-speaking Highlander John Brown is well attested; Constance Chatterley's proclivities were evidently

. . . (his) restless quest for advance led to his appointment as captain of the Inflexible

Fig. 3.2 [British] naval officers of the First World War, by Sir Arthur Stockdale Cope, 1921. Has the painter made some comments here? Beatty (14) is in the centre of the stage, the focus of the composition. Jellicoe (21) sits, in reflective mood, on the right, with his brother-in-law, Madden (20), seated on his right and Wemyss, the successful First Sea Lord, who followed him, standing on his left. Arbuthnot (5), Cradock (7) and Hood (8), of whom the first and last died at Jutland, and the second died at Coronel, are in the shadows on the left of the painting. Tyrwhitt (11), the commander of the Harwich Force, standing next to Keyes (12), by then the hero of the Zeebrugge Raid, adopts a confident pose. Battenberg (16), the former First Sea Lord, and de Robeck (9), formerly commander of the naval forces at the Dardanelles, are perhaps thinking of what might have been. Sturdee (18), the victor at the Falklands battle, on Battenberg's left, leans eagerly forward over the table. *(By courtesy of the National Portrait Gallery, London)*

shared by some of her real-life sisters. Fisher's blunt approach may well have endeared him to the King, just as some years later the similar approach of Mr J.H. Thomas endeared that Labour politician to King Edward's son and successor.

Fisher's power and passion leap at the reader from the pages of his letters: one can appreciate how wonderful it must have been to know him, and how terrible to have incurred his displeasure. He could indeed be ruthless: even Admiral Sturdee, the victor of the Falklands battle in 1914, suffered stinging reprimands and, later, humiliating treatment for his perceived failure to sink all the ships of von Spee's squadron *(Fig 3.2)*. Fisher expressed in conversation and on paper views which many held but were afraid to express; he persuaded by repetition; he was, of course, accused of exaggeration;

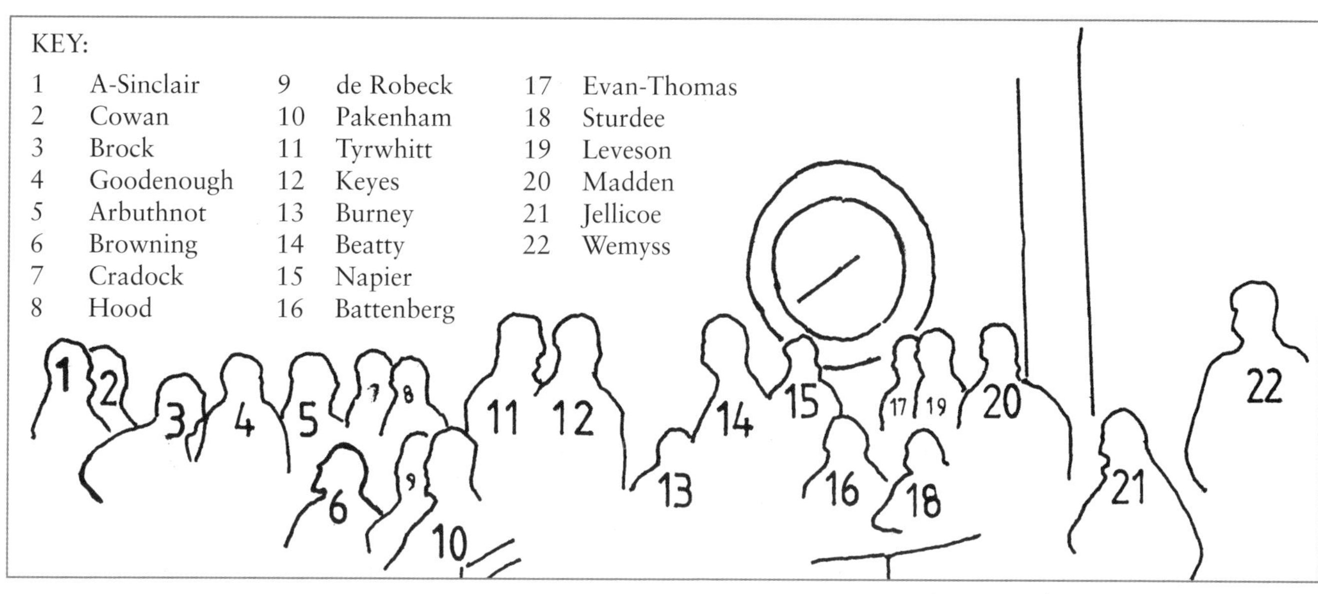
KEY:
1 A-Sinclair
2 Cowan
3 Brock
4 Goodenough
5 Arbuthnot
6 Browning
7 Cradock
8 Hood
9 de Robeck
10 Pakenham
11 Tyrwhitt
12 Keyes
13 Burney
14 Beatty
15 Napier
16 Battenberg
17 Evan-Thomas
18 Sturdee
19 Leveson
20 Madden
21 Jellicoe
22 Wemyss

but, in truth, he did not overstate his cases, he simply presented them clearly and forcefully. One of his more advanced suggestions, made in 1905 to King Edward VII, was that the Royal Navy should 'Copenhagen' the German Fleet: that is, reduce it to impotence by a surprise attack without a declaration of war, as, in effect, Nelson had done to the Danish Fleet in 1801 and Admiral Gambier did in 1807. 'My God, Fisher, you must be mad!' said the King. Fisher was popular with all but his enemies, a favourite with women, but not, so far as is known, a *coureur*; the sailors, though recognising in him a strict disciplinarian, saw that he did not spare himself and that he combined strictness with fairness; the general public saw in him on one hand the embodiment of the spirit of the Royal Navy and on the other the driving force for reform.

His religion was that of the Old Testament . . .

Few people, I suspect, would make an association between ballroom dancing and religion; nowadays, too, one might observe that both have altered out of recognition since Fisher's time. But he did indeed apply himself to both disciplines with equal vigour and enthusiasm. His religion was that of the Old Testament rather than of the New; he was a glutton for sermons; as a dancer he seems to have been indefatigable. The great achievement was, of course, to persuade the politicians and compel the administrators of the Navy to adopt the far-reaching reforms that were necessary. Anyone with even slight experience of the Service and of government departments must wonder at Fisher's success, which transcends that of Florence Nightingale and Sidney Herbert in their dealings with the Army. Nelson was and is the Navy's great exemplar. He aimed always at annihilation of the enemy, and his fighting tactics were highly original, but in the long Victorian afternoon and evening originality at least was far from the minds of those in charge of the great Service. Fisher's struggle against conservatives ashore and afloat was prolonged and bitter, and in the end resulted in his departure for the House of Lords, then as now the repository of men and women who have become an embarrassment to the government but whose achievements forbid relegation to complete obscurity. Before that, Fisher had achieved more for the Navy than had anyone else over so short a period of time. In this, he was undoubtedly helped by his friendship with the King and his skilful manipulation of the Press, but many of his reforms were opposed by the Prince of Wales, by a vocal section of the Navy led by Lord Charles Beresford, by a section of the Press and by politicians of both parties.

Fisher had achieved more for the Navy than had anyone else over so short a time

Much of Fisher's success must be attributed to his techniques of advancing his ideas by the repeated use of short and pithy aphorisms, nowadays known as 'sound bites', and by the skilful use of the national Press. 'Favouritism is the secret of efficiency' is a good phrase, so is 'la carrière ouverte aux talents', borrowed from Napoleon: we could do with their application now. 'Buggins' Turn' sums up all that we now observe in the appointment of mediocrities to posts of importance. We have indeed seen refinement of the use of the Press, but it has been used more often to produce personal and private advantage and to protect public figures than to advance the public cause. J.L. Garvin, a member of the political staff of the *Daily Telegraph* from 1899 to 1908 and Editor of the *Observer* from 1908 to 1942, was a steady and even inspired supporter of Fisher's ideas; W.T. Stead, Editor of the *Westminster Gazette*, who in 1912 was to die in one of the greatest catastrophes of British marine technology and seamanship, gave firm support in the campaign to increase the size and efficiency of the Fleet.

Fisher's remarkable prescience was shown by his forecast, years before the event, that a world war would start in October 1914; the combination of prescience and technical knowledge was shown too, by his early recognition that the land war in Europe would soon end in stalemate, and that some extraordinary method would have to be used if that stalemate were to be broken. It is all the more remarkable that a man with so full a grasp of the principles and practice of war should have failed to realise the need for a department dedicated to examining the tactical uses to which the weapon that he had forged should be put. It was Fisher's resistance to the formation of a Naval War Staff that led to his successor Wilson's humiliation when he appeared before the meeting of the Committee of Imperial Defence in 1911, and eventually to the replacement of McKenna by Winston Churchill as First Lord. In the event, the time available to the War Staff for forming its plans was inadequate: right up to the end of the war no one knew exactly how the Grand Fleet would best be employed.

The Fisher reforms

Fisher's contributions to the Royal Navy continued throughout his professional career, both in sea and in shore appointments. He was a gunnery enthusiast in the days when firing the guns was a nuisance in the Navy because it fouled the decks; he was an enthusiast for speed when cruising speeds were around 8 knots. Perhaps his most important contributions were made during his tenure of the offices of Second Sea Lord from 1902 to 1904 and of First Sea Lord from 1904 to 1909. They were concerned with training and conditions of service, the manning of the reserve fleet, the scrapping of obsolete ships, improvements in gunnery and in the speed of squadrons and fleets, the redistribution of the fleet and the introduction of Dreadnought battleships and battlecruisers.

Training

Fisher's great contribution to training was the introduction of common entry for aspirant executive, engineer and marine officers. The project did not come fully into operation until fifty years later, but the reforms of 1905 marked the beginning of the end for division between the gentlemen of the executive branch and the players of the engineer branch. Similarly, Fisher's proposal that all the costs of training naval officers should be borne by the State had to wait until 1947 for full implementation. The conditions of life and service for the lower deck were greatly improved: discipline was made less harsh, levels of pay were raised and conditions of life at sea were much changed for the better. The prospects of promotion from the lower deck to commissioned rank were improved. It is scarcely surprising that the nickname bestowed on Fisher by the sailors should have been an affectionate one – 'Jacky'. These nicknames tell a lot about the sharpness of the sailor and his perception of the character of his officers. One worthy and excellent admiral of the Second World War was styled 'Wrong-way Charlie' because, chiefly through faulty intelligence reports, he rather too often took his Fleet away from the enemy. Another suffered the indignity of having his sailors call their life-jackets after him, because he had had so many ships sink under him. The nickname 'Cutts', given to one of the most successful admirals of the Second World War, indicates, perhaps, respect and slightly unwilling admiration rather than liking.

Fleet Reserve

Fisher recognised that the enemy in the next war was certain to be Germany

Fisher's reorganisation of the Fleet Reserve had the object of providing a reserve of ships and men which could rapidly be brought to a state of readiness for war. Kipling's story 'Their Lawful Occasions' contains what is perhaps an almost true depiction of the state of the Reserve before Fisher got busy on it. Torpedo gunner Emanuel Pyecroft speaks: 'What with lying in the Reserve four years and what with the new type of tiffy [engine room artificer] what cleans dynamos with brick dust and oil, Two Six Seven's steam gadgets were paralytic.' Fisher changed all that *(Fig 2.4)*. A Reserve Fleet was established, manned by nucleus crews of two-fifths of the normal complement, including specialists and officers in key positions. It was based on the three home ports, Chatham, Devonport and Portsmouth; the nucleus crews lived on board; there were periodic practice cruises. On mobilisation, the crews would be completed by drafts from barracks and training establishments. Thus was formed a reserve of ships and men which would truly and quickly augment the fighting strength of the Navy in time of war.

The reorganisation of the Reserve was combined with the removal of many ships which 'could neither fight nor run away': ships which had been kept on foreign stations as token assertions of British power and, perhaps, to boost the self-esteem of the representatives of the British Foreign Service. Lastly, Fisher recognised that the enemy in the next war was certain to be Germany, and accordingly began the disposal of the Fleet to meet that threat. Its greatest strength had to be in the North Sea, in order to meet the challenge of the High Sea Fleet: ships and squadrons were redistributed to that end, with the result that when war came, the Grand Fleet was in position to command the North Sea and its exits through the channels between Scotland and the Orkneys, the Orkneys and Shetland, Shetland and Iceland, and Iceland and Greenland. That concentration was possible only if satisfactory arrangements were made with the French for the safeguard of the Mediterranean, so that the British presence there could be restricted to a few battlecruisers, cruisers and escort vessels.

Speed and gunnery

Speed and gunnery were obsessions with Fisher. He strove to increase the operational speeds of squadrons and fleets and to improve the accuracy of gunfire at long range. He was fortunate enough to have among his senior commanders Admiral Percy Scott, appointed commander of the gunnery school HMS *Excellent* in 1890. Scott was another enthusiast, another man of intellect and independent thought. Consequently, he too fell foul of Lord Charles Beresford, with the important difference from Fisher's case that he was junior to that Admiral. He received from Beresford a notable public reprimand for his tactless response to an order for his cruiser squadron to paint ship in preparation for a visit by royalty. Nevertheless, Scott's career prospered, and he was able to introduce techniques for aiming and for tackling the problems of shooting at a moving target from a moving, rolling and pitching platform. His most notable triumph was in gaining acceptance of the 'director firing' method, by which the whole main armament of the ship was aimed simultaneously through a director sight mounted in the foretop and fired in salvoes from the central control. Scott's career was crowned by his appointment in 1905 as Inspector of Target Practice: in that post he raised the percentage of hits made to rounds fired from 56 to 81. By the time of Jutland, most of the large ships of the Royal Navy were fitted for director firing: this advantage was denied to the Imperial German Fleet. In the event, neither side foresaw the great ranges at which battle would be joined, and accuracy at such ranges remained poor.

Scott was another . . . man of intellect. Consequently, he too fell foul of Sir Charles Beresford

The Dreadnought battleship

The best known of Fisher's innovations was of course the introduction of the Dreadnought battleship. The British battleship – the prime strategic weapon of the time – was typically armed with weapons of mixed sizes ranging from twelve-pounders to guns of 12-inch (30-cm) calibre *(Fig 3.3)*. The two latest ships of this type,

Overleaf: Fig. 3.3 HMS *Agamemnon*. She and her sister, *Lord Nelson*, were the last British battleships before the introduction of the *Dreadnought*, started before the *Dreadnought* but completed after her. Both were strong ships, but were never thought fit to operate with the Grand Fleet. (*Royal Naval Museum*)

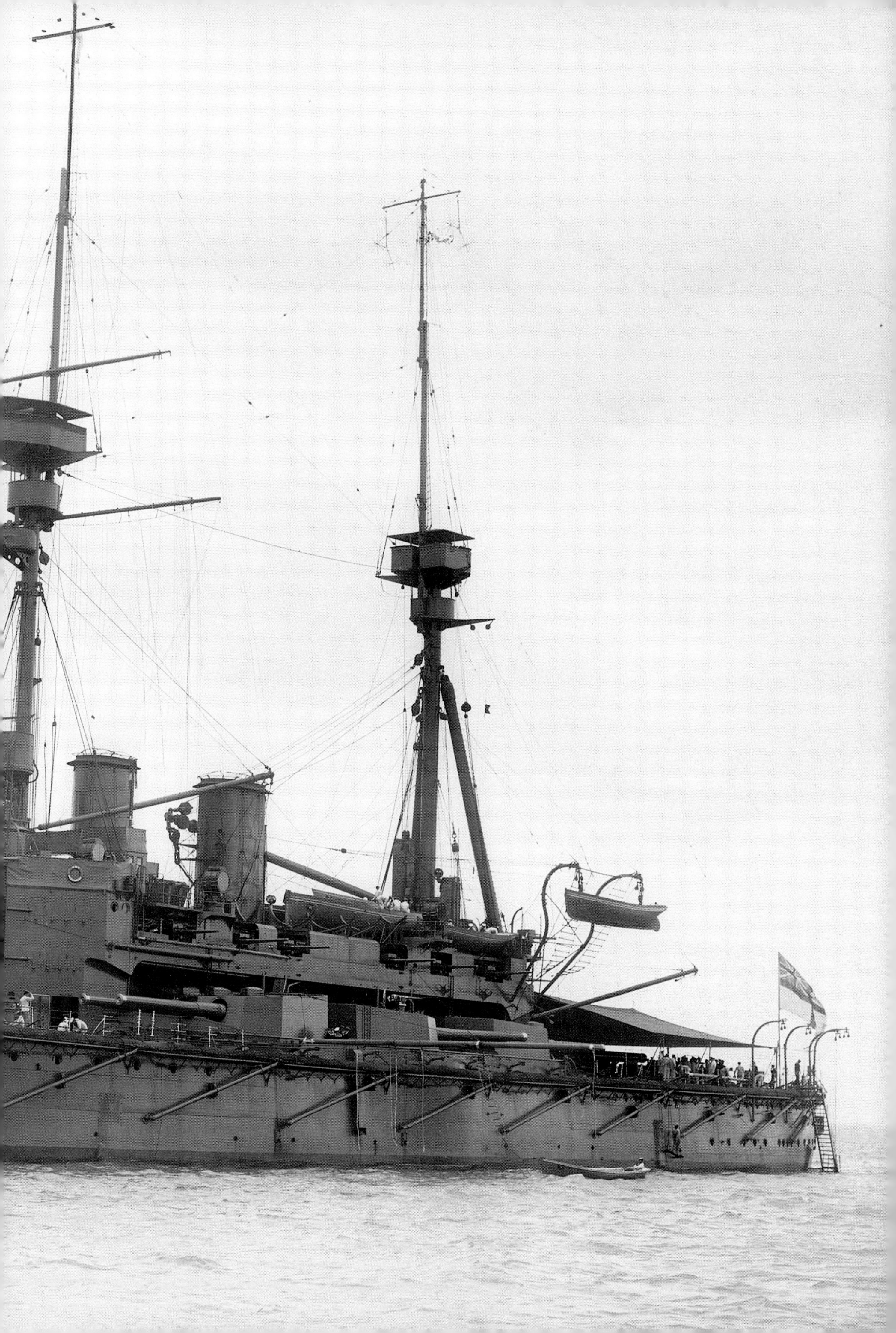

Fig. 3.4 HMS *Dreadnought* in 1910. (*Imperial War Museum: Q 38714*)

laid down in 1904 and completed in 1907, had a mixed heavy armament of 12-inch (30-cm) and 9.2-inch (23-cm) guns. Their heaviest guns were mounted in two turrets on the centre line; the ten 9.2-inch guns were mounted in six turrets, three on each beam. Maximum speeds of 18 to 19 knots were given by reciprocating engines. The idea of an 'all big-gun' ship was not original, and can be traced back to Vittorio Cuniberti, a civil engineer in the Engineer Corps of the Italian Navy. His ideas were studied in America, England and Japan, and indeed the navies of the first and last laid down Dreadnoughts before England did. Fisher's particular achievements were the speed with which HMS *Dreadnought*, the ship that gave her name to the whole class, was built, and the combination in the ship of speed, protection and heavy armament. With a normal displacement of about 18,000 tons, the ship was given a maximum speed of 21 knots by turbines producing 23,000 horsepower. The substitution of turbines for reciprocating engines gave an enormous advantage in reliability and in reducing the frequency and length of overhauls. The *Dreadnought* was the first turbine-driven large ship in any navy, and subsequently the turbine was the engine of choice for all ships designed to combine size with speed *(Figs 3.4 & 3.5)*.

Dreadnought's ten 12-inch (30-cm), 45 calibre guns were arranged in five turrets, three of which were on the centre line and two abeam of the foremast. A broadside of eight guns was thus achieved. It was not until five years later that the first British ships with superimposed turrets appeared, though the American Dreadnoughts completed in 1909 had them. Fisher pressed home his dictum of 'the biggest possible big gun and the smallest possible small gun': the *Dreadnought* carried only unprotected twelve-pounder guns to repel attacks by torpedo-boat. The maximum thickness of the armour belt was 11 inches (28-cm), and similar protection was given to the barbettes. The ship was laid down in December 1905 and completed in October 1906, the extraordinary rapidity of construction being made possible by prior manufacture and assembly on site of as many of the component parts as possible.

The appearance of the Dreadnought class at once made all existing battleships obsolete, including the two British battleships, *Lord Nelson* and *Agamemnon*, begun before but completed after her. She was the wonder of her time: almost as great a deterrent and a portent as the atomic bomb was in a later age. Her strength and power convinced admirals, their political leaders and the general public that this was the weapon on which national security chiefly depended. No government could afford to ignore this fearsome weapon: European countries were soon building Dreadnoughts in competition with one another; on the other side of the world the race began between the United States and Japan for control of the Pacific by fleets of capital ships; Argentina bought Dreadnoughts in the United States, Brazil in England. Chile ordered two Dreadnoughts in England, but in the event got only one: one of them was bought by Britain and converted into an aircraft carrier; the other was requisitioned and named HMS *Canada*, serving throughout the war and only getting to her purchasers in 1920. Even the coming of the aircraft carrier in the later years of the First World War did not check this enthusiasm: although the British *Vanguard*, completed in 1946, the last Dreadnought to be built, was scrapped in the 1950s, her near contemporary, the American *Missouri*, saw action as recently as 1992, during the Gulf War. A lifespan of almost ninety years does not seem too bad for such a weapon.

The appearance of the Dreadnought made it necessary for the German Admiralty to revise its plans and for the German Government to embark on a programme of building similar ships. So began the sad and unprofitable Anglo-German Dreadnought race, brought to an end only by the First World War; even more sadly, to be repeated in the 1930s during the rise to power of the Third Reich. The lessons taught by the fate of the Second Reich and the decline of British power and prosperity had not been learned by either side.

The battlecruiser

Fisher's restless mind had not stopped at the Dreadnought: he had conceived also vessels of great size and speed, armed with the heaviest guns, lightly protected, for action as powerful scouting cruisers, capable of destroying armoured cruisers and catching and destroying fast armed merchant cruisers, and acting as a fast and mobile wing of a battlefleet. The *Invincible*, completed in 1908, was the first of these battlecruisers *(Figs 3.6 & 3.7)*. She carried

Fig. 3.5 HMS *Dreadnought* in 1910. Note the absence of secondary armament apart from the twelve-pounders on the turrets and elsewhere. The placing of the foretop just abaft the fore funnel caused great inconvenience to those occupying the former. The ship steered badly at speeds of less than 10 knots. (*Royal Naval Museum*)

eight 12-inch (30-cm) guns mounted in four turrets, two of which were on the centre line and two on either beam. Sixteen 4-inch (10-cm) guns, lightly protected, were carried as secondary armament. The turbines developed 41,000 horsepower and on trials gave a maximum speed of 26 knots. Protection had to be sacrificed to gain speed: the maximum thickness of the armoured belt was 7 inches (17.7 cm). Properly used, as they nearly were at the Falklands battle in 1914, these ships could be of great value. The *Invincible* and her sister *Inflexible* accomplished their mission in 1914 by sinking the two powerful German armoured cruisers *Scharnhorst* and *Gneisenau* without themselves sustaining serious damage, but firing off most of their 12-inch (30-cm) ammunition in the process.

These early indications of the inaccuracy of British gunnery at long range and of the poor destructive effect of British projectiles may not, perhaps, have been appreciated: the magnitude of the victory appeared at the time so overwhelming that all but Fisher joined in lauding Sturdee, the victorious commander. Eighteen months later, at Jutland, the weakness of these ships when pitted against ships with a similar armament was tragically revealed: the *Invincible* and her successors *Indefatigable* and *Queen Mary* blew up when German shells penetrated their deck and turret armour to enter the magazines. A last and awful reminder of the fragility of the battlecruiser came twenty-five years later, with the destruction of the *Hood* by shellfire from the *Bismarck*. 'Speed', Fisher had said, 'is the best protection', but the margin of speed of a ship over that of its opponent or opponents has to be very large to make that true. One of the most remarkable aspects of Fisher's early reforms, before the pace of German expenditure on armaments compelled acceleration of the British programme, was that between 1904 and 1905 expenditure was actually reduced. This reduction was made possible by the removal of useless ships on useless missions and by increasing efficiency in the operation of the Fleet.

Fig. 3.6 HMS *Invincible* in 1910. Her high speed and heavy armament made her a prodigy of the time, but experience at Jutland showed that she and her sisters were not strong enough to withstand fire from heavy guns. Her proper function was the pursuit and destruction of armoured cruisers: at the Falklands in 1914 she and the *Inflexible* destroyed von Spee's *Scharnhorst* and *Gneisenau*, shooting away almost all their 12-inch shells in the process. (*Royal Naval Museum*)

Fisher's fall

By 1909 the Furies were on Fisher's track. His reforms had angered many naval officers and a section of the Press, and he was perceived, almost justly, as an obstruction to the formation of a Naval War Staff. His principle 'favouritism is the secret of efficiency' had in the end produced a schism between two sections of the Navy's officer corps the effect of which was to diminish the benefit produced by the temporary suspension of the principle of 'Buggins' turn'. Two factors made Fisher's departure from the Admiralty inevitable: the hostility of Lord Charles Beresford and the episode of the 'Bacon letters'.

Lord Charles Beresford, a younger son of the Marquis of Waterford, a Conservative MP and a mover in high society as well as a sailor, rose to be Admiral commanding the Channel Fleet. He had in earlier days famously quarrelled with the Prince of Wales, later King Edward VII, in a matter concerning a lady. The immediate *casus belli* between Beresford and Fisher may have been the publication of letters written to the latter by Captain Bacon, then serving in the Mediterranean Fleet commanded by Beresford. In these confidential letters Bacon commented sharply on various aspects of the conduct of affairs in the Fleet. Those comments were not favourable to Beresford's regime. Fisher was so much pleased by the content, force and relevance of the letters that, very rashly, he had some of them printed for circulation to the Fleet. That was, of course, an ultimately fatal step: Beresford and his friends in Society and in Parliament and in sections of the Press mounted a campaign of criticism of Fisher's methods and reforms. By 1909 the Prince of Wales, later King George V, himself a captain in the Royal Navy, had joined in the criticism of Fisher. Beresford, who had been a notably insubordinate Commander in Chief of the Channel Fleet, eventually took his complaints to the Prime Minister, H.H. Asquith, who decided that a sub-committee of the Committee of Imperial Defence should investigate the charges. Although the verdict of that sub-committee was in general favourable to Fisher, its implied criticism of Fisher's methods was in the end fatal. Fisher left the Admiralty early in 1910 with a peerage, condemned, apparently, to end his life in smouldering inactivity *(Fig 3.8)*. It was and is remarkable that he had lasted so long and had managed to do so much. If he had not dared and done so much, the Navy and the nation would have been the losers.

In the event, the nation had not done with Fisher: Winston Churchill was in regular correspondence with him after assuming the office of First Lord, and recalled him to the Admiralty in 1914 when Prince Louis of Battenberg was obliged to quit the office of First Sea Lord because of his German parentage *(Fig 3.2)*. This was a bold step: Fisher was then 74, and was known strongly to disapprove of many appointments and dispositions made since 1910. However, he proved to be a great war leader, almost certainly better than any of

Overleaf: Fig. 3.7 HMS *Invincible*. (*Imperial War Museum* Q39274)

Fig. 3.8 Admiral of the Fleet: Lord Fisher of Kilverstone, by Sir Hubert von Herkomer, 1910. Fisher is here at the height of his fame, though not at the end of his tremendous career. Von Herkomer was born in Waal, Bavaria, and did most of his work in England. The museums in Bushey, Herts, and Landsberg am Lech, Bavaria, show selections of his work and illustrate his varied life. (*By courtesy of the National Portrait Gallery, London*)

those who succeeded him during the war. The ill-planned and ill-fated Dardanelles expedition of 1915 was the rock on which both he and Churchill foundered: Churchill because of his perceived role as the initiator of the affair; Fisher because his reluctant initial approval gave way in the end to frenzied opposition and mental breakdown. Churchill was young enough eventually to make a comeback, but for Fisher time had run out. He was never again to excercise power. In spite of repeated calls by his supporters for his reinstatement, he was left to smoulder energetically as Chairman of the newly-formed Board of Invention and Research. It was and is typical of the techniques of official retribution for insubordination that Fisher, without whom there would have been no victory, was not asked to be present when in 1918 a large part of the German Fleet surrendered to the Allied, mainly British, Fleets in the Firth of Forth.

CHAPTER FOUR

WINSTON CHURCHILL'S CONTRIBUTION

Winston Spencer Churchill, the elder son of Lord Randolph Churchill and the former Miss Jeanette Jerome, was born in 1874. Lord Randolph was a younger son of the 7th Duke of Marlborough, the 1st Duke and Duchess having risen to direct the affairs of the nation in war and peace during the reigns of William and Mary and Queen Anne. Winston Churchill was destined to better his ancestor as a leader of the nation in war; his popularity with the British people far surpassed that of the 1st Duke; his importance as a world statesman greatly exceeded that of his ancestor; he made important contributions to the civil government of the country and to the study of history; and left behind him a reputation transcending those of most of his countrymen *(Figs 4.1 & 4.2)*. However, like his famous ancestor, he was not free from serious defects of character. Early in his career Winston Churchill was seen by many colleagues and opponents and by a section of the public as insincere, tricky and unreliable. The perception of these defects was never entirely eradicated, and even in his years of power Churchill displayed an uncertain touch in the selection of subordinates, made many errors of judgement and was less than frank in his dealings. Both Churchills possessed the ability to deceive – a quality not often appreciated in time of peace, but always useful in war. The 1st Duke deceived the French commanders most notably at Blenheim and Ramillies; the later Churchill successfully bluffed the German leaders after the defeat of the British and French armies in 1940.

Stanley Baldwin, perhaps the shrewdest prime minister of the years between the wars, remarked of Churchill that at his birth a

Fig. 4.1 Winston Churchill (1874–1965), by Ambrose McEvoy, in 1911, as he appeared in his time as First Lord. Is the mercurial temperament of the sitter suggested by the style of the painting? *(By courtesy of the National Portrait Gallery, London)*

good fairy had showered on him a profusion of gifts – among them, robust health, an active and questing mind, oratorical and literary powers, a capacity for sustained hard work and a devoted wife. A bad fairy had, however, seen to it that he was denied the gifts of wisdom and good judgement. Churchill was relegated to a marginal position during the years of his maturity, and came to the fore only when the country was in a desperate state. It was Churchill's misfortune that he took charge of the conduct of affairs at the time of the final decline of the British Empire, whereas the 1st Duke took control when the first British Empire was about to develop. The 1st Duke may indeed have been the shrewder man.

Lord Randolph Churchill attained prominence early, when he was appointed Chancellor of the Exchequer in Salisbury's administration of 1886. The prominence was of short duration: at the end of the year Lord Randolph rashly resigned, believing that the prime minister would not be able to find anyone to fill his place. Perhaps Churchill's judgement was even then impaired by the neurological disorder that disabled and eventually killed him: the calculation proved wrong, though it was at the time a near-run thing. This episode marked the end of Lord Randolph's political career, and surely made a deep impression on his elder son, who greatly admired his father and longed to emulate him. In the event, of course, he did very much better, but evidently the father's belief in 'Tory Democracy' persisted in the son.

Lord Randolph rashly resigned . . .

After bad experiences, only too common at the time at preparatory or private schools, Winston Churchill was sent to Harrow, a boys' school in the suburbs north-west of London. His account of his lack of academic progress there makes agreeable reading. Indeed, the education offered at that time and for the next fifty years to the upper classes at similar and even at better public schools was hardly calculated to prepare youths for careers other than in the Army, the Church, teaching and politics. These schools had their origin in royal, religious and secular foundations for the production of clerks able to read and write and conduct business for the illiterate ruling class. Later, members of the ruling class began to send their sons to such institutions to gain an education appropriate to the estate of a gentleman; with the development of the middle class in the nineteenth century prosperous merchants too began to send their sons to these schools. New schools modelled on the same pattern were founded to cater for this demand. In such academies there was for most students a heavy emphasis on the Classics, which were generally taught in an unimaginative manner: it was common practice to require pupils to convert English poetry into Latin verse of correct metre and to read versions of the Greek playwrights from which all material thought offensive had been removed, irrespective of its importance or relevance. The teaching of science was rudimentary; modern languages were taught in such

There was for most students a heavy emphasis on the Classics

a manner that few pupils emerged able to converse in any foreign language – even in French or German.

These defects of education were not important for youths who were destined to step into great fortunes and great estates or for whom arrangements had been made to be 'the next Prime Minister but three', but they must greatly have impaired the effectiveness of those less fortunately situated. The toughest and best persevered to rise to eminence in politics, the Army, the professions, the arts and even in the sciences, but many must have declined into lives of mediocrity. The education formerly provided by the public schools of Britain may have played a part in the long slow decline in the quality of industrial leadership and management: many entrepreneurs, enriched by their own exertions, sought to obtain gentility for their offspring by entering them at the major public schools. Unfortunately, neither then nor now did or does the education provided by the State regularly offer any compensating advantages: enterprise and originality can as easily be suppressed in a State institution as in a privately run one.

The public schools of Britain may have played a part in the long, slow decline . . .

It was Churchill's good fortune that his gaze was fixed on a career in the Army, so that he was after three years taken out of the main educational stream and put into the 'Army Class'. He brought one priceless asset away from Harrow: the ability to write English correctly, fluently and lucidly. He was generous enough to give the credit for this gift to his instructor, but inborn ability must have been chiefly responsible. Evelyn Waugh puts into the mouth of one of his characters the view that Churchill was a 'master of sham Augustan prose', but the verdict of posterity must surely be more generous than that. Churchill writes magnificently and persuasively: the reader has to beware of the latter facility, because by its use the author can, like a conjurer, deceive. Winston Churchill crowned his career at Harrow with triumphs in swimming and in the martial arts, but throughout he was obviously a persistent nuisance to authority. He was later to be a persistent nuisance in the Army, pestering his superiors in order to be involved in action, and enlisting the aid of persons of influence in Society to further that endeavour. He was indeed able to gain first-hand experience of war in Cuba, India, the Sudan and South Africa, behaving with conspicuous bravery and finding time to write admirable accounts of the campaigns and of his own part in them in particular. He obviously refused to be suppressed, and then and later the country had cause to be grateful for that characteristic.

He was later to be a persistent nuisance in the Army

Churchill entered Parliament in 1902 in the Conservative interest, but very soon was at odds with the Party leaders over the matter of Tariff Reform. He left the Party in 1904 to join the Liberals, and so was in position in 1906 to join the Liberal Government as Under Secretary of State for the Colonies. He was later transferred to the Home Office: even there, Churchill's enthusiasm for action found

Fig. 4.2 Churchill harangues a wartime audience. The officers in the foreground seem unappreciative. (*Hulton-Deutsch Collection/Corbis HU045874*)

expression in participation in the then-celebrated 'Sidney Street Siege', in which armed police attempted to arrest a gang of anarchists. That enthusiasm found a less agreeable outlet in the enlistment of the Army for help in dealing with striking coal miners. Even in these civilian posts, Churchill's interest in war and in the preparations for war was not abated; indeed, it would have been almost culpable in him to lose interest at a time when the requirements of national security were in sharp conflict with those of social reform. In alliance with Lloyd George, then at the Treasury, Churchill withstood the demands of the Admiralty, led by Reginald McKenna, for the construction of additional Dreadnought battleships to counter the German threat.

Although Churchill represented the change as having been dictated by the need to form a Naval Staff and a Naval War Plan, and precipitated by the disastrous showing of the Admiralty at a meeting of the Committee of Imperial Defence, it is possible that his move in 1911 from the Home Office to the Admiralty was a shrewd stroke by Prime Minister Asquith, designed to bring a poacher on to the side of the gamekeepers. Or, it may simply have been done to appease the radical wing of the Liberal Party, led by

Overleaf: Fig. 4.3 The 2nd Battle Squadron at sea. These were the ships completed in 1912 and 1913, of which *Audacious* had been one. (*Royal Naval Museum*)

Once in the Admiralty, Churchill became even more enthusiastic for naval expansion than his predecessor

Lloyd George: the appointment of one who had argued so strongly against expenditure on the Navy may have given the impression that this policy was to be followed. Once in the Admiralty, Churchill became even more enthusiastic for naval expansion than his predecessor had been. *(Fig 4.3)*

First Lord of the Admiralty

Churchill's tenure of office at the Admiralty was long remembered; indeed, when early in the Second World War a reluctant King and prime minister brought the still turbulent 65-year-old back into government, the Admiralty signalled all ships and shore establishments 'Winston is back'. There were difficulties: admirals resented Winston's tendency to listen to junior officers and himself to direct naval operations; his interference in the conduct of operations was notorious. Indeed, such interference in the Mediterranean in 1914 may have contributed to the escape to Constantinople of the German battlecruiser *Göben* and her attendant light cruiser *Breslau*. Of lesser importance, but characteristic of the man, was Churchill's running contest with King George V over the names selected for new battleships. The King, not unnaturally, thought that he should have a commanding voice in this process, and took particular objection to the proposal that a ship should be named *Oliver Cromwell*. Since the first English dictator had had a hand in the judicial murder of his ancestor, the King's reluctance was understandable. A lighter note entered the discussion with Churchill's proposal that a ship should be named *Pitt*: the King, having served in the Navy and knowing the sailor's tendency to produce and use derisive variants of ships' names, saw clearly the possibilities for rhyming slang here, and vetoed the suggestion. Showing a rare lack of appreciation of the humour of the situation, Churchill pompously protested that the King's reasoning was beneath the royal dignity.

He let it be known that his purpose was to make the Navy ready for war at the shortest possible notice

But Churchill's interest in and his enthusiasm and genuine feeling for the Navy surely excuse much. He took the steps necessary for the formation of a Naval War Staff; he let it be known that his purpose was to make the Navy ready for war at the shortest possible notice; he had a hand in the design and construction of the Queen Elizabeths, the finest Dreadnought battleships at the time and for many years afterwards; it was during his administration that the steps were taken that led to the introduction of oil as fuel for the big ships of the Royal Navy, and to the arrangements for its supply and storage.

Fisher was of course delighted by the prospect of replacing coal by oil, and took an important part in the development of sources and the creation of reserves. He may even have had a glimpse of the principles of the supply train and the strategic stationing of oilers for replenishment in case of war. It now seems odd that Churchill's agile mind did not light upon what was to be a serious strategic defect of the Navy, particularly in the Second World War – namely, the absence of a fleet train to sustain the fighting ships and supply them with provisions, fuel and ammunition. It was perhaps the ready availability in 1914 of overseas stations that led to neglect of this vital consideration. A.G. Macdonell, himself a Scot, put it well in 1933: '. . . in the days of coal, every coaling station was English; (that) in the days of oil, the only oil wells that did not already belong to people who selfishly wanted to keep them for themselves, became English . . .'

At the start of Churchill's work at the Admiralty his First Sea Lord was Admiral Sir Arthur Wilson, a 'salt-horse' of the most traditional type, thoroughly well versed in all aspects of his profession, hard-working, apparently impervious to wind and weather, and much admired by officers and men. Wilson was, however, wholly opposed to the formation of a Naval War Staff, and because of that was obliged to give way to a more compliant officer. Even then, Churchill was thinking of bringing Fisher back as First Sea Lord, but evidently he did not at that time feel sufficiently secure to take this bold step. He did, however, come to rely extensively on Fisher's comment and advice, tendered in conversations and correspondence. Admiral Sir Francis Bridgeman was appointed to the post, but did not last long: it is likely that he showed his disapproval of what he saw as Churchill's interference with matters properly the concern of the Sea Lords. He may have resented the reliance, which could hardly have been kept entirely secret, on Fisher's advice. 'Ill-health' was given as the reason for his departure early in 1913. His successor was Admiral Prince Louis of Battenberg. This remarkable man, a scion of the ancient house of Hesse, was the grandson of Prince Alexander, known as 'Sandro', who, having married as was thought beneath him, was deprived of his royal title and obliged to assume the name of Battenberg. An early meeting with Queen Victoria's sailor son Alfred, later Duke of Edinburgh, implanted in Prince Louis the desire to join the Royal Navy: his career, at first beset by difficulties, was distinguished by thorough professionalism and efficiency. After bachelor days in which he distinguished himself as a *coureur* hardly inferior to the Prince of Wales, Prince Louis married in 1884 Princess Victoria of Hesse, the daughter of Victoria's third child.

Wilson was wholly opposed to the formation of a Naval War Staff

Prince Louis of Battenberg was certainly a very able man, and no one can rightly question his entire loyalty to his adopted country. It was his misfortune to come to head the Navy just at the time when war against his homeland was imminent. When in the early months of 1914 the Navy ran into disasters, the suggestion by rumour and articles in the Press that these arose from having a 'German' in charge of the Navy proved too strong for the Government to resist, and led to Prince Louis's resignation. This was a hard blow to the man and to the country; it may, however, have contributed to the determination of Prince Louis's younger son, the future Lord Mountbatten, to vindicate by his own renown the reputation of his father.

The period of Churchill's rule at the Admiralty from 1911 to August 1914 produced important additions to Fisher's reforms. The greatest stroke was no doubt the formation of a Naval War Staff and the planning that flowed from that, though the amount of time granted to this body was insufficient to permit the development of a strategy beyond one simply of containment. The enemy was always going to be Germany, and dispositions had to be made accordingly. The concentration of the best units in the North Sea had been begun by Fisher, and was of course continued. The submarine and the torpedo had made obsolete the policy of close blockade of the enemy ports; for it was substituted that of remote blockade, with the Fleet based principally at Scapa Flow, with additional anchorages and port facilities at Invergordon, Rosyth, the Tyne and the Humber. The light forces were based at Harwich, and a force of pre-Dreadnought battleships was maintained in the Thames estuary. Churchill's vigilance produced important improvements in the pay and conditions of the lower deck; the attempt was also made to make easier the transition to commissioned rank and to improve the prospects of officers who had 'come aft through the hawse-hole'.

The concentration of the best units in the North Sea had been begun by Fisher

The Queen Elizabeths

A very important achievement was the formation of the 'fast division' of battleships (the 'Queen Elizabeths') *(Figs 4.4–4.6)*. The consequences of that step were, in effect, the substitution of oil for coal as the Navy's prime mover, and the development of Britain's oil industry. They were the last great ships designed by Sir Philip Watts, the Director of Naval Construction, who retired in 1912. They were completed during the tenure of office of his successor, Sir Eustace Tennyson-d'Eyncourt. Watts and Churchill had, perhaps, perceived the fearful defect of Fisher's battlecruisers: their speed and firepower gave them great advantages in attack, but the sacrifice of protection in the search for speed made them very vulnerable to fire from heavy guns. They sought to develop a ship which would combine high speed with heavy protection and formidable hitting power. The resulting five ships of the 1912 programme were destined to be famous in the Fleet during both world wars; they were among the most successful battleships ever built for any navy.

Watts and Churchill had perceived the fearful defect of Fisher's battlecruisers

The five Queen Elizabeths each mounted eight of the then new 15-inch (38-cm), 42 calibre guns, disposed along the centreline in four turrets and firing a broadside of 16,000 pounds. The maximum thickness of the armour belt was 13 inches (33 cm). Turbines driving four shafts produced an estimated 75,000 horsepower and gave a speed of 24–5 knots. The 1914 Jane's *All*

Fig. 4.4 to 4.6 The Queen Elizabeths. All five of these ships were well-armoured and had an armament of eight 15-inch guns, all mounted on the centre line. Speed was said to be 25 knots, but this was probably an overestimate. The *Queen Elizabeth*, *Valiant*, and *Warspite* were virtually re-built in the 1930s; the *Malaya* and *Barham* underwent a rather lesser reconstruction.

Fig. 4.4 The *Queen Elizabeth* on her way down the Channel in 1915, on the way to the Dardanelles, where she was to fire her main armament against the Turkish positions. (*Painting by Charles Dixon, 1915, in the author's possession*)

Fig. 4.5 HMS *Malaya* at Cowes in the 1930s. She had by then been much modified and had her protection increased. Note the anti-torpedo 'blisters'. She ended up at the end of the Second World War as a target for torpedoes in Loch Long. (*Author's collection*)

the World's Fighting Ships gives a horsepower of 58,000, but that was clearly a deliberate understatement. The boilers were oil-fired: that gave a better power/weight ratio than did coal firing; the advantage over coal in refuelling was tremendous; the back- and heart-breaking task of 'coaling ship' was no longer necessary; the dreadful labour of stoking coal-fired boilers and of shovelling coal from one bunker to another was removed. Oil offered too, the

Fig. 4.6 HMS *Warspite*. She had the most adventurous career of the Queen Elizabeths. In the Second World War she intervened in Norwegian waters and in the Mediterranean, and at the end avoided the breakers at Faslane by going aground in Mounts Bay. (*Royal Naval Museum*)

convenience of refuelling of ships at sea, but it was long before the Royal Navy took full advantage of this.

It was a bold decision to rely on oil as fuel for these large and important ships: previously, only the smaller ships of the Royal Navy had depended on this source of energy, which was then unobtainable in Britain or in home waters. It was to meet this need that a Royal Commission on Oil Supply headed by Fisher worked to secure the

It was a bold decision to rely on oil

sources and transport of oil and to make arrangements for its storage. The Anglo-Persian Oil Company, later British Petroleum, was one of the results of this work. Churchill presents the arrangements for transport and storage as standing the tests of war. So they did, but in fact stocks of oil ran dangerously short during both world wars, and the cost of transport in lives and *matériel* was fearful. Certainly, though, a Navy wholly dependent on coal-fired ships could not easily have survived either war. It was bold, too, to place so much reliance on the 15-inch (38-cm) gun, which represented a large step forward from the 13.5-inch (34-cm) gun, then the standard armament of the most advanced British battleships. The performance of the new gun in practice and later in battle was fully to justify the confidence of Churchill and his advisers among the British armourers.

It is, or was then, necessary for departmental ministers to maintain their positions in Cabinet and Parliament by retaining touch with affairs outside their departments. Churchill, as First Lord, was in the position of having to make large demands for money while remaining a member of a government dedicated to disarmament and social reform. He therefore sought to limit the naval rivalry between Britain and Germany and so to lessen his department's demands on the Treasury. At the same time, Asquith's Government was moving towards a solution of the long-running problem of the government of Ireland by introducing Home Rule. That proposal of course aroused the deep hostility of the Protestants of Northern Ireland and by 1914 had led almost to civil war. Early in his tenure of office, Churchill thought it necessary in support of his position to brave the anger of the people of Belfast by speaking there in favour of Home Rule. It is possible that a little later, when civil war seemed more than likely, he would have been willing to use a battle squadron to cow the 'loyalists' of Belfast. The Irish problem was to prove as intractable as that of friendship with Germany, and indeed remains so to this day. The necessities of war obliged the government to postpone its scheme for Home Rule; in the event, that postponement became indefinite, and the failure became the cause of slaughter as yet immeasurable.

The Irish problem was to prove as intractable as that of friendship with Germany

The introduction of the German Navy Law of 1912 effectively dashed British hopes of coming to an understanding about restriction of naval armaments, though attempts were made through intermediaries to come to an agreement. Sir Ernest Cassel, then aged 60, had been born to a Jewish family in Köln and after a stint with the bankers Eltzbacher had worked in England for a year, moving to Paris in 1870. Obliged to leave France because of the onset of the Franco-Prussian War, he moved back to England to start work with the financial house of Bischoffsheim and Goldschmidt and there to lay the foundations of an enormous fortune and to take British nationality in 1878. Cassel's wealth and financial acumen, his contributions to worthy causes and his interest in horse-racing brought acquaintance with the Prince of Wales and his circle and with the ruling class. Cassel's familiarity with the German language and his acquaintance with the Jewish head of the Hamburg-Amerika shipping line, Albert Ballin, made him an obvious choice as an emissary to discuss the naval rivalry with Ballin and the German Chancellor and Kaiser. Cassel's reception in Germany was cordial, and in February 1912 R.B. Haldane, the Germanophile Secretary for War and an alumnus of the University of Göttingen, visited Germany for further discussions with the Chancellor and Kaiser.

The negotiations were not helped by the publication in Germany, on the day after Haldane's arrival in Berlin, of a report of a speech made in Glasgow by Winston Churchill, in which the First Lord characterised the German Fleet as being in the nature of a luxury. The Germans, the Kaiser and von Tirpitz in particular, did not appreciate having their hard-won Fleet being described as a '*Luxus-Flotte*'. Partly because of this, and partly because of disagreement on the question of Britain's neutrality in the event of Germany becoming involved in war, the Haldane mission failed in its main purpose – namely, a reduction in the pace of German naval construction. Nevertheless, Haldane was given a copy of the draft of the Supplementary Navy Law, which provided for, *inter alia*, a fleet flagship and five squadrons each of eight battleships. At this remove one wonders whether Churchill was so naïf in the matter of the Glasgow speech as he represents: it was, after all, ultimately in his interests to provoke the Germans so as to bolster his own plans for naval expansion. Hopes for limitation of armaments were in the event proved vain, and from this time both sides went forward with preparations for the coming deadly clash. It is interesting to observe that Cassel's contributions to his adopted country included the provision of a grand-daughter who, as Lady Louis (and later Countess) Mountbatten, did no mean service to the nation and the world and, it is said, to a number of gentlemen too.

Churchill's fall

For Churchill, as for Fisher, the war was to bring triumph and disaster and, as did not happen to the Admiral, success at the last. The failure in 1915 of the ill-planned Dardanelles expedition gave to Churchill's enemies the ammunition for which they had been waiting, and in May he was obliged to leave the Admiralty with criticisms by his former colleagues ringing sharply behind his back. After service on the Western Front, he was brought back by Lloyd George and given the important post of Minister of Munitions, but he was to wait more than twenty years for his greatest triumph. Churchill's successor at the Admiralty was the former Prime Minister, Arthur Balfour, whose distinguished presence in the Cabinet was no doubt desired by

The failure of the . . . Dardanelles expedition gave Churchill's enemies the ammunition for which they had been waiting

Asquith. Balfour, raised to the peerage in 1922, brought to the office a fine mind, an imperturbable personality and great personal courage, but not Churchill's energy or inspiration. During his term of office Gallipoli was evacuated and Jutland was fought and the German submarine campaign was re-activated. Balfour's distinction of character and habit of authority evidently made him an admirable chairman of committees and expeditor of business, but he was not a great initiator and he certainly lacked Churchill's dynamism.

The question of Fisher's successor had indeed been difficult

Churchill, falling, took Fisher with him. It seemed plain that the Admiral was no longer up to the demands of the post of First Sea Lord: his eccentric behaviour over the Gallipoli crisis cast doubts on his mental stability, and he was allowed to go. However, Fisher's departure in this fashion did not prevent Churchill from proposing, in a debate in the Commons in 1916, that the old Admiral should be reinstated. Balfour had little difficulty in disposing of this suggestion. The question of Fisher's successor had indeed been difficult: the two obvious choices, Jellicoe and Beatty, were doing jobs from which they could not be spared. The choice, perhaps influenced by Balfour, fell on Sir Henry Jackson, then aged 61. Jackson, who entered the Navy at the age of thirteen, was perhaps a scientist *manqué*: at the age of thirty he developed an interest in wireless telegraphy and in the use of the coherer for the reception of electro-magnetic radiation. A year later he met Marconi, and with him went on to improve the techniques and extend the use of wireless telegraphy in the Navy. Jackson's work was recognised in 1901 by his election to fellowship of the Royal Society, and a year later he published in the Proceedings his most notable paper, 'On some phenomena affecting the transmission of electric waves over the surface of the sea and earth'. Jackson's only important sea-going appointment was in command of the Third Cruiser Squadron in the Mediterranean in 1908, after which he took on the direction of the newly created Naval War College at Portsmouth. The intellectual Balfour may have found or expected to find a congenial collaborator in Jackson, a man whose career had been dedicated to exploration of new ideas and new techniques in naval warfare, and who was among admirals of the day the furthest removed from the conventional 'salt-horse'. There was little enthusiasm in the Admiralty or Fleet for the combination of 'philosopher and scientist', however, and it seems clear that neither benefited from it. So it was that the Navy faced its greatest test under the leadership of two men whose personalities were wildly different from those of the two who had prepared it for war. Jackson was succeeded at the Admiralty in December 1916 by Jellicoe, but the Balfour/ Jellicoe combination was short-lived, being terminated by Balfour's departure for the Foreign Office at the time of the fall of Asquith's administration.

CHAPTER FIVE

THE GERMAN REACTION

The growth at the end of the nineteenth and beginning of the twentieth century of Germany's foreign trade, most of which was seaborne, and the development of the German overseas empire, clearly indicated to its government the need for protection by a High Sea Fleet. The earliest German venture on to the high seas had been that of the Hanseatic League in the fourteenth century. The League's enlargement was necessarily accompanied by the deployment of naval and military forces. Its decline began with the migration of the herring shoals of the Baltic to the North Sea, and by the time of the Thirty Years' War Lübeck, Bremen and Hamburg were the only constituents. At the time of the Thirty Years' War the question of a revival of German power on the sea was again raised, and indeed the Bohemian power-broker Wallenstein styled himself 'General of the Ocean and Baltic Sea'. His hopes of making headway against the Danes and the Swedes remained illusory. Friedrich-Wilhelm, the 'Great Elector' of Brandenburg and the originator of Prussian hegemony in Germany, encouraged German seafaring during his reign from 1640 to 1688. A hundred years later Friedrich II, King of Prussia (Frederick the Great), evidently thought about extending Prussian power to the high seas.

It was Napoleon's activities that later gave justification for such thoughts: during the time of the blockade of Europe and Prussia's forced alliance with Imperial France, Prussian ships became the easy prey of the British Fleet. The lesson was not lost on leaders such as Gneisenau, but it was not until 1848 that a start was made on the development of a German Fleet, based at Bremerhaven. The rise of Prussia led in 1853 to the formation of a Prussian Fleet and the supersession of the original German force, but after the defeat of Austria and her allies nominal control reverted to the North German Federation. Wilhelmshaven, the naval base on the Jade, was opened in 1869. When, after the defeat of France in 1871, the German states were finally united and the Second Empire was proclaimed, the Imperial Navy succeeded to a well-prepared inheritance. By 1906 Germany possessed twenty battleships of over 10,000 tons, mostly armed with 11-inch (28-cm) guns and heavily protected (*Fig 5.1*).

The defeat of Denmark in 1864 placed in German hands the city of Kiel, with its excellent harbour, and the flat land intervening between the Elbe estuary and Kiel Fjord. The completion in 1895 of the 'Kiel' or 'Nord-Ostsee' or 'Kaiser Wilhelm' Canal gave Germany a protected passage for the largest battleships of the time between the North and Baltic Seas and between two of her principal ports. It was later to become vulnerable to attack from the air, but in the early part of the twentieth century it was virtually unassailable. It offered the German Fleet the opportunity to pass safely from a North Sea made dangerous by the presence of the British Fleet to its much safer training waters in the Baltic. The strategic advantage of this link can be compared with that which might have been offered to the British Fleet by a ship canal linking the Firths of the Forth and Clyde along the line of the present cut from Grangemouth to Clydebank.

The introduction . . . of the Dreadnought battleship came as no surprise to the German Government

Provocation from across the North Sea was not lacking. Fisher's succession to the office of First Sea Lord in 1904 brought the concentration of British naval power in home waters against Germany and signalled the continuation and intensification of the antagonism begun by the differences arising in the Boer War. German apprehensions were voiced by influential figures in Government and Press, and were shared by the general public. Scare stories about sudden, unprovoked attack were common to both countries: in this field the palm for literary merit went to Erskine Childers' *The Riddle of the Sands* (1903); that for imaginative writing to August Niemann's *Der Weltkrieg; Deutsche Träume*. Matters were not helped by tensions arising at King Edward's state visit to the Kiel egatta in 1904, and during the return visit of a German squadron to Plymouth two weeks later. Early in 1905 Arthur Lee, Civil Lord of the Admiralty in Balfour's government, went so far as to state publicly that in any war against Germany the Royal Navy 'would get its blow in first, before the other side had time even to read in the papers that war had been declared'. It is not surprising that the German people and their leaders were fearful of Britain's intentions; it is perhaps surprising that when, nine years later, the crisis arrived, the Germans appeared to discount the liklihood of British intervention. The launch of the Dreadnought marked a raising of the stakes.

The introduction by the Royal Navy of the Dreadnought battleship came as no surprise to the German Government: the principles underlying the construction of such ships had long been

* This figure is taken from Jane's *All the World's Fighting Ships*, 1914.

Fig. 5.1 The Second Squadron of the High Sea Fleet (pre-Dreadnoughts) puts to sea, led by SMS *Preussen* (1905). (*Corbis NA006884*)

canvassed; and similar steps were being taken by the American and Japanese navies. German engineering and shipbuilding firms were fully competent to produce their own Dreadnoughts. However, the larger ships posed difficulties for the Kiel Canal: the early ones had beams of 90 feet and drew 27 feet at full load, and the later ones were to have beams of up to 96 feet. This was too wide for the canal, and a start had to be made on enlarging it. Germany would not fully be ready for war until her Dreadnoughts could pass the Kiel Canal. That would be achieved in 1914. Germany's first Dreadnoughts, the *Nassau* and her three sisters, laid down in 1906 and 1907 and completed in 1909 and 1910, were ships of 19,000 tons powered by triple expansion reciprocating engines and fuelled mainly by coal. They were strongly protected: each mounted twelve 11-inch (28-cm), 45 calibre guns in six turrets, two on the centre line and two on each beam. It was not until 1908 that the Germans recognised the advantages of turbine propulsion for their large ships; and not until 1911 that they recognised the advantage of having all the turrets mounted on the centre line.

It was in their response to the Invincible class of battlecruiser that the German engineers and constructors showed their true mettle. Their first battlecruiser, *Von der Tann*, a ship of 20,000 tons completed in 1910, was powered by Parsons turbines giving at least

Fig. 5.2 SMS *Von der Tann*. Named after the Prussian general of the Franco-Prussian War, this very strong and well-armed vessel was the first large ship of the German Fleet to be powered by turbines. She stood up well to fire at Jutland. (*Royal Naval Museum*)

50,000 horsepower and 25 knots, with a 'best recent speed'* of 28.1 knots; there was an armour belt of 10 inches (25 cm) at its thickest, and there were 8 inches (20 cm) of armour on the turrets; eight 11-inch (28 cm), 45 calibre guns were carried in four turrets, two of which were on the centre line and one on either beam, and there was a secondary armament of ten 6-inch (15 cm) guns *(Fig 5.2)*. It was, for the German designers and builders, a triumph to have produced a ship so formidably armed and well protected, that could steam at 28 knots. Considerable care was taken to reduce weight, for instance by the use of small tube boilers; at the same time, minimal use was made of flammable materials such as wood. This ship and her even more formidable successors were to form the Scouting Group which, under the command of Admiral Franz Hipper, did so much damage to the British Fleet.

Alfred von Tirpitz, State Secretary at the German Ministry of Marine from 1897 to 1916 and the virtual creator of the Imperial Navy, had witnessed the impotence of the Prussian Navy at the time of the Franco-Prussian War, and was determined that imperial Germany should not suffer in the same way *(Fig 1.8)*. His methods and personality were to some extent similar to Fisher's: Tirpitz was intolerant of criticism, used propaganda to persuade the German taxpayer of the necessity for a strong Navy, and sought ceaselessly to increase and improve the *matériel*, methods and training of the Fleet. He had clear ideas about the role of the Navy in a war against England: the High Sea Fleet was to be strong enough to inflict on the Royal Navy damage sufficient to take from Britain her position as the strongest naval power in the world. This was the 'risk theory' or 'Risikogedanke' that underlay German preparations. In addition, Tirpitz, originally a torpedo specialist, developed Germany's force of submarines, provided escort vessels for the High Sea Fleet, and made preparations for attacks on commerce by cruiser squadrons, individual cruisers and armed merchant ships. These preparations were very thorough; one cannot help thinking that the same care must have gone into the planning for the employment of the Fleet.

By 1914 the German Fleet was composed of formidable vessels, had a highly efficient officer corps and excellent ratings and petty officers, was well drilled and had assigned to it a clear role in the event of war. It had in the Baltic a protected area of sea for manoeuvres, with a short route to the North Sea provided by the Kiel Canal. Even so, its officers and men never quite lost their feeling that the Royal Navy was superior, not only in size but also in construction and technique and in the operations of war. The High Command and even the Kaiser seem to have shared this view. Germans recalled the part played by the Royal Navy in the Napoleonic wars, noted the facility with which in 1854 it had penetrated Russian waters to land an expeditionary force in the Crimea, and remembered the command of the seas that had prevented interference from outside during the South African war. They saw the vast Fleet, with a tradition of victory, officered by men confident of their role and confident in the men they commanded, and manned by the hardy men of a seafaring race. Perhaps they thought about it as now, with much greater justification, we think about American power and as we used to think of Russian superiority. Yet the figures were there to show them that their ships were certainly the equal of and probably superior to those of the British. Their gunnery was supported by the best optical industry in Europe and probably in the world; their fleet was operating on interior lines of supply, from good harbours, well protected by the fortifications of the island of Helgoland. But Germany had no tradition of naval victory; only one of humiliation in the wars against Denmark and France. Her ally, Austro-Hungary, did indeed have a tradition of victory at sea derived from the famous encounter off Lissa, but the Austro-Hungarian fleet was needed in the Mediterranean to balance those of France and Italy. It was this feeling of inferiority that more than anything else confined the operations of the German surface fleet and eventually gave victory to the Royal Navy.

CHAPTER SIX

THE OUTBREAK OF WAR 1914

It is now customary to regard the First World War as 'the unnecessary war', though some have argued – not too convincingly – that the atrocities committed by the German Army in Belgium and France in 1914 contradicted that view. Most wars are indeed unnecessary, except for those few who profit from them. Very few had in 1914 realised, and few even now realise, that, in C.V. Wedgwood's words, 'war breeds only war'. On the other hand, it is hard to see how war could then have been avoided. France earnestly desired revenge for her defeat and the restitution of her provinces lost in 1870; Germany had prepared an unbeatable army and a formidable navy, and at that time generals and admirals often thought of war as the desirable culmination of their preparations. Three times in the last century Germany had, it seemed to her leaders, gained in power and prestige by short and decisive wars. The Slavic populations of the southern parts of the Austro-Hungarian Empire dreamed of liberation; Austro-Hungary desired the suppression of Serbian aspirations for pan-Slavic union; Russia looked for control of the Dardanelles as a warm-water outlet to world oceans; Britain looked with apprehension at growing German sea-power and industrial might. There were understandings between the German and Austro-Hungarian Governments and to a lesser extent between them and the Italian Government, while military conversations had taken place between the British and French General Staffs, and it was understood that in the event of war with Germany the British Fleet would assume the responsibility for the protection of the Channel and Atlantic coasts of France. Arrangements for mutual support in the event of war with Germany existed between the French and Russian

Governments. Although continental politicians and military leaders knew something of what modern war might mean, the effects of the newest and most frightful weapons were not known, nor was the impact of modern war on civilian populations recognised. Fisher had, indeed, advocated making war as frightful as possible, so that no one would be tempted to use it as an instrument of policy. No one else in authority took any notice. All thought that he was exaggerating; in the event, the reality proved much more frightful than the estimate. It was only much later that the theory of the 'deterrent' for the prevention of war was widely proclaimed.

Sarajevo

On 28 June 1914 the Austrian Archduke Franz Ferdinand, heir to the imperial throne and Inspector-General of the Austro-Hungarian armed forces, and his wife Sophie were murdered while on an official visit to Bosnia, annexed by Austria six years previously. They were being driven through the capital, Sarajevo, when Gavrilo Princip, a young pro-Serbian nationalist and member of the Black Hand secret society, shot them at point-blank range. The complicity of Serbia, and in particular of its Prime Minister Nicholas Pašić, was instantly and probably correctly assumed. Assured by Kaiser Wilhelm of Germany's support in 'punishing' Serbia, and contemplating the virtual abolition of Serbia as an independent state, the Austrian Government on 23 July demanded *inter alia* the right for Austro-Hungarian officers to collaborate in the suppression of subversive organisations in Serbia and the actual participation of Austrian representatives in judicial proceedings against the conspirators. The sanction of war was threatened, and the Serbian Government was given twenty-four hours in which to reply.

The Serbian Government was given 24 hours to reply

Pašić replied, just within the time limit, that the right of official Austrian participation in the investigation could not be conceded; he was evasive about four other demands, but agreed all the others. In our days we have seen just such Serbian responses to equivalent demands. We have seen too, similar claims for intervention in the trial of foreign nationals thought to have been implicated in acts of terrorism.

Confident of Germany's support and therefore discounting the certainty that action against Serbia would bring Russia into the field, the Austrian Government went forward with preparations for invasion. The near-certainty that the involvement of Russia in war would bring France into the field on her side seems also to have been discounted. Mobilisation began on 25 July. The aged Emperor, who had seen enough of disaster involving the Austrian army, is said to have commented: '*Also, doch*' (So, after all); the Hungarian Prime Minister was similarly unenthusiastic. Kaiser Wilhelm, observing the present and likely future effects of his support, swung rapidly to a more pacific posture. A major though not absolute constraint on the actions of the German Government was provided by uncertainty about Britain's attitude and actions in the event of war with France.

The British response

The British Foreign Secretary was Sir Edward Grey, a Wykehamist, who exhibited to an extraordinary degree the convolution of mental processes that was and remains a common characteristic of the alumni of Winchester College, William of Wykeham's famous foundation. Alongside Grey, von Holstein, until 1906 senior counsellor and *éminence grise* of the German Foreign Ministry, and Bethmann-Hollweg, until 1917 Chancellor, appear to be models of straightforwardness and clarity of thought. Indeed, many Britons to this day find it difficult to penetrate the meaning of Wykehamist utterances or to fathom their Byzantine modes of thought. We can see that it was too much to expect that simple German politicians would or could accomplish such a feat. Yet Grey would surely have been horrified by any suggestion that his conduct and utterances lacked frankness or that he practised dissimulation. Indeed, no one who has read *Fly Fishing* or seen the place on the Northumbrian hills above Fallodon where Grey sat to muse and watch the birds can doubt the man's sincerity. No one can read without pain the story of the progressive deterioration of his vision or the tragic account of the death of his beloved wife in an accident.

Grey would surely have been horrified by any suggestion that his conduct . . . lacked frankness

Yet Grey's agonised – and agonising – dissection of the events that led up to the declaration of war, and his examination of his speeches and actions during that time, reveal to us a mind delighting in complex analysis, and apparently unable to comprehend the springs of action of those with lesser intellects. He believed, for instance, that in invading Belgium, Germany had discounted the importance of British intervention, in the belief that they would win a decisive victory before British power could be mobilised effectively. Consequently, he dismissed the proposition that Germany would not have invaded if she had been certain that infringement of Belgian neutrality would bring Britain into the war against her. But of course, it did. The events of 1914 were to show that Germany's calculations, though not far off the mark, were fatally incorrect. Grey's Permanent Secretary, Sir Eyre Crowe, counselled a clear and early warning to Germany that, in any struggle between Germany on one hand and France and Russia on the other, she would find Britain against her. That counsel was rejected, yet not only was the intervention of Britain eventually Germany's nemesis, but it brought to the prescient Kaiser foreknowledge of that doom. Grey's later warning to Lichnowsky, the German Ambassador, came too late to do more than provoke the Kaiser into an outburst of fury against Britain: Grey was abused as a 'common cur', and 'mean and

Mephistophelean'. Even now, few would go so far in denigrating a Wykehamist; the Kaiser had, of course, had scant experience of dealing with products of the famous academy. As late as 1 August a telegram from Lichnowsky indicating a probability that Britain would remain neutral if France were not attacked brought from Wilhelm an exuberant and exaggeratedly joyful response which elicited from his generals a gasp of horror and disbelief. Austria declared war on Serbia on 28 July; Russia began mobilisation on the 29th; Germany declared war on Russia on 1 August; Belgium was invaded on the 3rd, making inevitable the involvement of France; Britain's ultimatum to Germany expired at midnight on 4 August, and most of Europe was at war.

The initial moves

All the combatant nations had made their preparations. Germany relied on the plan of General von Schlieffen, chief of the German General Staff from 1891 to 1906: the French Army was to be broken by a massive thrust through Belgium and Luxembourg by the major part of the German Army, while the Russian Armies were to be warded off by a fighting retreat, during which parts of East Prussia would temporarily be abandoned. Once France was subdued, the attention of the German Army would be turned to the Russian front. Twenty-six years later the Wehrmacht, having less to fear from Russia, would succeed with a rather similar plan.

British preparations were no less impressive. On 28 July the First Fleet was at Portland after a trial mobilisation. Churchill and Battenberg decided that it should go without delay to its war station in Scapa Flow, and accordingly the Fleet left Portland and steamed first south and then east up the Channel to pass the Straits of Dover during the hours of darkness. We have from Hilaire Belloc a view of this event observed by him from the *Nona*, off the coast of Devon: 'Like ghosts, like things themselves made of mist, there passed between me and the newly risen sun, a procession of great forms, all in line, hastening eastward. It was the Fleet recalled.' On hearing of Germany's declaration of war on Russia Churchill anticipated Cabinet approval in ordering the mobilisation of the whole Navy. The necessary though ruthless step was taken of superseding Sir George Callaghan, in command of the Grand Fleet and due to leave that post in October 1914, by his second in command, Sir John Jellicoe. The regular Army of seven divisions, though deficient in machine-guns, was very well trained and well equipped. Lord Kitchener, the most famous British soldier of the time, had been kept in England in order that, if war came, he might replace as Secretary for War Haldane, who was naturally distrusted by sections of the Press and public because he could read and speak German and knew Germany well.

British preparations were no less impressive

The events of the early part of the war took most participants by surprise. Most well-informed persons thought that hostilities would last a few months only: in fact, they were to last for four years. The German Army found the British Army a tougher opponent than had been expected, and underestimated its ability and that of the French Army to recover from the shattering blow of the retreat from Belgium and northern France: just when German success seemed assured, a decisive check was administered at the Marne. The large Russian Armies rolling forwards into East Prussia were decisively defeated at the battles of the Masurian Lakes. At sea, the instructions given to the commander of the British battlecruiser force in the Mediterranean envisaged the probability that the German battlecruiser *Göben* would attack the ships transporting the French forces from North Africa; instead, her commander Admiral Souchon took her to the Dardanelles and eventually to Constantinople and the Black Sea. His later actions contributed materially to bringing Turkey into the war on Germany's side. The decision by Rear-Admiral Troubridge, commanding a squadron of four armoured cruisers in the Adriatic, not to engage the *Göben* as she steamed east was perhaps to influence the tactical thinking of British commanders. Troubridge, who was later to prove that his decision did not originate in cowardice, was court-martialled on a charge of failing to engage an 'enemy then flying'; although he was acquitted, the episode was clearly a factor influencing decisions about engaging an enemy of superior force.

The decision . . . not to engage the Göben *was perhaps to influence the tactical thinking of the British commanders*

The Germans found the British Fleet vulnerable: von Müller's light cruiser *Emden* inflicted massive damage on British shipping in the Indian Ocean before she was destroyed; an inferior British cruiser force was sunk by von Spee's cruiser squadron off the coast of Chile; three British armoured cruisers were sunk by a single submarine in the waters between Harwich and the Dutch coast. British battlecruisers scored early successes against much weaker opponents: a home thrust into the Helgoland Bight sank three German cruisers and damaged three more, and the *Invincible* and *Inflexible* under Sturdee's command sank von Spee's armoured cruisers in the South Atlantic.

After the initial war of movement the Western (from the point of view of the Germans) Front stabilised into attrition by trench warfare; the Eastern Front too became stabilised; an attempt to give aid to Russia by forcing an entry to the Sea of Marmara and the Black Sea through the Dardanelles failed owing to lack of planning. At sea, the severity of the submarine war against Allied shipping was for a time mitigated by American anger at the loss of American lives in the torpedoing of the *Lusitania* of the Cunard Line off the southern coast of Ireland in May 1915 *(Figs 6.1 & 6.2)*. No combatant nation desired to offend the 'Great Neutral' more than was absolutely necessary. It was to be nearly two more years before German provocation and Mexican aspirations overcame Isolationist, anti-British and pro-German sentiment sufficiently to bring the United States into the War on the side of its hereditary for, the British Empire.

The British Government 1914–16

Fig. 6.1 Cunard liner *Lusitania*. The sister of the much longer lived *Mauretania*, she was driven by turbines and was capable of 26 knots. On 7 May 1915 she was torpedoed and sunk by U-20 (Kapitän-Leutnant Schwieger) while steaming at 18 knots off the Old Head of Kinsale on the last part of her voyage from New York to Liverpool. Over 1,200 lives were lost, including those of 128 American citizens. It has been surmised that she was carrying munitions not declared in the manifest. The sinking aroused great feeling against Germany not only in England but also in the United States, where it might have become a *casus belli*. *(Imperial War Museum: Q 43227)*

During, respectively, the first eight and the first nine months of the First and Second World Wars the ruling party continued in power in Britain, not reaching out to the opposition parties to form coalitions for the more effective conduct of affairs. In the later war it took the débâcle of the Norwegian campaign and the imminent prospect of further such disasters in France and the Netherlands to propel Winston Churchill into power in May 1940. He at once saw that the energies of the nation could not fully be mobilised under party government, and that members of the opposition parties ought to be included. Churchill's first Cabinet contained nineteen Conservative, eight Labour, three Liberal and five non-party ministers.

Herbert Asquith KC *(Fig 2.5)* took over in 1908 from Henry Campbell-Bannerman the leadership of the Liberal Party and the Premiership. He was, perhaps, one of the most gifted of the British prime ministers of the twentieth century, presiding over a government which introduced long-overdue measures of social reform, limiting the power of the House of Lords and tackling boldly the question of how Ireland should be ruled. It was his and the nation's misfortune that the German challenge came to disrupt

Overleaf: Fig. 6.2 The sinking of the *Lusitania*, May 1915. One of the mass graves of victims in Old Church Cemetery, near Cóbh (formerly Queenstown). *(Hulton-Deutsch Collection/Corbis HU040606)*

his plans for reform, and that he and other advocates of peace were obliged to prepare for a European war. When in 1914 the time for decision came, it was the Conservative Opposition that was to the fore in advocating a declaration of war on Germany, but even the ablest Conservative politicians – and there were many of them – were not formally invited to join the administration. That would, it seems, have been a step too far. With some prodding from Churchill, Asquith appointed the non-party Lord Kitchener as Secretary for War, but that was as far as he went.

It took the acute shortage of shells . . . to compel Asquith to seek an accommodation with the Conservatives

The events of 1914 were sufficiently catastrophic: the Russian Army suffered defeats that would have put a lesser nation out of the war; in the West, the German armies very nearly broke through to Paris and to early victory. It took the acute shortage of shells and the disaster of the attack on the Gallipoli peninsula of European Turkey in May 1915 to compel Asquith to seek an accommodation with the Conservatives, one of the conditions of which was the removal of Churchill. Even that was not enough: at the end of 1916 Asquith was replaced by David Lloyd George *(Fig 2.5)*, formerly one of the ablest advocates of social reform, and in war a strong and capable leader. In *Mein Kampf* Adolf Hitler, himself a veteran of the First World War, paid tribute to the 'Welshman's towering political capacity'. Sadly for humanity, he was well qualified to make such a judgement. In the event, Asquith's failure and Lloyd George's triumph were to lead to the virtual extinction of the Liberal Party and its replacement by Labour as the alternative to Conservatism.

In 1939 most Britons were resigned to the inevitability of war and to the prospect of a long hard slog, whereas in 1914 many Britons and many French and Germans looked forward to an early victory. Some of the ablest and best in Britain welcomed the prospect of war: Rupert Brooke thought of himself and others going to war as 'swimmers into cleanness leaping'. Keeping his illusions despite his experiences with the Royal Naval Brigade, he rejoiced in the prospect of going to fight near the antique battlefield of Troy. Sadly, he succumbed to septicaemia before he arrived there. In 1914 Lord Kitchener *(Fig 3.2)*, the veteran of Sudan, South Africa, Egypt and India, apprehended well the nature of the war to come, and almost alone among the leaders of the nation both foresaw and predicted that it would last for years and demand mobilisation of all the resources of the State. His comment was of course disregarded: it was one thing to lead the nation into a short and victorious war; quite another to lead it into a long and demanding conflict with an uncertain outcome. Now we can wonder whether Kitchener's prescience was after all so remarkable; whether other leading men foresaw the nature of the coming struggle and kept quiet for fear of discouraging others. Germany was, after all, a formidable power and was known to be so, and Austro-Hungary had never been a minor player. Of such miscalculations was courage made.

CHAPTER SEVEN

THE WAR AT SEA

Early in the war the Royal Navy was given a decisive advantage by the partial penetration of the German naval codes and cyphers. In September 1914 the German light cruiser *Magdeburg* was wrecked off Odensholm at the entrance to the Gulf of Finland in the Baltic, and a few hours later the Russians picked up the body of an under-officer of her crew holding cipher and signal books of the German Navy. Churchill says that he and the then First Sea Lord, Battenberg, 'received from the hands of [our] loyal allies these sea-stained, priceless documents'. The true story may be rather less picturesque: Warner tells us that 'The Russians set to work at breaking down the codes, and by November they were able to give information of importance to their naval allies'. In any case, the British were able to penetrate the German codes and ciphers as, very early on in the war, a number of codebooks fell into their possession. One contemporary account which was almost certainly apocryphal but achieved widespread circulation, possibly for the purposes of misleading German Intelligence, concerned the finding in 1915 of an intact German submarine, U31, washed ashore at Yarmouth with her crew dead aboard and her codebooks intact. For, earlier the same year, the British had obtained another important source of information about the movements of the German fleet: Captain Hall, Director of Naval Intelligence, placed radio direction-finding stations along the east coast which intercepted radio signals and thus enabled him to plot by cross-bearings the position of any German ship making a signal. In the early part of the war, certainly, radio signalling was used very freely, without much appreciation of how such a signal could betray the position of the ship making it. Had it not been for the foreknowledge of the movements of the German Fleet given by these intercepts, the Grand Fleet would have been hard put to arrange a meeting with it.

Fig. 7.1 HMS *Audacious* sinking, having hit a mine in the waters north of Ireland. The sinking was witnessed by the passengers and crew of the White Star liner *Olympic*, which attempted to take the stricken ship in tow. Censorship succeeded for a long time in keeping from the Germans definite intelligence of the loss of this important ship. (*Royal Naval Museum*)

The prime functions of the Royal Navy – the defence of the islands against invasion, the protection of shipping bound for and leaving Britain, the interception of war supplies bound for Germany and the containment of the German Fleet – were faithfully performed. The transport of the main Expeditionary Force and its equipment to France was not interrupted; later, men and equipment were brought safely to the bases from which the Dardanelles expedition was to proceed. Thoughtful and inquiring minds may have noticed the poor standard of British gunnery and the inferior destructive effect of the British 12-inch (30-cm) shell at the Falklands battle; they may have noticed too, the excellence of the German gunnery at Coronel and the stern resolve of the German crews in the Falklands encounter. The loss of the new battleship *Audacious* in October 1914 to a single mine or torpedo may have caused some to reflect on the soundness of British warship design and construction *(Fig 7.1)*. Very serious questions should have been asked about the efficiency of the battlecruisers' signalling after the errors during the action of December 1914 and the Dogger Bank action of January 1915, which will be discussed later. Neither Churchill nor Fisher was to have the experience of presiding at the Admiralty during the culminating battle of May 1916: both were obliged to leave during the crisis that followed the withdrawal from the Dardanelles in 1915.

Fig. 7.2 & 7.3 Scapa Flow. This splendid anchorage was and is protected by the tricky currents produced in the Pentland Firth by the tides running through the narrow strait.

Fig. 7.2 Light cruisers at anchor. (*Royal Naval Museum*)

The British Grand Fleet

Most of the units of the Grand Fleet that encountered the High Sea Fleet in May 1916 were in commission early in the war. In August 1914 Sir John Jellicoe commanded a fleet of twenty Dreadnought battleships and nine Dreadnought battlecruisers. By 1916 these were to be augmented by the five ships of the Queen Elizabeth class, by two ships of the later Royal Sovereign class and by three ships originally constructed for Brazil, Chile and Turkey respectively. About one-third of the battleships were armed with guns of 12-inch (30-cm) calibre; one-third with 13.5-inch (34-cm) guns and seven with 15-inch (38-cm) guns. The *Canada*, originally constructed for the Chilean Navy, was armed with 14-inch (35-cm) guns. The four most modern battlecruisers were armed with 13.5-inch guns; the other five with 12-inch guns. Scouting for this battlefleet were the older protected cruisers and the later light cruisers, faster but thinly armoured. Protecting it from submarine attack were numerous destroyers and submarines.

The main body of the fleet operated from Scapa Flow, the protected area of water in the Orkneys *(Figs 7.2 & 7.3)*. There were good anchorages in the Cromarty Firth at Invergordon, in the Firth of Forth at Rosyth and in the Humber: in May 1916 the battlecruisers were stationed at Rosyth *(Map 1)*. Alternative anchorages were available in Loch Ewe on the west coast of Scotland and of course at the great naval bases at Chatham, Portsmouth and Devonport.

The battle fleet was organised into six divisions, each of four ships, comprising the First, Second and Fourth Battle Squadrons. There were

Fig. 7.3 Battleship anchorage, Scapa Flow. (*Royal Naval Museum*)

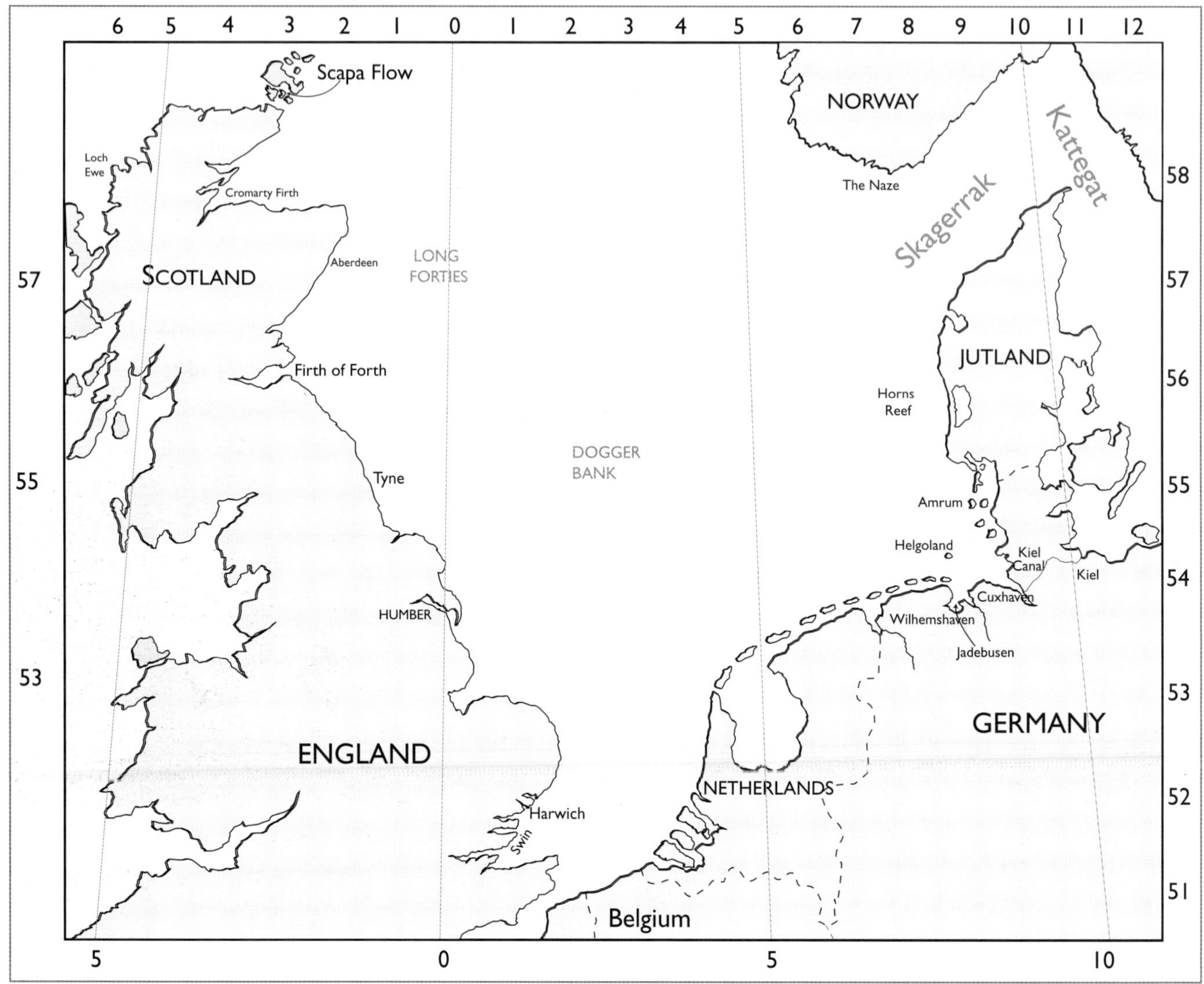

Map 1 The North Sea bases.

also the fast battleships of the Fifth Battle Squadron – the Queen Elizabeths (*Figs 4.4–4.6*) whose construction owed so much to Watts and Churchill. The battlecruiser fleet was organised into three squadrons, the first comprising the sister ships *Lion* and *Princess Royal* of 26,500 tons, the rather later *Queen Mary* of 27,000 tons and the much improved *Tiger* of 28,000 tons *(Figs 7.4–7.8)*. All were armed with eight 13.5-inch (34-cm) guns on the centre line; the armour protection of the first three was known to be defective. All could steam at over 30 knots. The second squadron comprised the second-generation ships *Indefatigable* and *New Zealand* which were later to be characterised by Hough as 'the worst ships built for the Royal Navy during the Fisher era' *(Fig 7.9)*. These 19,000-ton ships could steam at 28 knots and carried eight 50 calibre 12-inch (30-cm) guns. Their high freeboard and poor armour protection made them very vulnerable. The third squadron was composed of the three original battlecruisers, *Invincible*, *Inflexible* and *Indomitable*, each of 17,000 tons and carrying eight 45 calibre 12-inch (30-cm) guns. Battle was to show that these ships were no match for their German counterparts.

Fig. 7.4 HMS *Tiger*. The last and most satisfactory of the 'Cats'. Eight 13.5-inch guns in four turrets all on the centre line, well-disposed armour, 28 knots. (*Royal Naval Museum*)

Fig. 7.5 HMS *Tiger* entering Portsmouth Harbour. (*Painting by H.M. Swanwick, 1915, in the possession of the author*)

Fig. 7.6 HMS *Lion*, Admiral Beatty's flagship at Jutland. Here she is shown at the very end of her life, just before being broken up at a yard on the Tyne. (*Etching by Norman Wilkinson, 1924, in the possession of the author, reproduced by permission of Mr Rodney Wilkinson MC*)

Fig. 7.7 HMS *Lion*, Beatty's flagship at the Dogger Bank and Jutland. (*Royal Naval Museum*)

Fig. 7.8 HMS *Queen Mary*, the ship with the best gunnery record in the Battlecruiser Fleet. She was to be destroyed at Jutland by fire from the *Derfflinger*. (*Royal Naval Museum*)

Fig. 7.9 HMS *Indefatigable*. She, *New Zealand* and *Australia* were 'improved' versions of the *Invincible*. She was to be destroyed at Jutland by fire from the *Von der Tann*. (*Royal Naval Museum*)

The German High Sea Fleet

On 31 May 1916 Admiral Scheer had under his command a battlefleet of sixteen Dreadnoughts and six 'pre-Dreadnought' ships and a battlecruiser scouting force of five ships. The battleships were organised into three squadrons: two of eight ships each and one composed of the six pre-Dreadnoughts. The First Squadron was composed of four 20-knot ships (Westfalens), each mounting twelve 45 calibre, 11-inch (28-cm) guns, and four slightly later and faster ships (Helgolands), each mounting twelve 50 calibre, 12-inch (30-cm) guns. The Third Squadron included four 23-knot ships of 25,000 tons (Kaisers), each carrying ten 50 calibre, 12-inch guns, and four ships of over 25,000 tons (Königs), each mounting ten 12-inch guns on the centre line *(Figs 7.10–7.12)*. The last of these had been completed in 1915; their horsepower of 34,000 gave them speeds of over 22 knots. All the six pre-Dreadnoughts were formidable ships. Five of them had been completed between 1906 and 1908: each carried four 40 calibre, 12-inch (30-cm) guns; these ships of 13,000 tons were capable of 19 knots *(Fig 7.13)*. The sixth had been completed in 1905: her tonnage and armament were similar, but she could not manage more than 18 knots.

Fig. 7.10 & 7.11 SMS *König*. This strongly armoured ship, completed in October 1914, mounted ten 12-inch guns and could probably steam at 22 knots. She was heavily hit by fire from the Grand Fleet during the first encounter at Jutland. Surrendered on 21 November 1918, she was scuttled at Scapa on 21 June 1919, and was still on the bottom in 1986. She is shown at anchor (Fig 7.10) and at speed, from the air (Fig 7.11) *(Royal Naval Museum)*

The battlecruisers too were formidable ships: the latest two were almost certainly better than the *Tiger*, the best of the British ships of this class. The oldest, *Von der Tann*, was a very strong ship of 21,000 tons, armed with eight 45 calibre 11-inch (28-cm) guns and

Fig. 7.11 SMS *König*. (*Royal Naval Museum*)

Fig. 7.12 SMS *Friedrich der Grosse*. Scheer's flagship at Jutland, she was completed in August 1912, could probably steam at 24 knots, and was armed with ten 12-inch guns. (*Royal Naval Museum*)

Fig. 7.13 SMS *Hessen*. Completed in 1903, she was the oldest of Scheer's Second Battle Squadron: one of the 'Five-minute ships'. (*Royal Naval Museum*)

Previous pages: Fig. 7.14 SMS *Seydlitz*. Although capable of 29 knots and strongly protected, she was always an unlucky ship, sustaining at the Dogger Bank damage which could easily have been fatal, and very nearly being lost at Jutland. Note how closely placed are Caesar and Dora turrets. (*Royal Naval Museum*)

capable of 28 knots. The *Moltke*, a sister ship of the famous *Göben*, displaced 23,000 tons, mounted ten 50 calibre, 11-inch guns and was capable of 28 knots; the *Seydlitz*, at 25,000 tons, was similarly armed and slightly faster (*Fig 7.14*). The *Derfflinger* and *Lützow*, completed in 1912, were ships of 28,000 tons, carrying eight 50 calibre, 12-inch (30-cm) guns on the centre line *(Fig 7.15)*. Both were capable of 29 knots.

Most of the men of the High Sea Fleet's heavy ships spent much more time ashore in barracks than did their opponents in the Grand Fleet. Scapa was of course a very different anchorage from Wilhelmshaven and Cuxhaven: in spite of all attempts to provide recreational facilities it remained a usually cheerless place. Yet the morale of the men of the Grand Fleet was clearly more robust than that of their opponents: there were serious disorders in the German Fleet in the summer of 1917, partly political in origin and derived from doubts about the conduct and progress of the war expressed by Erzberger, a leading member of the Centre Party in the Reichstag. These disorders were doubtless due too, to lack of sympathy between officers and men, to the rigorous style of German discipline and to the opportunities for subversion offered by life in barracks. In the last months of the war, when the British blockade had produced general demoralisation, morale declined catastrophically, discipline was lost and the symptoms of mutiny appeared.

Fig. 7.15 SMS *Derfflinger*. With the *Lützow*, Hipper's flagship, she was the strongest and best of the German battlecruisers, and did terrible damage to the British battlecruisers. Surrendered on 21 November 1918, she was scuttled at Scapa the following June, and was later raised and towed, bottom-up, to Faslane on the Gareloch for breaking up. (*Royal Naval Museum*)

CHAPTER EIGHT

THE SEA COMMANDERS

The British commanders

The British Commander in Chief, Sir John Jellicoe, was 56 at the time of the battle of Jutland *(Fig 8.1)*. He was the second son of J.H. Jellicoe, a captain in the service of the Royal Mail Steam Packet Company, and the former Lucy Keele, whose family had produced notable Navy officers. Jellicoe entered the Navy in 1872 through the cadet training ship *Britannia*, and was soon marked out as a promising officer. He continued to do well in sea-going appointments, and in 1884 came to the notice of the then Captain Fisher when appointed as a lieutenant to the *Excellent* gunnery school. He followed Fisher to the *Minotaur* as a staff officer, and after further sea-going appointments returned to the *Excellent*. In 1889 Fisher, then Director of Naval Ordnance, plucked Jellicoe from his ship and took him to the Admiralty to help in the expansion and modernisation of the Fleet. Further sea-going appointments in the Mediterranean Fleet followed, culminating in that of commander in the *Victoria*, flagship of Admiral Sir George Tryon. In 1893 the *Victoria* was rammed and sunk by the *Camperdown* in the course of a manoeuvre involving ships of each of two lines steaming parallel to the other, six cables (1,200 yards) apart, turning inwards. The turning circles of the ships were such that execution of the order was virtually certain to result in collision, but no officer in either ship had the hardihood to indicate as much to the Admiral. Almost all those who have served in any organisation know, often to their cost, how unwise it can be to suggest to a superior that he or she may be mistaken. Jellicoe, ill in the sick bay at the time, was lucky enough to survive, but 321 men including the Admiral were lost. Orders given in a ship at sea must almost always be obeyed without hesitation or demur; that is specially so in a ship of war and very particularly so on active service in wartime. Certainly, no officer nor rating obeying orders is likely officially to be blamed, even if the consequences are catastrophic. Sometimes, though, it is right to demur or even to disobey: Nelson disobeyed the order to break off action at Copenhagen in 1801 and emerged triumphant; Dalrymple-Hamilton technically disobeyed orders by reversing course during the final action against the *Bismarck* in 1941, and neither merited nor suffered blame. As Fisher said: 'Any fool can obey orders.' However, much knowledge and skill are needed to know when to question orders; much courage is required of him or her who does it. We do not know the effect of the destruction of the *Victoria* on Jellicoe's thinking about the delegation of authority.

Jellicoe had a further three years in the Mediterranean as commander of the flagship of Admiral Culme-Seymour. He was again at the centre of events as chief of staff to Admiral Seymour commanding the China Station: the Boxer rising of 1900 led to the siege of the foreign legations at Peking (Beijing) and to the despatch of an expeditionary force from Wei-hai-wei under his command. Jellicoe was seriously wounded while leading an attack, but survived and in 1902 was appointed naval assistant to the Controller at the Admiralty. It was during that appointment that he met and married Florence Cayzer, the second daughter of the shipping magnate. Fisher brought Jellicoe back to the Admiralty in 1904 as Director of Naval Ordnance, in which post he was concerned with the armament of ships and in particular with the planning and construction of the Dreadnoughts. It was during Jellicoe's term of office that control of naval ordnance was wrested from the War Office. A further sea-going appointment as a flag officer was followed by a return to the Admiralty in 1908 as Third Sea Lord, responsible for new construction at a critical time in the rivalry with Germany. Jellicoe was at sea again in 1910, as vice-admiral commanding the Atlantic Fleet and later in command of the second division of Dreadnoughts of the Home Fleet. He returned to the Admiralty in 1912 as Second Sea Lord, marked then as the future Commander in Chief of the Grand Fleet on the outbreak of war.

This small, modest, imperturbable and very brave man, known in the Fleet as

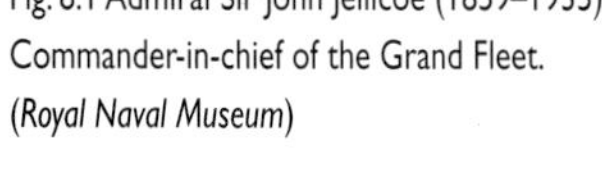

Fig. 8.1 Admiral Sir John Jellicoe (1859–1935), Commander-in-chief of the Grand Fleet. (*Royal Naval Museum*)

'Silent Jack', and much liked and respected by all ranks, was a master of his profession in technical knowledge, ability in handling ships and fleets, leadership and tactical and strategic thinking. *Si fractus illabatur orbis, impavidum ferient ruinae.** Jellicoe knew well the strengths and weaknesses of the force that he commanded and of the men who led it; he was fully aware of the burden that the Government and nation had placed upon his shoulders: it was no less than the security of the country and the choice between victory and defeat. If the Grand Fleet were lost, Britain would be isolated from her allies and sources of food and materials and open to an invasion which she could not hope to resist. Yet even before the war started, Jellicoe was deeply distrustful of the quality of British technology. Correlli Barnett quotes what he wrote on 14 July 1914: 'It is highly dangerous to consider that our ships as a whole are superior or even equal fighting machines.' Jellicoe had good reason: he had visited Germany in 1910 and 1913, and knew well the quality of the German officers and men and of the ships in which they served. Nevertheless, the test of battle was to show that, through the effort directed by Jellicoe, the morale of the men of the Grand Fleet had not adversely been affected by the twenty-two months of waiting for action.

Sir David Beatty

The admiral commanding the battlecruisers was a man of altogether different personality *(Fig 8.2)*. David Beatty was born in 1871, the second son of Captain Beatty of the 4th Hussars and the former Katherine Sadleir, daughter of Nicholas Sadleir of Dunboyne Castle, County Meath. The Beattys were of old Irish stock, with estates in County Wexford. The young Beatty entered the Navy in 1884 through the *Britannia*, where he did not do well, and went thence as a midshipman to the *Alexandra*, flagship of the Duke of Edinburgh, commanding the Mediterranean Fleet. His first great chance came in 1896, when the commander of the *Trafalgar*, in which Beatty was serving as a lieutenant, chose him as second in command of a small force of gunboats operating on the Nile in support of Kitchener's operations against the forces of the Mahdi in the Sudan. Colville, the commander of the force, was wounded in action against the Sudanese, and the command devolved on Beatty. He took three gunboats above the third cataract, and after continuing action was able to occupy Dongola and to pursue the rebel troops as far as the fourth cataract. For these actions Beatty was awarded the DSO. He greatly distinguished himself in further action against the Mahdists in 1897 and 1898, commanding a rocket battery ashore at the battle of Atbara and taking part in his

It was during this advance that his name came to the attention of the young Winston Churchill

* Were the world to fall to bits, its ruins would strike him unafraid.

Previous pages: Fig. 8.2 Man of power. Admiral Sir David Beatty (1871–1936), now Commander-in-Chief, on the quarter-deck of HMS *Queen Elizabeth*. (*Royal Naval Museum*)

ship in the advance to Omdurman. It was during this advance that his name came to the attention of the young Winston Churchill, then a lieutenant in the 4th Hussars attached to the 21st Lancers in Kitchener's army. These brave and successful actions brought Beatty special promotion to commander at the age of 27. They brought him too to the China Station as commander of the *Barfleur* at the time of the Boxer rebellion. He was involved in operations to rescue the expeditionary force commanded by Admiral Seymour, was wounded but was able later to command the naval detachment that finally extricated Seymour and his force. For these services he received special promotion to captain, at the age of 29.

While at home in the interval between the Egyptian and Chinese campaigns, Beatty had met Ethel, the wife of Arthur Tree and the daughter of the immensely rich Marshall Field of Chicago, a pioneer of the chainstore system. She was three years younger than he; evidently, the two were much attracted to each other. In 1901 Arthur Tree divorced his wife on the uncontested grounds of desertion, and soon afterwards she and Beatty were married by special licence. Beatty thus became financially independent, but he paid a price for that by committing himself to a woman who was, to say the least, demanding and who could and did sometimes make home life miserable for her husband. One may speculate on the extent to which these characteristics were a result or a cause of Beatty's affairs outside his marriage. Few who marry for money are so fortunate as was Disraeli with Mary Anne. The strong disapproval of Society might have been expected, because at that time divorce was viewed unfavourably, and to marry a divorcée might mean social suicide. Such rules were of course infinitely flexible when one of the parties concerned was very rich indeed, and in any case high society in England was at the time leaving behind the rigidities of the Victorian age for the more relaxed customs of a Court over which presided the genial figure of Edward VII. Even so, Ethel's presentation at Court was delayed until 1910.

Such rules were of course infinitely flexible when one of the parties was very rich indeed

Between 1902 and 1910 Beatty commanded in succession four cruisers and the *Queen*, a battleship completed in 1904. Although he had not completed the six years of service in captain's rank necessary for promotion to flag rank, he was in 1910 promoted rear-admiral by special Order in Council, at the age of 38. In 1911 Beatty took a step which could have been fatal to his career: he refused the offer of an appointment as second in command of the Atlantic Fleet. The rejection of this important appointment caused Beatty to miss the vital experience of handling a fleet at sea. He remained on half pay from 1910 to 1912, except for a period attending the Senior Officers' War Course at Portsmouth. It was lucky for Beatty that in 1911 Churchill went to the Admiralty to replace McKenna: the former recalled the young Beatty's exploits in the Sudan and, in conversation with him, was so much impressed by his quickness of thought and strategic insight that he appointed him as his 'Naval Secretary' at the Admiralty. Churchill and his advisers evidently realised that Beatty had had little or no experience of command of a fleet; accordingly, he was given command of a squadron of six old cruisers for the period of an exercise in the summer of 1912. Beatty evidently did well, for next year, when the command of the battlecruiser squadron fell vacant, Churchill appointed him, over the heads of many more senior and perhaps more suitable admirals, to this critical post. The squadron was later to become the battlecruiser fleet. In spite of the magnitude and importance of the appointment, Beatty does not seem to have been in any hurry to take it up – an oddly casual approach at so critical a time.

Fig. 8.3 Captain, later Rear-Admiral, Sir Robert Arbuthnot, commanding the First Cruiser Squadron, whose flagship *Defence* was destroyed by fire from *Derfflinger*. (*Royal Naval Museum*)

Churchill's selection of men was often at fault, as was seen in particular during the Second World War. He was less often at fault in perceiving failure and ejecting men who had or were likely to fail than in choosing men for high command. Thus, his love for the aggressive leader led him during the Second World War to appoint Admiral Sir Henry Harwood, the victor in the difficult action against the *Graf Spee*, to the Mediterranean command. He failed to appreciate the merits of Admiral Andrew Cunningham, whose command of the Mediterranean Fleet was very successful, and did all he could to prevent Cunningham becoming First Sea Lord. The Admiral's mistake was to fail to confine his aggressive instincts to action against the enemy: Churchill did not appreciate an admiral who was immune to his own aggression. The most notorious example of Churchill's hostility to men who not only had minds of their own but let him know it is provided by his attitude to Charles de Gaulle, the leader of the Free French during the Second World War and the leader of France after it. In picking Beatty for the very important appointment to command the battlecruisers, Churchill was obviously influenced by his memory of the Sudan campaign and by the young admiral's aggressive spirit and grasp of strategic principles. Indeed, the two had a good deal in common, and Beatty came from a class not far inferior to that to which Churchill belonged. Through his wife, he was of course much richer than was his political superior, though the poverty of which Churchill from time to time complained was, at the most, relative. Fisher's initial reaction to Beatty's elevation to flag rank may have been unfavourable. Filson Young describes an incident of the time when Beatty was Churchill's Naval Secretary. Mentioning and commending Admiral Beatty to Fisher, he received the answer: 'Really? Never met him.' Perhaps Fisher found something about the younger admiral that did not ring quite true?

Beatty's lack of experience in the command of fleets and his relative lack of interest in the technical side of his profession were clearly not overlooked, but evidently they were thought less important than his moral and inspirational qualities and his grasp of the problems of war. In the event, they were to lead to what might have been disaster. Those who worked with Beatty were devoted to him, and he was obviously popular with the men of the battlecruiser fleet *(Figs 8.3–8.5)*. Like other great leaders, he cultivated personal and sartorial characteristics to mark himself out as a leader. A photograph of Beatty with his aides shows him in the pose of the dashing admiral, with the monkey-jacket worn, in defiance of regulations, with three buttons, the cap with the enhanced peak worn tilted to the left, and the thrusting lower jaw. He looks like an actor playing the part of a dashing admiral, and beside him his companions look like bit-players. Twenty-four years later one of Britain's most successful soldiers, General Bernard Montgomery, helped his own personality cult by wearing, in defiance of regulations, two cap badges. It is curious how these small touches of insubordination do so much to attract the attention and even the admiration of those who, if they did the same, would firmly be told to get properly dressed.

Beatty, like almost everyone else, had his faults

Beatty, like almost everyone else, had his faults. He was clearly vain; he was a 'snob' in the sense that he liked to associate with people of aristocratic birth; he seduced or was seduced by the aristocratic wife of his aristocratic friend Godfrey-Faussett, an Equerry to three successive monarchs. Some thought of him as a cad or bounder; the more common view in the Navy was that he was a 'show-off'. It is indeed likely that, were any of us now to be afforded the privilege of meeting Nelson, he or she would think of him as a show-off and a 'bounder' or something even more impolite. In fact, many if not most of our great men have been endowed with exceptional sexual urges. Nelson himself seduced or was seduced by the wife of his good friend Sir William Hamilton. Others who come to mind are Charlemagne, Henry VIII, Henry of Navarre, Charles II, Louis XIV, Goethe, Byron, Simón Bolívar, David Lloyd George, Mao Tse Tung and J.F. Kennedy. Doubtless Second and Third XIs of scarcely less renown could readily be produced. It is not clear whether this sexual prowess reflects an innate characteristic of great men, an unusual range of opportunities, or simply the revelation by biographers of a talent not confined to famous men. Famous women do not seem regularly to share with men this characteristic: even her most dedicated detractors have not yet sought to impute to Florence Nightingale a sexual relationship with Sidney Herbert.

Beatty was superstitious to an extraordinary degree, sometimes basing important decisions on the predictions of a clairvoyant. On the other hand he was, in the early part of his career, remarkably lucky – though most of the luck deserted him in 1916. His extraordinary bravery was of course a quality shared with many other officers and men of the Fleet. Beatty showed evidence of courage of a different sort in tackling his professional superiors and political masters on matters concerning the Fleet and, later, the Navy. It is true that much later he was out-manoeuvred by Trenchard over naval aviation, to the lasting disadvantage of the Navy and the country, but he was then fighting an opponent far more ruthless and devious than he could ever be. He was, it appears, a good judge of men: he recognised that the dashing Keyes did not have too much in the way of brains, and that Burney, commanding the First Battle Squadron, was hardly an inspiring leader. Unfortunately, Beatty's judgement clearly failed him in his choice of Ralph Seymour, a well-connected and obviously likeable scion of the British nobility, as Flag Lieutenant – at that time, in effect, Signals Officer to the battlecruiser fleet. The effect of this misjudgement will be examined later.

Rear-Admiral Evan-Thomas

The third British leader to play a crucial part in the battle of May 1916 was Rear-Admiral Hugh Evan-Thomas *(Fig 3.2)*. He had started in the Navy as Hugh Thomas, but later extended that to Evan-Thomas when his father added his own father's first name to the surname. Evan-Thomas was in the *Britannia* in 1877 with Albert Victor ('Eddy') and George, the sons of Edward VII, and was regarded by them as a friend and mentor. He was with the princes and their tutor, Canon Dalton, in their training cruises in the old corvette *Bacchante* from 1879 to 1882. It appears that towards the end of the period Evan-Thomas showed Dalton letters written to him by his sister Catherine, and that this chance led later to her marriage with the Canon. From this union sprang the Hugh Dalton who was later to be Chancellor of the Exchequer in the Labour Government of 1945–50. Evan-Thomas's later appointments owed much to his Court connections: in 1892 he was taken from the flagship of the Mediterranean Fleet to become First Lieutenant of the *Melampus*, commanded by Prince George, by then Duke of York. *Melampus*, a handsome protected cruiser of 3,400 tons, completed in 1890, could steam at 19 knots and was a

Evan-Thomas's later appointments owed much to his Court connections

fitting command for a royal prince. In 1897 Evan-Thomas went to the Admiralty as secretary to the committee charged with revision of the Signal Book, and after this was appointed to take over the Signal School at Portsmouth. Here he was again at the centre of high social life, mixing with influential officers and their wives.

Fig. 8.4 Commander Sir Charles Blane, lost in the *Queen Mary* at Jutland. (*Royal Naval Museum*)

Evan-Thomas held commands in the Mediterranean and Channel Fleets, and in 1903 was appointed flag-captain to Lord Charles Beresford in the Channel Squadron. He secured the admiration and respect of Beresford, who was then approaching the climax of his struggle against Fisher. There followed a short period in command of the Admiralty yacht *Enchantress*, and three years as Naval Secretary to the First Lord of the Admiralty. In 1908 Evan-Thomas was appointed captain of the new Dreadnought *Bellerophon* in the Home Fleet, commanded by Sir William May. It was during that appointment that the *Bellerophon* was chosen to test Percy Scott's director-firing equipment: Evan-Thomas reported unfavourably on the system. He must have known that his commander May viewed the system unfavourably, and that the Director of Naval Ordnance shared this view. Scott's system was later shown conclusively to be the essential corollary to the standardisation of heavy armament in a ship. It was almost certainly the influence of the new King, George V, that brought Evan-Thomas to the command of the Royal Naval College at Dartmouth in 1910: the Princes Edward and Albert were being sent there to follow in the footsteps of their father. Promotion to rear-admiral followed in 1912, and, after a period as second in command of the Home Fleet's First Battle Squadron, Evan-Thomas was given command of the Fifth Battle Squadron, composed of the best ships in the Navy. This was a splendid command: the ships were new, they employed a system of propulsion relatively new in the Navy, they were the most heavily armed ships of the Fleet, and they represented a then unique combination of speed, protection and armament. Beatty evidently recognised their quality when he asked for the squadron to be permanently attached to the battlecruisers at

Rosyth. He even went to the Admiralty behind Jellicoe's back in trying to secure this augmentation of his force.

The relations between the commanders

Jellicoe, coming to the chief command in 1914, would not necessarily have had any say in the choice of Beatty to command the battlecruisers or that of Evan-Thomas to command the Fifth Battle Squadron. The latter had been known to him personally for many years, but Beatty would have been more of an unknown quantity, except in so far as Jellicoe would have known him as a rising star and as part of the extended family of the Navy. Jellicoe and Beatty evidently got on well together, though there were episodes when the former's patience was sorely tried, as for example in the matter of the transfer of the Fifth Battle Squadron to Rosyth and, later, in an episode during the battle of Jutland. Jellicoe must have admired the younger man for his actions in the Sudan and China, and for the manner in which he handled his command. He was, however, rightly critical of the standard of gunnery of the battlecruisers; in fact, the presence of the Fifth Battle Squadron at Rosyth at the end of May 1916 arose from the temporary withdrawal of Hood's Third Battlecruiser Squadron (the 'Invincibles') to Scapa Flow for gunnery practice. The more confined waters of the Firth of Forth and the potentially dangerous waters outside it severely restricted the opportunities for gunnery practice by the battlecruisers. Beatty, perhaps conscious that Jellicoe was riding him on a light rein, and certainly aware of and admiring the older man's record and deep professional competence, kept to himself any reservations he might have had about Jellicoe's qualities as a leader in battle. He may indeed have thought that the command of a battle fleet required of its commander qualities other than those required of the commander of a fast scouting force. Beatty was certainly aware that any overt criticism of his chief would almost certainly lead to the loss of his command, even though he had the ear of the First Lord and had by 1916 gained a place in the affections of the public as the

Fig. 8.5 Rear-Admiral Hon. H.L.A. Hood, commanding the Third Battlecruiser Squadron, who was lost with his flagship *Invincible*. (*Royal Naval Museum*)

Jellicoe's place was secure up to the time of Jutland

dashing leader of the battlecruisers. However, Jellicoe's place was secure up to the time of Jutland: there was no one else fitted to assume his terrific responsibilities. The singular story of Beatty's relations with Evan-Thomas will be examined later.

The German commanders

Reinhard Scheer, commander in chief of the High Sea Fleet, was born to middle-class parents in 1863 in Hesse-Nassau, in the heart of Germany and a long way from the sea *(Fig 8.6)*. His imagination was

Fig. 8.6 Vice-Admiral Reinhard Scheer (1866–1928), commanding the High Sea Fleet. *(Imperial War Museum: Q 20348)*

engaged by a book on the German Navy, and he entered the service at the age of 15, to rise to become Chief of Staff of the Fleet in 1909. At the outbreak of war he was in command of the Second Squadron, composed of pre-Dreadnought battleships. The Fleet had since February 1913 been commanded by Admiral von Ingenohl, who was in 1915 succeeded by Admiral von Pohl, largely because of the perceived failure at the Dogger Bank encounter. Von Pohl was even then suffering from the illness that was in January 1916 to enforce his resignation. Scheer succeeded him in command. His photographs show a rugged, determined face: one would not trifle with such a man. All his professional energy was committed to the struggle against 'England': Scheer advocated a ruthless assault by submarines on Britain's sea trade; he favoured a policy towards the Grand Fleet much more aggressive than that pursued by his predecessors, though he recognised that there was little likelihood of decisive victory in a battle against the whole of it. Rather, he seems to have had in mind the entrapment of detached squadrons of the Grand Fleet with the object of whittling away its superiority and rendering it vulnerable to rival naval powers such as Japan and the United States. There was, after all, considerable irritation in America at the British policy of blockade of Germany, and Japan could hardly continue indefinitely to accede to the promotion of British interests in the Pacific.

Scheer advocated a ruthless assault by submarine on Britain's sea trade

Well trained in seamanship and in the use of torpedoes by his service in torpedo-boats and in the handling of a squadron by his command of the pre-Dreadnoughts, Scheer was a very competent leader of the High Sea Fleet, well versed in its technicalities and in the principles of communication and manoeuvring; aggressive but careful. The man was as formidable as the force that he commanded; it is likely that, had his policy for the war at sea been earlier adopted, Britain would have been knocked out before it became convenient for America to intervene. In the event, political objections to unrestricted submarine warfare delayed its implementation until February 1917, by which time the intervention of the United States and the consequent defeat of Germany were inevitable.

Admiral Hipper

The commander of the scouting forces was Franz Hipper, born in 1863 in Weilheim, Upper Bavaria, to parents of the middle class *(Fig 8.7)*. Weilheim is far from the sea; Bavaria was at that time an independent kingdom distinctly hostile to Prussian ambitions. Indeed, it was in 1866 to go to war against Prussia as an ally of Austria and was itself to suffer defeat at the hands of the Prussians. Von Tirpitz was clearly right in saying 'The Navy is the melting-pot of the German people'. As a youth Hipper was, it seems, an avid reader of the novels of Frederick Marryat (Captain Marryat), who had served with the dashing Cochrane and had been admitted to the Royal

Fig. 8.7 Vice-Admiral Franz von Hipper (1863–1932), commanding the German Scouting Groups. (*Imperial War Museum: Q 20352*)

Society in recognition of his work on the compilation of a code of signals. Marryat left the Navy to write novels such as *The King's Own*, *Peter Simple* and *Mr Midshipman Easy*, which enjoyed a great vogue from the time of their publication to the present day. These evidently fired the young Hipper's imagination and turned his mind to the Navy. Inadvertently, Marryat nursed the pinion that impelled the steel: his disciple lived to do greatly for his country, to do great damage to the Royal Navy, and incidentally to be responsible for the death of Fleet Surgeon Norris, Marryat's grandson, lost with most of his shipmates in the *Indefatigable* sunk at Jutland. It does not seem that Hipper ever considered entering the Austrian Navy; rather, he joined in 1881 the Navy of the ten-year-old Second German Empire through the cadet school in Kiel. He had a record of a tendency to disregard regulations, but nevertheless made headway as a torpedo specialist and had a steady rise through service in cruisers to command in 1913 the splendid Scouting Force of the High Sea Fleet.

Hipper was a man of vigorous, possibly aggressive, temperament, occasionally abrasive in his intercourse with his fellow officers, but

Fig. 8.8 The destruction of the *Blücher* by gunfire at the Battle of the Dogger Bank in January 1915. The ship is on her beam ends, and men are clambering over her side in the desperate scramble to get clear. Attempts at rescue were interrupted by the appearance of a German airship. (*Corbis NA006784*)

well liked and generally lucky. Determined to strike home, he led the battlecruisers in an attack on Yarmouth in November 1914 and in another, on Hartlepool and Scarborough, in December of that year. Curiously enough, Osbert Sitwell's father, Sir George Sitwell, a near-contemporary of and an admirer of Kaiser Wilhelm, was at the time at his house in Scarborough and experienced the bombardment. A fragment of shell penetrated the front door and was retrieved by Lady Sitwell, who seized the opportunity to take it to Osbert, at the time about to depart for France, as a good luck token. Perhaps it worked? At any rate, Osbert survived the slaughter, to the enduring advantage of literature and art.

In January 1915, through superior British Intelligence, Hipper's force was caught by Beatty's battlecruisers in a raid on British patrols over the Dogger Bank. Hipper had – unwisely as it turned out – taken with his force of three battlecruisers the heavy cruiser *Blücher*, a ship of 15,500 tons armed with twelve 8.2-inch (20.5-cm) guns and capable of 25 knots, but insufficiently protected against shells of the heaviest calibre. Beatty, with five battlecruisers, engaged at long range. The *Blücher* was soon hit and slowed down, to become the object of target practice by four of the British battlecruisers *(Fig 8.8)*. Hipper did not hesitate to abandon her to her fate, and made his escape with his remaining ships. That was, indeed, the correct decision, for the *Seydlitz* had been badly damaged and might well have fallen victim too. The actions against ill-defended British ports occasioned civilian casualties, and gave the British Press the opportunity to characterise Hipper as 'the baby-killer'. Certainly, both the German commanders waged war in deadly earnest.

CHAPTER NINE

MATÉRIEL AND METHODS

The operation of the battlefleet of capital ships was, and perhaps still is, one of the chief functions of naval warfare. The qualities required of a capital ship of the time, and even perhaps of today, were and are protection, firepower and speed. Protection was *intrinsic*, in the construction of the ship, and *extrinsic*, by measures outside the ship, such as intelligence, escort and manoeuvring. It was directed against shellfire from surface ships, underwater attack and, late in the war, attack from the air.

Construction

A ship of the early twentieth century was protected by armour plating and by subdivision into watertight compartments. Armour plating was disposed so as to cover the ship's vitals: the boilers and engines, the control sections and the guns and their magazines. It was vertical, protecting against missiles with a horizontal trajectory, and horizontal, protecting against missiles with a more vertical, or plunging, terminal trajectory. More armour meant more weight and so less speed for a given horsepower. Subdivision was by watertight bulkheads across and along the ship, pierced at intervals by apertures which could be closed by water-tight doors secured by clips. In the British Navy of the 1940s the doors were colour coded: some were kept permanently closed, others were closed according to the ship's state of readiness for action. The more bulkheads and the more doors there were, the more difficult it was for the men to move around the ship and for stores, fuel and ammunition to be loaded. An additional protection was given to coal-fired ships by the placing of bunkers on the beam: the mass of coal limited the destructive effect of torpedoes and shells.

The extent and thickness of armour protection were in general greater in German ships than in British; German compartmentation was more intricate, and their damage control systems were more advanced. It has been averred that the advantage of intricate compartmentation was available to the Germans because one of its disadvantages – poor accommodation for the crews – was not an important factor in ships which were not expected to remain at sea for long periods. In fact, of course, the British had since at least 1906 been building their ships for action in the North Sea against the Germans: they too could have adopted intricate compartmentation without inflicting intolerable hardship on their seamen. In addition, the Germans built their docks to accommodate their ships, whereas the British tendency was to build the ships to fit the docks. So, the beam of the German ships was generally greater than that of the British: the beam of the early British battlecruisers was under 80 feet; that of the *Von der Tann* was 85. The beam of the British flagship *Iron Duke* was under 90 feet; that of the *Kaiser* was over 95. Increase of beam gave better opportunities for compartmentation and armour protection.

The torpedo

During the assault on Mobile in 1864, in the American Civil War, Rear-Admiral Farragut spoke one of the most enduring throwaway lines of the United States Navy: 'Damn the torpedoes. Captain Drayton, go ahead!' The 'torpedoes' of those days were floating explosive devices, not the auto-dirigible self-propelling weapons ('locomotive torpedoes') of today. It was the work of the Englishman Robert Whitehead with the Austrian Navy that led to the development of the submarine weapon carrying an explosive warhead, powered by compressed air and fitted with mechanisms to maintain depth and direction that in the twentieth century has done so much damage to ships and those who serve in them. Initially, torpedoes were fired from shore stations or from fast torpedo-boats designed to approach an enemy at high speed, if necessary behind a smokescreen. The development of the submarine produced the vessel ideally suited for the use of the weapon: it could in theory approach the target unseen and attack after sighting through a periscope (*Fig 9.1*). Later still, of course, the torpedo-carrying aircraft was developed into a weapon more formidable still.

It was the work of an Englishman, Robert Whitehead . . . that led to the development of the submarine weapon

At the time of Jutland the torpedo was an effective though occasionally unreliable missile, the principal weapon of the submarine and the torpedo-boat. Its effective range was about 5,000 yards (4,500 metres), though that might be stretched to 10,000. Both British and German capital ships of the period were fitted with torpedo tubes, but few encounters were so close that these could be used with much hope of success. Some German capital ships did in fact fire torpedoes at Jutland, but none hit. The only instance of one

battleship torpedoing another occurred twenty-five years later, when the *Rodney*, completed in 1927, hit the *Bismarck* with a torpedo fired at a range of 3,000 yards (2,700 metres).

Protection against torpedo attack

The battlefleet array had to be protected against torpedo attack by submarine or torpedo-boat, and had to be warned of the approach

Fig. 9.1 'A' class submarines moored at Dover in 1909. Eight of these boats, the oldest then in the Royal Navy, were in commission in 1914. A3 (foreground) and A7 had been lost. The rudimentary 'conning-towers' are covered. (*Hulton-Deutsch Collection/Corbis HU048669*)

of the opposing battlefleet by scouting cruisers. Torpedo-boats, light, fast and 'expendable', attacked at speed under cover of artificial smoke or the smoke of battle; they were repelled by the fire of the secondary armament of the battleships or by counter-attack by torpedo-boat destroyers ('destroyers'). In this respect, British battleships in general carried secondary armament of smaller calibre than that carried by the Germans. This defect was the result of one of Fisher's earlier pronouncements: 'The biggest

As the size of torpedo-boats increased, it became necessary to fit secondary armament of progressively larger calibre

possible big gun and the smallest possible small gun.' Indeed, the *Dreadnought* carried only twelve-pounder guns as secondary armament. As the size of torpedo-boats increased, it became necessary to fit secondary armament of progressively larger calibre and range. Submarines had to attack at periscope depth, and were kept down by the screening destroyers and cruisers. The track of a torpedo running towards a ship could at this time usually be seen. The ship could then be turned away to present a smaller target and to outrun the torpedo, or its course could be altered to present only the narrow target of its bow to the advancing threat. 'Combing the tracks' was the phrase used to describe these evolutions.

Battleships and battlecruisers at anchor could be protected against torpedo attack by torpedo-nets hung on booms projecting from the ships' sides and hinged at the base so that they could be folded back against the side when not in use. The nets were furled and stowed above them. By the time of Jutland the potential danger of damaged torpedo nets fouling propellers in battle had been appreciated in the British Fleet and the nets and booms had been removed. The Germans, however, retained nets and booms until after the battle: during it the German battlecruiser *Derfflinger* was forced at a critical stage to stop to clear away the after torpedo net which had been shot away and was hanging over the port screw. It was only later that the expedient of using 'torpedo bulges' – great metal blisters attached to the sides of the ship – was used. These bulges were designed to explode the torpedo and dissipate its main force before it reached the ship's true side. Tennyson-D'Eyncourt relates how these bulges were initially filled with water, but notes that the later use of steel rods for filling proved successful. Interestingly enough, it seems that the fitting of bulges did not diminish speed by more than half a knot.

Although during the war effective weapons for destruction of the submerged submarine were developed, the key to control of submarine attack depended mainly on detection of the submerged boat. There never was during the First World War any really effective method of doing this. The usefulness of the ship-mounted hydrophone, whose development began in the latter part of 1916, was much restricted by the need to avoid interference by noise from the sea and from the ship's engines by keeping stationary. Furthermore, the earlier hydrophones had no directional capability. The development of ASDIC (the acronym for the device being supposedly derived from the Allied Submarine Detection Investigation Committee of 1917), which depended on bouncing supersonic waves on to a submerged object and recording their reception, came too late in the war to be of practical use in it. Thus, for almost all of the war detection of a submerged submarine depended simply on observation of its periscope.

The mine

The marine mine was and is, essentially, a floating bomb. It was devised during the American War of Independence by an American, David Bushnell: kegs of gunpowder were floated down the Delaware in the hope that they would explode against the ships of the British squadron. The Russians later refined these weapons to create floating bombs fired on contact by a chemical fuse activated by the breaking of a glass phial of sulphuric acid. By the time of the First World War two types of mine were in use: the contact mine fired mechanically by contact with the hull of a ship, and the mine fired electrically from a shore station. Towards the end of the war the British developed a mine fired by the magnetic field of a passing ship. Mines were distributed by ships (minelayers) or by submarines (and, much later, by aircraft). They were moored, floating at a pre-determined depth, and planted in fields strategically planned to deny certain areas of sea to the enemy. Free-floating mines were banned by international agreement, but of course from time to time the moorings of mines broke and the devices floated free. The explosive charge of mines was large enough to inflict serious damage even on a Dreadnought battleship.

The explosive charge of mines was enough to inflict serious damage even on a Dreadnought

Little enough could be done to guard against the mine danger. Passages through fields could be cleared by the difficult and dangerous work of minesweeping; in clear and shallow water the presence of mines could be detected from aircraft. The 'paravane', invented by Commander Burney and introduced in the Royal Navy in 1916, consisted of an 'otter', towed on each side of the ship by a cable attached to the bows and floating at a fixed depth. The pressure from the advancing ship pushed the mine aside so that it was deflected down the cable to reach the paravane, where cutters severed the mooring wire. The mine then floated to the surface and could be destroyed by gun or rifle fire. Mines exacted a heavy toll of shipping in both world wars; they were, in effect, the nemesis of the British naval assault on the Dardanelles in 1915.

Smoke

The Germans were more advanced than the British in the use of smoke produced by increasing the proportion of incompletely burnt fuel to obscure ships and confuse the enemy's rangefinders. This was a tactic for the weaker fleet, used to enable it to retreat unseen from a more powerful enemy. Scheer was to find it of help on two critical occasions at Jutland; twenty-five years later, the *Prince of Wales* was to use it to obtain a respite from the accurate fire of the *Bismarck*.

Scouting by cruisers

At the time of Jutland there were two types of cruiser: armoured and light. The battlecruiser had made the armoured cruiser virtually

Fig. 9.2 HMS *Falmouth* and other ships of Third Light Cruiser Squadron. All were to be very active at Jutland; *Falmouth* was torpedoed and sunk in August 1916. *(Painting by Arthur Burgess, 1914, in the author's possession)*

obsolete, and the chief burden of forward scouting fell on the fast, lightly armoured and lightly armed light cruisers *(Figs 9.2 & 9.3)*. The cruiser's function was to scout for enemy ships and to report their number, sizes and bearing and their estimated course and speed to the commander, while keeping out of the way of enemy fire. The armoured cruiser was of course able to press observation into the range of the fire of the smaller guns, but, with its lesser speed and light armour protection, was an easy victim for the battlecruiser or battleship.

Firepower

The ability to sink enemy ships depended on the weight of shell fired, on the speed of the projectile as it left the gun (muzzle velocity), on the distance to which it could be fired (the range), on the penetrating and explosive power of the missile, on the rapidity of fire and on the accuracy of delivery. The great naval powers had during the nineteenth and twentieth centuries steadily increased the size of the missile fired, by increasing the diameter (or calibre) of missile and gun *(Fig 9.4)*. At the time of Jutland, the largest shell was that of 15-inch (38-cm) calibre, weighing about 2,000 pounds and propelled by the explosion of cordite, whose principal ingredients were nitroglycerine and nitrocellulose, electrically ignited. The guns had rifled barrels, of 45 or 50 calibre – that is, with a length 45 or 50 times the calibre of the gun. British guns were 'wire-wound': built up by windings of wire round a central steel

Fig. 9.3 HMS *Falmouth*. (Royal Naval Museum)

tube, with an outer steel tube. German guns were built up from tubes and hoops shrunk on to central tubes. They were, weight for weight, stronger than the British guns and wore better. The calibres of the German guns and shells were less than those of the British, but their higher muzzle velocity gave them comparable ranges and penetrating power. All the guns were mounted on trunnions, which allowed them to be elevated and depressed, in turrets surmounting barbettes, which allowed rotation *(Fig 9.5)*. The motive power was generally hydraulic. The cordite in British ships was contained largely in silk bags, whereas the most proximal part (that furthest from the muzzle of the gun) of the German cordite was contained in brass cartridges. In the magazines the cordite charges were kept in metal magazine cases. The turret communicated with a working chamber below it, and with the 'handing room' and magazine below that, by a hoist, whose apertures were to a varying extent protected by metal doors and screens.

The principal types of shell were capped armour-piercing nose-fused high-explosive and, in the British Navy, capped 'common'. The British used a lyddite burster and the Germans one of TNT (trinitrotoluene) in their armour-piercing shells. The bursting charge in the capped pointed common shell was of black powder. The high-explosive shell was designed to burst on contact and shower the area with destructive fragments of metal; its function was to kill and disable men and wreck unprotected gear. The

Fig. 9.4 Krupp heavy shell that pierced the side of HMS *Defender* (destroyer) at Jutland and did not explode. (*Royal Naval Museum*)

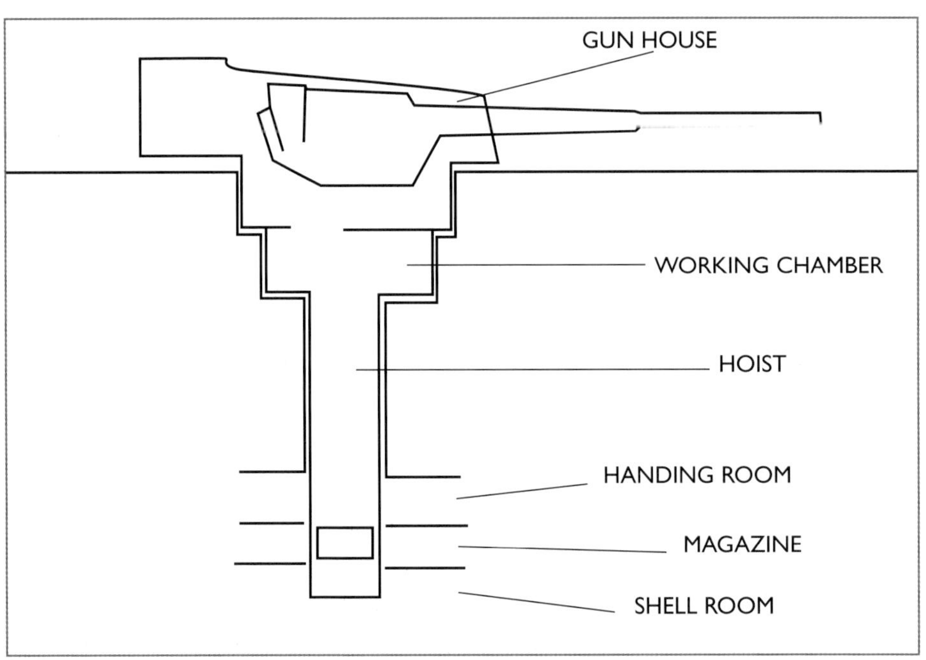

Fig. 9.5 Much simplified diagram of turret and barbette of a heavy gun.

armour-piercing type was intended to pass through the armour before exploding: its function was to cause massive damage to the ship and if possible to sink it by igniting flammable materials and ammunition. British heavy ships at Jutland carried about 100 shells for each heavy gun, while German ships carried about 90. The preference in the heavy ships was for armour-piercing shells: their role was, after all, to damage and if possible sink similar armoured ships.

The blast effect of the firing of large-calibre guns was known to be so severe as to damage structures anywhere near the muzzle of

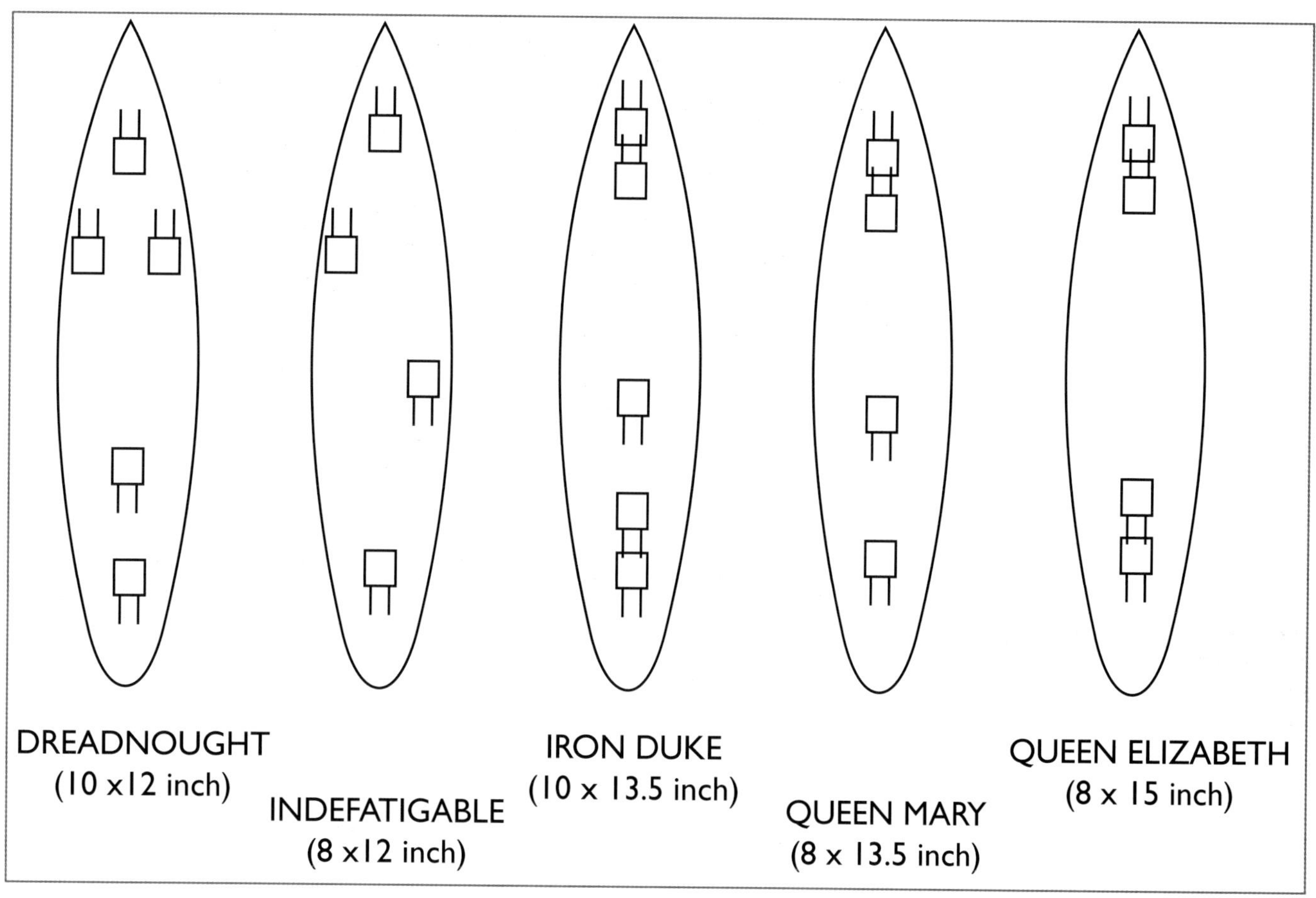

Fig 9.6 Arrangement of heavy guns in five British capital ships, *Dreadnought* (1906) to *Queen Elizabeth* (1914).

the gun firing. Consequently, both British and German Navies were slow to adopt the superimposition of turrets pioneered by the United States Navy. Instead, turrets were mounted on the beam as well as on the centre line. With turrets mounted on the beam, a degree of cross-deck firing was required to give maximum firepower to the broadside. It was not until 1912 that, with the completion of the Orions, British designers produced a ship with all the main armament mounted on the centre line. In these ships, there were two forward turrets, one midship turret and two after turrets, giving a ten-gun broadside *(Fig 9.6)*. In British ships the two forward turrets were designated 'A' and 'B', the amidships turret was 'Q' and the after turrets were 'X' and 'Y'. The Germans named their turrets respectively 'Anna', 'Bertha', 'Caesar' and 'Dora'. The firing of a complete broadside of all guns caused so much strain on the ship that 'broadside firing' usually indicated the firing together of all left or all right guns. The biggest guns could fire their projectiles to distances of 25,000 yards (22,860 metres). The effective range of the largest British guns was greater than that of the generally smaller German ones, though the *Von der Tann*'s 11-inch (28-cm) guns could be elevated to range to 22,000 yards (20,100 metres). The German rate of fire was generally higher than the British: the

It was not until 1912 that . . . British designers produced a ship with all the main armament on the centre line

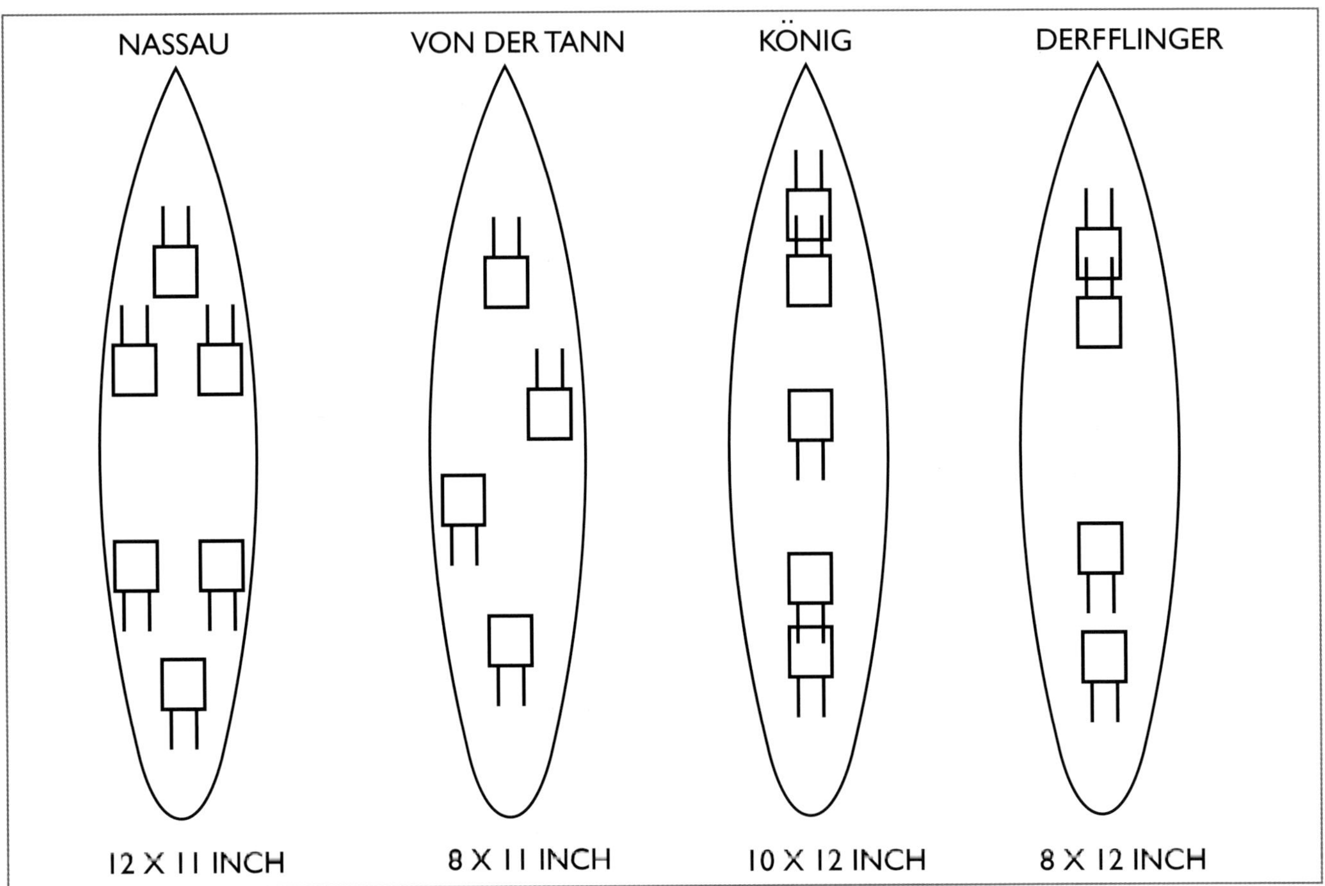

Fig. 9.7 Arrangement of heavy guns in four German capital ships, *Nassau* (1909) to *Derfflinger* (1914).

interval between salvoes in the German ships ranged from 30 to 40 seconds, while that in the British ships ranged from 40 to 50 seconds *(Fig 9.7)*.

Accuracy of fire

The great problem of naval gunnery before the development of guided missiles was how to hit an object moving at a speed and in a direction that had to be estimated, at a distance which again had to be estimated, from a variably steady platform moving in a direction and at a speed which could fairly accurately be gauged, allowing for deflection by wind and for resistance by an atmosphere of altering density. The British used coincidence rangefinders whose accuracy depended greatly on the distance between the two lenses through which the images were refracted. The longer the distance, the more accurate was the estimation of range. In this particular, the German rangefinders were generally more advanced than were the British. Spotting on a vertical object such as a mast or funnel, the operator saw an image split horizontally, and adjusted the angles of the lenses with knurled knobs until a single image was seen. The Germans used stereoscopic rangefinders, products of their advanced optical industry, with which the operator adjusted the lenses until a 'Wandermark' such as a cross or arrow appeared to him to be on the target. It is pretty certain that the German system was more accurate than the British. On the other hand, the introduction in the Royal Navy of Admiral Scott's 'director firing' system gave it a clear advantage over the Germans. Scott's system, introduced slowly, reluctantly and against considerable opposition, consisted in vesting the control of all the main armament in an operator placed in the foretop or gunnery control tower, both placed above smoke from guns and funnels, so that continuous observation of the fall of shot could be maintained from a position above the smoke of battle. The range was adjusted by the 'bracket' system based on observation of shell splashes and hits, being altered by fixed distances until some shells of one salvo fell short of the target and some went over. The rate of fire on that range was then increased.

The German director system was less advanced than the British: a director-pointer in the gunnery control tower gave the recommended training angle to the individual turrets, and the guns were laid and fired from the turrets. On the other hand, the Germans used a 'ladder' system for initial ranging. Fire was opened by a rapid succession of three salvoes, each being fired before its predecessor had landed. If the target were within the ladder, the correct range was rapidly found and steady firing on that range could be started.

Both navies struggled with the problems of allowing for changes of range and of rolling of the gun platform. It was in particular necessary, with the help of the calculators of the day, to adjust elevation and bearing to allow for constant alterations of range and bearing and for the rolling of the ship. In Kipling's parody 'The Ballad of the Clampherdown' there is a reference to the last problem:

> And the great stern gun shot fair and true
> With the heave of the ship to the stainless blue
> And the great stern turret stuck.

In both navies the principle of the transmitting station, into which information was continuously fed, was used. Early in the twentieth century Arthur Pollen, an inventor and business executive with a particular interest in the problems of naval gunnery, started the development of the 'Argo Clock' system, which in its final form produced, as Roskill says, 'constantly up-to-date ranges and bearings . . . and corrected them automatically for the changes produced by the movements of both sides' ships during the projectiles' time of flight'. Fisher of course supported enthusiastically Pollen's system; Jellicoe, Director of Naval Ordnance from 1905 to 1907, also backed its adoption. It was in the upshot unfortunate that at about the same time Captain (later Admiral Sir) Frederic Dreyer was working on a similar but cheaper and clearly inferior scheme. It is no longer surprising that the naval officer's

It is no longer surprising that the naval officer's scheme should have gained approval in preference to that of a civilian

scheme should have gained official approval in preference to that produced by a civilian inventor. The Dreyer 'Fire Control Table' was fitted in almost all the British capital ships that were involved in the First World War, and continued in use in certain ships up to the time of the Second. Indeed, the *Hood* was equipped with this apparatus when in 1941 she was sunk by gunfire from the *Bismarck*. As Roskill says, 'it was not until the 1920s, when the "Admiralty Fire Control Table Mark I" was fitted in the Nelson class battleships and . . . in all later capital ships and cruisers that the navy obtained the degree of "helm free gunnery" offered to it before the 1914–18 war'.

Von Hase gives a good, though guarded, description of the German system of adjustment of elevation and bearing to take account of continuing alterations of both factors. He also describes cautiously the gyroscopically controlled apparatus for allowing for the rolling of the firing ship, saying that at the time of the Jutland battle this system was not available in the German fleet. In gunnery, then, the Germans had the advantage in the field of range-finding; the British had it in the field of fire control from a central point. Neither side had yet come to terms with the difficult problem of allowing for changing ranges and bearings.

Speed

'Speed', Fisher had said, 'is the best protection.' The rate of fuel consumption went up sharply as speed increased, and very large increases in horsepower were needed to give an additional two or three knots. On the other hand, the faster ship or fleet was able to place itself in an advantageous position in relation to that of its opponent; it was able to choose and maintain a range; it could catch and damage or destroy a slower and less powerful ship; in the last resort, it was able to run away to fight another day. Of course, battles are not often won by running away or just by keeping out of range; good gunnery is necessary if the advantages of speed are to be exploited. The faster ship could also steer a zig-zag course while under fire and so confuse the enemy range-finders, without losing too much bearing on its opponent. At the battle of Tsushima in 1905 the Japanese commander Togo used the superior speed of his ships to place them ahead of the Russian line and to concentrate fire on its leading ships. After the disastrous battle off Coronel in 1914 the light cruiser *Glasgow* was able through superior speed to escape destruction after two British armoured cruisers had been sunk by the gunfire of von Spee's ships. At the Falklands Islands battle six weeks later Sturdee was able to keep his battlecruisers far enough away from von Spee's ships to avoid serious damage from their fire; at Jutland, as will be seen, Beatty was able through superior speed to head off Hipper's ships from perception of the

Sturdee was able to keep his battlecruisers far enough away . . . to avoid serious damage

Grand Fleet; twenty-four years later the new *Scharnhorst* and *Gneisenau* used their superior speed to escape from the accurate gunnery of the old *Renown*. At the time of Jutland the British Fleet in general had the advantage over the German of slightly superior speed. This advantage was of course less in the confined waters of the North Sea than in the broad stretches of the South Atlantic: there just was not enough space for exploitation of a four-knot difference in speed.

The arrays were directed and controlled by communications and, so far as battle conditions permitted, by standing orders.

Communication

This proved to be the Achilles' heel of Beatty's campaign. Orders could be conveyed over short distances by flag hoists or by light signals. The ratings and petty officers of the signals branch developed rare skill in the rapid interpretation of these signals, and their officers were not far behind them. The hoisting of the signal was preparatory: it called for acknowledgement; the order was to be obeyed when the signal was hauled down. Flag signals could be difficult to read if the wind were blowing the flags directly towards the recipient, so they were usually repeated by lamp. In battle, signal halyards might be shot away, so that messages had to be sent by lamp or wireless telegraphy. At longer distances wireless telegraphy could be used, the messages being encoded before transmission and decoded on reception. This was, of course, an efficient method, but it carried the risk of giving away the position of a ship or fleet, and during action signals offices were liable to be so much encumbered with traffic as to cause delay in decoding and presentation. The advantages of flexibility offered by wireless telegraphy to commanders of ships, squadrons and fleets were to some extent offset by the simultaneous facility it gave to the Admiralty of controlling those commanders. At least some of the confusion that at the beginning of the war enveloped the movements of the British battlecruisers in the Mediterranean could have been avoided had the Admiralty left the conduct of affairs to the discretion of the man on the spot.

Aircraft

Both sides were experimenting with the use of air power: the Germans principally with dirigible airships; the British with seaplanes, land-based aircraft and aircraft-carrying ships (*Figs 9.8, 10.3 & 10.4*). The value of the airships in bombing and reconnaissance was much impaired by their vulnerability to incendiary projectiles; that of aeroplanes in scouting and spotting the fall of shell was lessened by their short endurance and the unreliability and low power of their

Fig. 9.8 Short 184 Seaplane: the type of aircraft flown by Rutland and Trewin at Jutland. (*Imperial War Museum: Q 68423*)

engines. No one in high position, except perhaps Fisher, foresaw that the aeroplane would twenty-five years later become the nemesis of the battleship. No one at the time took any notice of Fisher's comment.

Tactics

The Grand Fleet was to be decoyed out over a submarine ambush . . .

It was hardly likely that the Germans, with their numerically inferior fleet, would conform to British expectations by drawing it up in line on a course parallel to that of the British Fleet and abiding the verdict of a broadside gunfire duel. Scheer's and Hipper's principal object was to come upon an isolated squadron of the Grand Fleet when they had numerical supremacy, and to destroy or seriously damage it before a superior force could arrive. Or, the Grand Fleet or a part of it was to be decoyed out over a submarine ambush by the appearance of a squadron of the High Sea Fleet. Both British and German commanders hoped that in the event of a battle it would be possible to lead their fleet across the head of the opposing line and so concentrate fire on the leading ships. This was the 'crossing the T' that Togo had achieved at Tsushima. Nelson had, of course, done just the opposite at

Trafalgar, aiming his two columns of ships at the line of French and Spanish ships and relying on British morale and rapidity of fire to surmount the dangerous phase when his leading ships came in succession under fire from numerous enemy ships. Nelson had advised that the order of sailing should be the order of battle, but the Grand Fleet cruised in squadrons abeam of one another, and was obliged to 'deploy' into line to meet the enemy.

Rules for the Grand Fleet's conduct in battle were laid down in the Grand Fleet Battle Orders, begun by Jellicoe in 1914 and thereafter from time to time amended. Marder tells us that the revised version issued in December 1915 was that in force at the time of Jutland; his impression from them is that Jellicoe's principal consideration was that of preserving the Fleet: it was, after all, the only one the country possessed, and Britain could not at the time expect any important assistance at sea from France, Italy or Russia. The first two were obliged by the presence of the Austro-Hungarian Fleet to maintain strong forces in the Mediterranean; one of Russia's fleets was effectively confined to the Black Sea, and the other to the Baltic. Certainly Jellicoe stressed the likelihood of a turn away by the enemy under cover of attack by torpedo-boats, and indicated the cautious line to be followed in that event. The importance of maintaining the integrity of the battle line was stressed, and little encouragement was given to independent thought and initiative. Vice-Admiral Sturdee, commanding the Fourth Battle Squadron, who had had experience of battle in the war, was inclined to criticise the rigidity of Jellicoe's tactics, but it does not appear that his ideas were acceptable. Jellicoe may have reckoned that the man whose immensely superior squadron had taken so long to sink von Spee's inferior force was not one to give him lessons in battle tactics. This may have been a misjudgement.

Sturdee . . . was inclined to criticise Jellicoe's tactics

At the time of Jutland both Beatty and Hipper had had experience of the frightful power of modern naval weapons. The experiences of their respective navies in the first two years of the war were available to all commanders. Lessons about coordination of plans had to be learned from the action in the Helgoland Bight in 1914, in which Beatty's battlecruisers had intervened successfully in an action between British and German cruisers and destroyers. The loss in 1914 of the modern battleship *Audacious* to a mine indicated all too plainly the vulnerability of British ships to submarine weapons. The amount of ammunition used and the time taken by the *Invincible* and *Inflexible* to sink the *Scharnhorst* and *Gneisenau* at long range with the fire of their 12-inch (30-cm) guns showed the defects of British gunnery and the insufficiently destructive effect of British heavy shells. It was in this battle in particular that the fierce resolve and bravery of the crews of the German ships in the face of overwhelming odds were shown. Defects in the signalling department of his flagship *Lion* were

The fierce resolve and bravery of the German crews in the face of overwhelming odds were shown

forced on Beatty's attention by incidents during the encounters with German battlecruisers in 1914 and 1915.

At the end of 1914 Hipper's battlecruisers, supported by the High Sea Fleet under von Ingenohl's command, raided Scarborough, Hartlepool and Whitby. British Intelligence came to know of the plan, though the imminent presence of the High Sea Fleet was not thought likely. The force assembled to meet the Germans included four battlecruisers under Beatty's command, accompanied by Commodore Goodenough's First Light Cruiser Squadron and supported by the six modern battleships of the Second Battle Squadron under the command of Admiral Warrender. Had von Ingenohl not sustained the impression that the Grand Fleet was out in force and early turned for home, the British squadrons might have been damaged very severely. As it was, the *Southampton*, the advance ship of Beatty's light cruiser screen, wearing Commodore Goodenough's broad pendant, sighted the cruisers and destroyers screening Hipper's force, and with the *Birmingham*, the ship next in line, opened fire. Beatty, not wishing entirely to be deprived of his cruiser screen, wanted to signal to the *Nottingham*, the third cruiser in line, that she and the *Falmouth* should retain their screening position. At this time the Flag Lieutenant acted as signals officer, so it fell to Seymour to interpret Beatty's intentions. Making to the *Nottingham* by searchlight the signal to resume station, and being uncertain of *Nottingham*'s identity, he prefaced the signal with 'light cruiser' instead of the ship's name. The signal was seen by the *Southampton*, and was probably relayed to Goodenough as 'Light cruisers resume station'. Goodenough, though in action and aware of the situation, felt that he could not do other than comply. Accordingly, the whole of his squadron broke off action and disengaged. In the event, diminishing visibility and further misapprehensions prevented any further contacts between the opposing forces. It was not altogether creditable on Beatty's part to blame Goodenough for this error.

Had von Ingenohl not . . . turned for home, the British squadrons might have been damaged very severely

Two more lessons about signalling were given in the action off the Dogger Bank in January 1915. Beatty, with the *Lion*, *Tiger*, *Princess Royal*, *Indomitable* and *New Zealand*, was enabled by superior British Intelligence to catch Hipper with the *Seydlitz*, *Moltke*, *Derfflinger* and *Blücher* in a reconnaissance of the Dogger Bank area. In the stern chase that followed, superior speed enabled the three most modern British ships, *Lion*, *Tiger* and *Princess Royal*, to get within long range of the Germans and to open fire on the last in line, the *Blücher*. Later, the *New Zealand* also got within range of that doomed ship; *Indomitable*, the oldest of the British ships, lagged behind. Beatty intended that his four ships within range should engage the four German ships in order from the right. The signal that was made was evidently open to misinterpretation, and indeed the *Tiger*, which should have fired on the *Moltke*, fired

The Tiger, *which should have fired on the* Moltke, *fired instead at the* Seydlitz instead at the *Seydlitz*, with which the *Lion* was engaged. Thus the *Moltke*, second in the German line, was not fired upon, and was able with the *Seydlitz* to concentrate fire on the *Lion* which, hit by three heavy shells, fell back. Half an hour later submarines on the starboard bow were reported to Beatty, and an eight-point (90°) alteration of course to port was signalled. By this time the *Lion*'s ability to signal had been seriously impaired by the loss of electrical power and damage to her halyards. She fell out of line *(Fig 9.9)*. The subsequent signals 'Course North-East' and 'Attack the rear of the enemy' were taken by Rear-Admiral Archibald Moore in the *New Zealand*, on whom the overall command now devolved, to mean that the whole British force should break off the action and concentrate its attack on the wretched *Blücher*, now fallen behind and abandoned by Hipper. The *Blücher*'s men fought to the last against overwhelming force, and the rest of Hipper's squadron escaped. So for the second time that day Seymour failed to communicate Beatty's intention.

In this contest the Germans suffered badly and learned a lesson. Hipper's flagship *Seydlitz*, always an unlucky ship, sustained a hit on the quarter-deck by a 13.5-inch (34-cm) shell from the *Lion*. In *Seydlitz* the two after turrets were close to each other rather than separated as was the case in her more modern sister ships. The shell penetrated the armour of the barbette of the aftermost turret and ignited charges in the working chamber. In turn the fire spread to the hoist and handing room and to the handing room of the adjacent turret, the flames shooting up to a height of 200 feet. Only the quick thinking of the commander in flooding the magazines averted a catastrophic explosion. The lesson drawn from this concerned the need to avoid having a train of cordite leading from

Fig. 9.9 HMS *Lion* being towed back into Rosyth after the Dogger Bank action. Here she and her destroyer escort are approaching the Forth Bridge. *(From a painting by W.L. Wyllie, Royal Naval Museum)*

the turret to the magazine, by reducing the quantity of charges out of their cases in the working chamber and handing room and, so far as possible, by keeping apertures in the train between magazine and turret closed by doors or screens. The custom of having ready-use ammunition in quantity in the working chamber and of disregard of anti-flash precautions had grown up because of the desire to increase the rate of firing. Campbell concludes: 'If the *Seydlitz* had had British charges at the Dogger Bank she would unquestionably have blown up.' Nevertheless, the *Seydlitz* suffered a similar turret catastrophe at Jutland sixteen months later.

The British were to pay at Jutland the price of the vulnerability of the train from turret to magazine. They failed to profit from the lessons taught at the Dogger Bank concerning the defects in the *Lion*'s signalling department. They failed too, to learn the lesson from the Falklands battle about the insufficiently destructive effect of their heavy shells, and compounded that failure by over-estimating the damage done to the German ships in the Dogger Bank engagement. It could not have been known at the time, but it might have been suspected, that the standard of British gunnery was well below that of the German. The British landed six heavy shells on the German ships excluding the *Blücher*; the Germans landed over thirty on the British. Once again, German bravery and resolve were clearly shown: neither the men nor their ships were going to be any pushover.

Jellicoe was aware of the vulnerability of British capital ships to underwater attack

In May 1916, after almost two years of war, Jellicoe was certainly aware of the vulnerability of British capital ships to underwater attack, of the strength of the German ships and the discipline and resolve of their crews, and of the poor shooting of the British battlecruisers. He was aware, too, of the tactics that would probably be used by the Germans. Bennett records a strikingly prescient letter to Beatty written by Jellicoe in the light of the Dogger Bank encounter:

> I imagine that the Germans will try to entrap you by risking their battlecruisers as a decoy. They know that the odds are that you will be a hundred miles away from me, and can draw you down to the Helgoland Bight without my being in effective support. This is all right if you keep your speed, but if some of your ships have their speed badly reduced in a fight with their battlecruisers, or by submarines, their loss seems inevitable if you are drawn into the High Sea Fleet with me too far off to extricate them before dark. The Germans know you very well and will try to take advantage of that quality of 'not letting go when you have once got hold', which you possess, thank God. But one must concern oneself with the result to the country of a serious decrease in relative strength. If the game looks worth the candle the risks can be taken. If not, one's duty is to be

> cautious. I believe you will see what is the proper course, and pursue it victoriously.

Beatty was aware of German strength and to some extent of the vulnerability of his ships; he was certainly aware of the defects in the *Lion*'s signalling department. It was, perhaps, stretching loyalty to a subordinate too far, to permit Seymour to continue in charge when so much was at stake. A man of Beatty's character would not find Jellicoe's advocacy of caution easy of digestion, though later in the war he was to be forced by events to adopt his policies.

Officers and men of the Grand Fleet and Battlecruiser Fleet were consumed by the desire to meet the High Sea Fleet, which had not been seen from any British surface ship since the beginning of the war. Among the members of the German high command, eagerness to meet the Grand Fleet was tempered by the realisation of numerical inferiority and by the unfounded belief in the technical superiority of the British array. Officers and men were, however, eager to meet their enemy and take their revenge for what was perceived as British treachery in turning on a nation so nearly related in race and so recently a valued ally.

PART TWO

ENGAGEMENT

CHAPTER TEN

THE EVE AND FIRST PHASE OF THE ENCOUNTER

Jellicoe's fleet was disposed in three anchorages: Scapa Flow, Cromarty Firth and Rosyth on the Firth of Forth *(Map 1*, page *84)*. With Jellicoe at Scapa were the sixteen ships of the First and Fourth Battle Squadrons, together with most of the Grand Fleet cruisers and destroyers (*Figs 10.1 & 10.2*). There was also the seaplane carrier *Campania*, a 22-knot, twin screw, twenty-three-year-old former Cunarder *(Figs 10.3 & 10.4)*. The Third Battlecruiser Squadron (the Invincibles) commanded by Rear-Admiral Hood was at the time at Scapa, having temporarily been detached from Beatty's command for gunnery practice. The eight ships of the Second Battle Squadron under the command of Vice-Admiral Jerram were at Cromarty with the four armoured cruisers of the First Cruiser Squadron under the command of Rear-Admiral Arbuthnot. With them was part of the 11th Destroyer Flotilla. Beatty had with him at Rosyth the four modern battlecruisers of the First Squadron and the two 'improved' Invincibles of the Second *(Fig 10.5)*. Also at Rosyth under Beatty's command were four Queen Elizabeths of the Fifth Battle Squadron: the *Queen Elizabeth* herself was in dock, but her sister ships were a massive addition to the strength of the squadron *(Figs 10.6 & 10.7)*. The *Barham*, *Malaya*, *Valiant* and *Warspite* were under the command of Rear-Admiral Evan-Thomas, the former shipmate and mentor of King George V. They had been at Rosyth since 21 May, having been sent by Jellicoe to make up for the temporary loss of the three Invincibles.

It remains a mystery why Beatty and his staff did not early – nor

Fig. 10.1 The *Iron Duke*, Jellicoe's flagship at Jutland. Completed in 1914, she could steam 21 knots, and mounted ten 13.5 inch guns in five turrets, all on the centre line. She survived as a gunnery training ship into the Second World War, being hit by German bombs in Scapa Flow. (*Royal Naval Museum*)

Fig. 10.2 The Grand Fleet at sea. (*Royal Naval Museum*)

Fig. 10.3 & 10.4 HMS *Campania*. Former Cunarder converted to seaplane carrier.
Fig. 10.3 Seen from the starboard side: the forward ramp is shown. (*Imperial War Museum: SP 352*)

Fig. 10.4 Note the doubling of the formerly elegant forward funnel. *Campania* seems to have been a rather unlucky ship: she missed the signal to proceed with the Grand Fleet on 31 May 1916, and in Scapa Flow in 1917 was rammed and sunk by *Furious*, one of Fisher's three 'large light cruisers'. (*Royal Naval Museum*)

for that matter, ever – before Jutland seek a meeting with Evan-Thomas and his staff, so that the former could make clear to his subordinate his intentions in the event of a clash with the enemy. Indeed, Gordon notes that Evan-Thomas was not even sent a copy of the Battlecruiser Fleet Standing Orders. After all, Beatty had sought, even intrigued for, the move of the Fifth Battle Squadron to Rosyth for combined action with his fleet. Did he, perhaps, think that in the event of battle Evan-Thomas's powerful squadron might take from his battlecruisers some of any glory that might be on offer? It is remarkable too, that in his account of the battle Chatfield does not mention the presence of the squadron until he comes to the point about which there is controversy. Certainly, there was some feeling between the ships' companies of the battlecruisers and those of the battlefleet, arising, no doubt, from

Top: Fig. 10.5 The battlecruisers leaving the Firth of Forth, probably in 1915. The *Lion* leads, followed by the *Princess Royal*. In the background, Edinburgh and Arthur's Seat and a ship of the Third Battle Squadron (then, the King Edwards). (*Drypoint by W.L. Wyllie in the possession of the author*)
Above: Fig. 10.6 The Fifth Battle Squadron at sea. (*Drypoint by W.L. Wyllie in the possession of the author*)

the impression that up to then all the fighting had been done by the battlecruisers and the belief, expressed by Chatfield, that they were 'the spear-point of the Grand Fleet'.

Beatty had with him the First, Second and Third Light Cruiser Squadrons, each of four ships, commanded by, respectively, Commodores Alexander-Sinclair and Goodenough and Rear-Admiral Napier, and three flotillas of destroyers. In addition, he had the seaplane carrier *Engadine*, a 21-knot cross-Channel steamer modified for her new function *(Fig 10.8)*. The seaplanes were hoisted out with a crane, and took off from the sea. They were recovered in the same way after landing on the sea.

Most of the High Sea Fleet was at Wilhelmshaven, in the Jadebusen, the enclosed estuary of the River Jade, or off Schillig on the north-east point of East Friesland. The Second Squadron, of six pre-dreadnoughts ('Deutschlands') under the command of Rear-Admiral Mauve, was in the Elbe, off Cuxhaven. Scheer was prevailed on to take these comparatively weak ships (the German sailors, grimly humorous, called them the 'Five-minute ships') with him, and in the event that decision was justified. He had with him the sixteen battleships of the First and Third Squadrons, the five battlecruisers

Fig. 10.7 Fifth Battle Squadron (foreground) and battlecruisers at Rosyth just before Jutland. (*Royal Naval Museum*)

of the First Scouting Group under Hipper's command, the nine light cruisers of the Second and Third Scouting Groups, and six and a half flotillas of torpedo-boats led by two light cruisers.

Jellicoe had planned for early June an incursion into the Kattegat by light cruisers, in the hope of drawing the High Sea Fleet out to be caught by the waiting Grand Fleet. Scheer at about the same time conceived a rather similar plan for drawing the British Fleet out over an ambush of submarines by a raid by his battlecruisers on Sunderland. The scheme, planned for 17 May, was in the event postponed to the 30th because of delay in repairs to the *Seydlitz*, but by the 23rd eighteen submarines had taken up their positions off the bases of the Grand Fleet. So placed, they could keep watch and be ready for offensive action, but they could not stay at these stations beyond 2 June. Scheer had planned reconnaissance by Zeppelins to make sure that the British battlecruisers were not supported by the Grand Fleet, but the weather proved unsuitable for that. So, it was decided instead to sail the battlecruisers to the Skagerrak with the battlefleet in support and between 40 and 50 miles astern. Scheer hoped to get the Grand Fleet out over his submarine ambush and to entice Beatty's force into action with Hipper's ships, which would fall back on the High Sea Fleet and so bring the British battlecruisers under the fire of his guns. The first part of the plan failed; the second might have succeeded had the Fifth Battle Squadron not been with Beatty's ships. Hipper's ships put to sea from the Jade

Fig. 10.8 The *Engadine* (completed 1911) returned to civil use after wartime service. She is shown in the early 1930s, under way in the Thames. (*National Maritime Museum*)

at 0100 on 31 May, and Scheer's followed them from the Jade and the Elbe ninety minutes later.

The increased German signal traffic told British Naval Intelligence that something was afoot; by noon on 30 May the Admiralty was able to warn Jellicoe and Beatty that the High Sea Fleet would probably put to sea the next morning; at about 1800 the same day Jellicoe was ordered to take the Grand Fleet to sea and to concentrate his forces eastward of the 'Long Forties' – that is, about 100 miles east of Aberdeen (latitude about 57 deg. N) *(Map 2)*. By 2230, before the High Sea Fleet left harbour, the Grand Fleet was at sea, and an hour later the Second Battle Squadron with its armoured and light cruisers and destroyer flotillas joined it from Cromarty. The battlecruisers and Fifth Battle Squadron from Rosyth were at sea by midnight. Ahead of Beatty's array was his slowest ship, the seaplane carrier *Engadine (Fig. 10.8)*. The Grand Fleet's seaplane carrier *Campania* was not with the Fleet. She lay in a rather remote part of the Flow, and may initially have missed the signal to raise steam. According to Captain Harper's record she was unable to raise steam in time to sail with the Fleet, but left Scapa at 0130, only to be ordered back with defects at 0430. She would, certainly, have been vulnerable to submarine attack. Marder gives a slightly different account of this episode, but the fact remains that this potentially useful ship was not with the Fleet at the time of the encounter. Morale in both British and German fleets was high: the British, though not hoping for too much from this particular sweep, always looked forward to the day when they would engage 'the Hun': the Germans too hoped for 'der Tag' when the treacherous English would feel the weight of righteous German anger. The weather was fair, the sea calm, and visibility limited only a little by

The treacherous English would feel the weight of righteous German anger

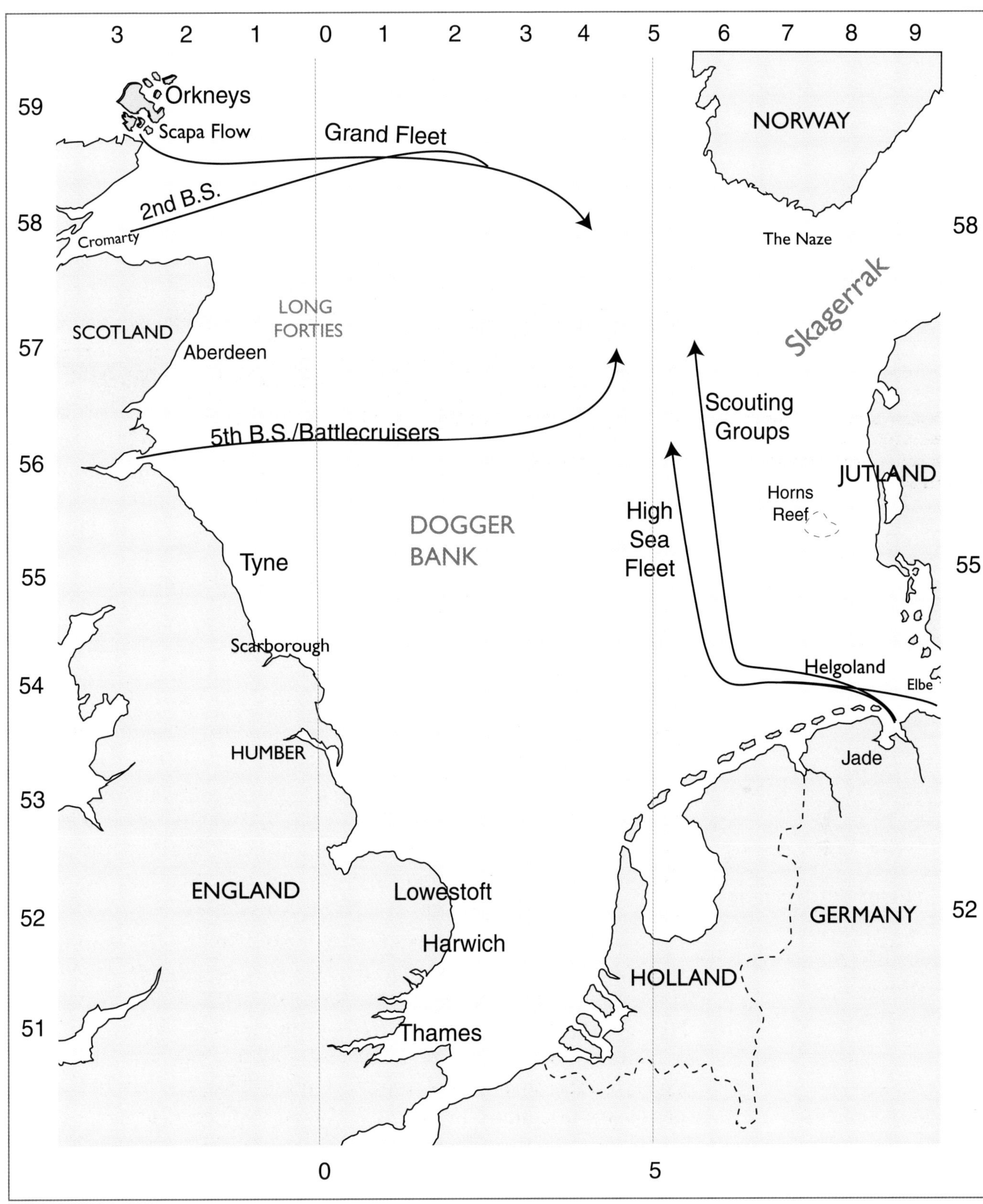

Map 2 Courses to the scene of action: Grand Fleet; Second Battle Squadron; Battlecruisers and Fifth Battle Squadron; Hipper's Scouting Group; High Sea Fleet.

mist. The mortal storm to come was to be created by man: for thousands of those who sailed there was to be no return.

At noon on the 31st the Second Battle Squadron and its attendant cruisers and destroyers met Jellicoe's main force and took up their appointed station. The battlefleet then steamed on a course ESE towards the point 57 deg. 45′ N and 4 deg. 15′ E. appointed by Jellicoe for reaching at 1430. The battleships were in six columns of four ships each, abeam of one another, the Fleet flagship *Iron Duke* leading the third column from the left. Ahead and on the same course were the three ships of the Third Battlecruiser Squadron, accompanied by the light cruisers *Chester* and *Canterbury*. The battlecruisers, with the Fifth Battle Squadron 5 miles away to the north-west, steamed E by N to reach their 1430 point at 56 deg. 40′ N and 5 deg. E. That point was about 70 miles S by E of Jellicoe's planned position for that time. The plan was that, if by 1430 the enemy had not been encountered, the battlecruisers would turn to meet the battlefleet and the whole array would steer for Horns Reef, about 25 miles off the west coast of Denmark. It was unfortunate that, on account of lack of cooperation between the Operations Division and 'Room 40' of the Intelligence Department, a signal was made, to reach Jellicoe at about noon, suggesting that the main German Fleet had not left harbour. About three and a half hours later Beatty's battlecruisers were in action with Hipper's squadron, and an hour after that the whole High Sea Fleet was seen by the battlecruisers' scouting cruisers. It is not surprising that after that, Jellicoe placed less than full trust in intelligence reports.

The first encounter

The cruiser screen was disposed obliquely some miles ahead of the heavy ships

Beatty's heavy ships were in three sections. The First Battlecruiser Squadron, *Lion*, *Princess Royal*, *Queen Mary* and *Tiger*, with Beatty's flag in the *Lion*, was about 2 miles abeam and to the south of the Second Battlecruiser Squadron (*New Zealand* and *Indefatigable*); the Fifth Battle Squadron (*Barham*, *Valiant*, *Warspite* and *Malaya*, *see Fig 10.9*), with Evan-Thomas's flag in the *Barham*, was about 5 miles astern. The cruiser screen, of twelve vessels in three squadrons, was disposed obliquely some miles ahead of the heavy ships, the First, led by Commodore Alexander-Sinclair in the *Galatea*, to the north, the Third, led by Rear-Admiral Napier in the *Falmouth*, in the middle, and the Second, led by Commodore Goodenough in the *Southampton*, to the south. The *Engadine* was ahead of the array *(Map 3)*.

The High Sea Fleet was, meanwhile, advancing on a course approximately North by East, to the east of the British. Hipper's battlecruisers were about 50 miles ahead of the battlefleet, screened ahead by five light cruisers. Scheer was aiming for a point in the mouth of the Skagerrak about 80 miles east of Jellicoe's proposed 1430 position. The encounter came about because, just after Beatty turned his ships northward at 1415 as arranged, the *Galatea*, on the port wing of the advancing screen of twelve light cruisers, reported 'Enemy in sight, consisting of one destroyer', and turned towards the enemy. Her lookouts had seen the Danish steamer N.J.

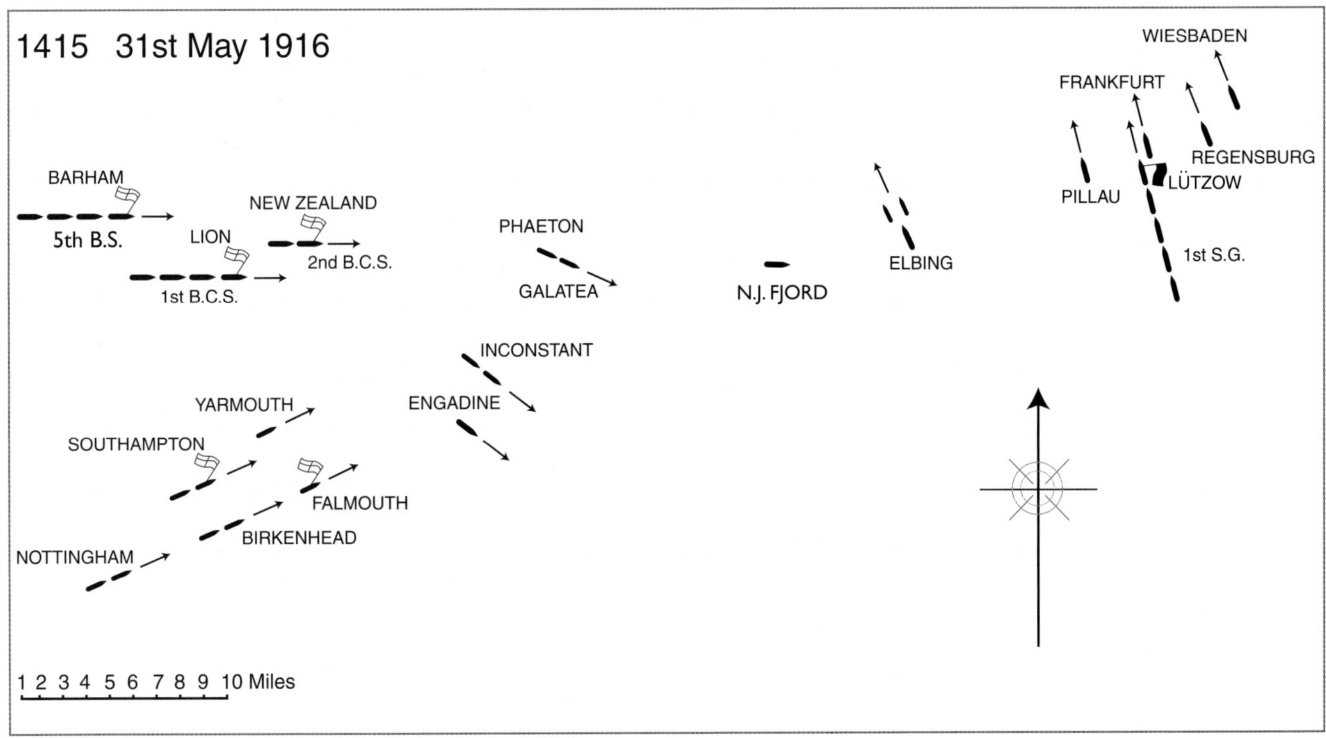

Map 3 Position of Battlecruisers and Fifth Battle Squadron at 1415, just before the turn to the north from their eastward course. The ships are not to scale. To the east, the *Elbing*'s escorting destroyers are about to turn to examine the (neutral) Danish steamer N.J. Fjord.

Fjord and the German destroyer that had been detached from Hipper's light cruiser screen to examine this ship. Beatty, in the *Lion*, had made to all ships the signal to turn to a course N by E for the rendezvous with the Grand Fleet, and this signal was taken in by the *Barham*, flagship of Rear-Admiral Evan-Thomas, and by the light cruiser squadrons. Thus, all the heavy ships and the Second and Third Cruiser Squadrons turned to the new course. In the *Galatea*, Alexander-Sinclair ignored the order to turn north and took his squadron east towards the enemy. Alerted by the *Galatea*'s signal, all the light cruisers altered course without further orders and steamed in her direction. *Galatea*, of 3,500 tons, with two 6-inch (15-cm) and six 4-inch (10-cm) guns, was soon in action with the German light cruiser *Elbing*, of 4,900 tons, with twelve 4-inch guns, which had turned in support of the German destroyers (*Map 4*). The *Galatea* was soon being hit, and with her consort *Phaeton* and the other two ships of the squadron turned away to the north-west. Hipper altered course to support his light forces.

Beatty's 'turn towards'

The action between the light forces brought the big ships to the scene. At 1432 Beatty made a flag signal to all ships to turn to a course SSE. Because of funnel smoke and the direction in which the flags were flying, the *Barham* did not take in this signal, and the four ships of the Fifth Battle Squadron continued in a general northerly direction for almost ten minutes, until the signal was repeated from the *Tiger*

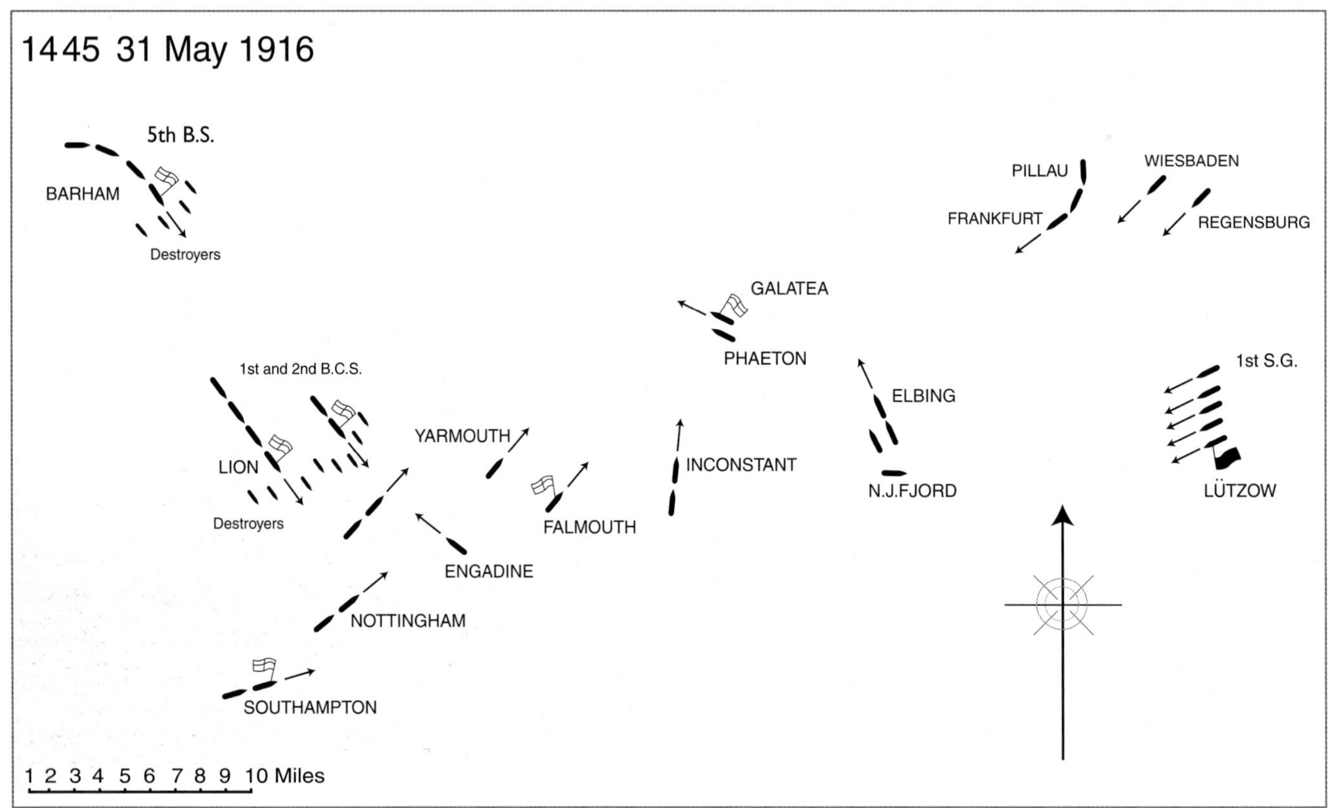

Map 4 *Elbing* turns in pursuit of *Galatea*. British battlecruisers have turned to course SE and are followed by the Fifth Battle Squadron. German battlecruisers and cruisers turn to close the *Elbing*.

by searchlight and received by the *Barham*. Because the combined speed of separation of the ships was almost 40 knots, this delay increased the distance between the battlecruisers and their powerful consorts to 10 miles *(Fig 10.9)*. The consequences of this signalling error were to be very serious for the ships, for the men and for the country: they determined that Beatty's battlecruisers should meet Hipper's deprived in the early stages of the support of the Fifth Battle Squadron. Hipper, with his flag in the *Lützow*, was leading the German battlecruisers on a course N by E some miles to the east of the mêlée between the *Elbing* and the British light cruisers. At 1427, as soon as he knew from the *Elbing* of her engagement with the enemy, he turned his ships to WSW and increased speed to 18 knots. An attempt at aerial reconnaissance was made by the British: a seaplane was hoisted out from the *Engadine*, and at 1508 Flight Lieutenant F.J. Rutland, with Assistant Paymaster G.S. Trewin as observer, took off from the water and steered N 10 deg. E. Rutland closed to a mile and a half at 1,000 feet and saw the German ships steering a northerly course. The seaplane was the target of fire from the secondary armament, but the later turn by the German ships to a south-easterly course was noted. The signal from the aircraft got through to the *Engadine* but was not received in the flagship. At 1545 the fuel pipe to the left carburettor broke, the aircraft lost height and Rutland was forced to land on the sea. Having repaired the pipe with a length of rubber tubing, he took off again and returned to his ship. The aircraft was hoisted in, and no further aerial

The consequences of this signalling error were to be very serious

Fig. 10.9 *Warspite* and *Malaya* seen from *Valiant* just before the action of 31 May 1916. (*Royal Naval Museum*)

reconnaissance was attempted. The *Engadine* had not, however, finished her work for that day: later, she was able to take in tow the frightfully damaged *Warrior* and transfer her survivors, including the wounded. Rutland had not finished either: during the transfer one of the wounded fell down between the ships. Braving the extreme peril of being crushed, Rutland went overboard and rescued this man. History had not even then done with Lieutenant Rutland: ten years later, alas, this bold and resourceful officer was to betray his countrymen and the Americans to the Japanese.

At 1525 the German ships were sighted by the *New Zealand*, then about 2 miles north-east of the *Lion*, on her starboard bow, and at about the same time Beatty's six battlecruisers were seen by the Germans. The distance between the squadrons was about 17 miles; the British were steering NE and the Germans NW by W. At this stage the ships of the Fifth Battle Squadron were not visible to the Germans. At 1530 Beatty altered course to E, and Hipper, seeing this change of course, turned to starboard to bring his ships to a course SE, later changed to SSE, in order to close the High Sea Fleet *(Map 5)*. A few minutes later Beatty ordered the *New Zealand* and *Indefatigable* to take station astern of the First Battlecruiser Squadron, increased speed to 24 knots and altered course to SSE, with his ships on a line of bearing NW *(Figs 10.10 & 10.11)*. 'Action Stations' had been sounded in the battlecruisers at about 1445.

Particular preparations were necessary in the *New Zealand*: when the ship visited New Zealand in 1913 she was toured by Maoris, whose Chief predicted that she would be involved in a great battle

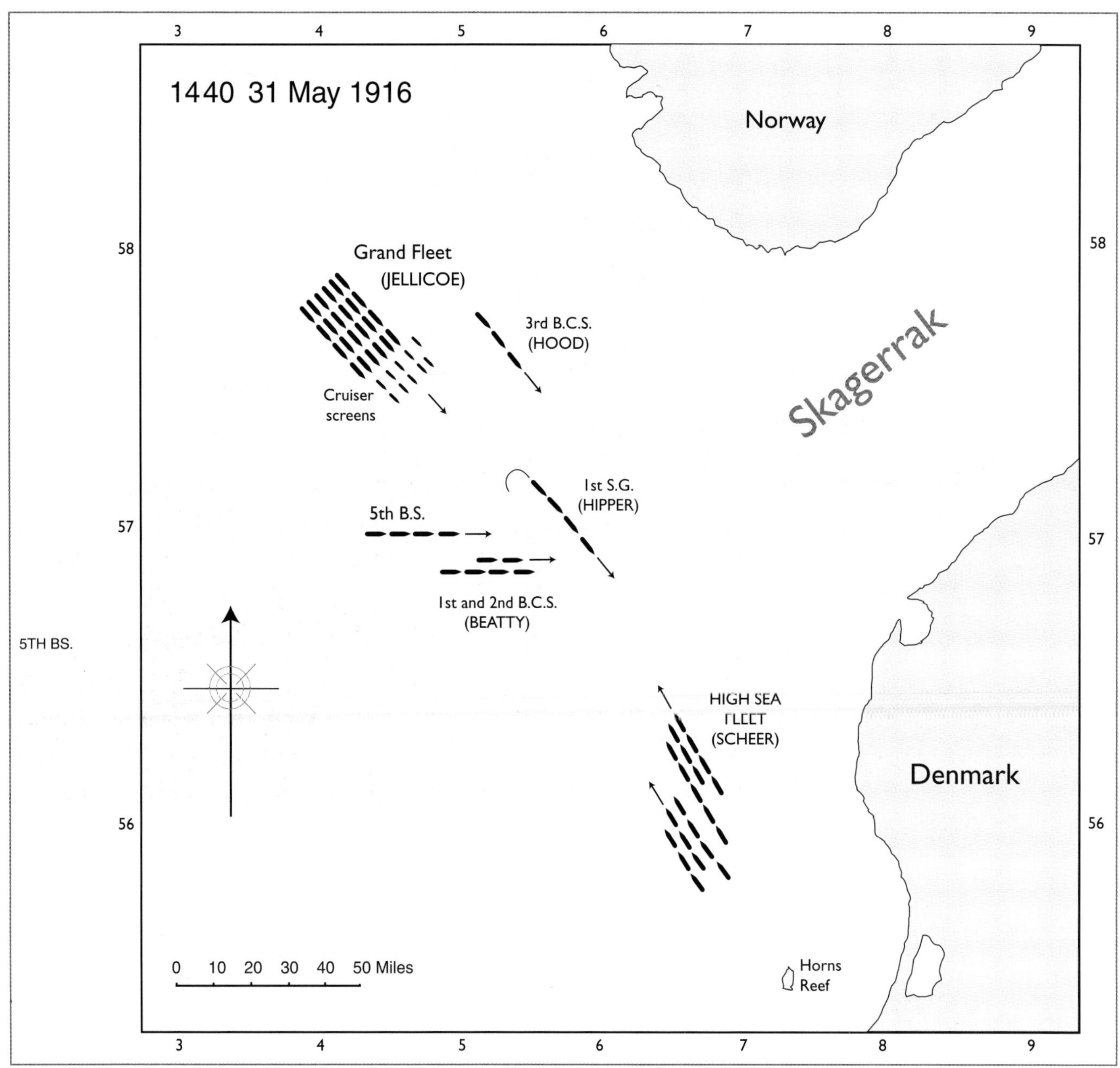

Map 5 The position of the fleets at about 1440. Hipper is turning to close the High Sea Fleet. Beatty attempts interception.

and that officers and men then serving in her would also be involved. The Chief further indicated that although the ship would be hit, there would not be any casualties. He gave the ship a *piu-piu*, or Maori war mat, something like an apron, and a green-stone *tiki*, both to be worn by the captain on the day of battle in order to ensure the safety of the ship and ship's company. In the event, most of those serving in the ship in 1913 were still serving in her in 1916; Captain Green faithfully donned the protective tokens, and the *New Zealand* sustained only one hit and no casualties. It is not surprising that when the ship was next in action, in 1917, her crew exhibited a lively interest in the donning of the *piu-piu* and *tiki*.

The Germans were the first to open fire, when the distance between the squadrons had decreased to 16,500 yards (15,100

Fig. 10.10 HMS *Indefatigable* steams into action on 31 May 1916. (*Imperial War Museum: SP 799*)

Fig. 10.11 HMS *Lion* in action. Note the smoke from hit on Q turret. (*Imperial War Museum: SP 1706*)

metres). The British opened fire at about 1548. The advatages of speed of ship, of range of gun and of weight of projectile, so long and so earnestly sought, so hardly won and achieved at so much cost, had been cast away. The Fifth Battle Squadron was then 8 miles away to the north-west, and the only cruiser screen was provided by the Second Squadron. Visibility was good, but the sun was behind Beatty's ships, giving the German gunners a clear advantage in ranging and spotting.

Battlecruiser encounter

Tactical advantage had been ceded to Hipper, whose ships had engaged within the range of their guns without having had to endure long-range fire from the British guns, to which they could not reply. Von Hase in the *Derfflinger* noted that during the first minutes of the engagement the British were not firing on his ship. Both sides initially over-estimated the range, but the Germans were soon on to their targets: within the first few minutes the *Lion* and the *Tiger* were both hit *(Figs 10.12–10.14)*. The best shooting by the British ships was that of the *Queen Mary*. She hit the *Seydlitz* twice: the second hit, on 'C' turret, caused a flash fire like that at the Dogger Bank, but rapid flooding of the magazine prevented an explosion. Meanwhile, the *Tiger* had been hit again, and the *Princess Royal* suffered a damaging hit. At 1600 a heavy shell from the *Lützow* hit the *Lion* on 'Q' turret, entered it at the junction of the face and roof armour and burst inside the turret *(Figs 10.14–10.17)*. Almost all in the gun-house and working chamber were killed and a fire was started. The Officer of the Turret, Major Francis Harvey RMLI, though frightfully and indeed mortally wounded, was able to give the order by voicepipe to the

Fig. 10.12 Light cruiser *Champion* leads the Thirteenth Destroyer Flotilla ahead of the Battlecruiser Fleet in the early stages of the 'run south'. (*Drypoint by W.L. Wyllie, courtesy of David Dawson Esq.*)

Fig. 10.13 British battlecruisers in action. (*Royal Naval Museum*)

Figs 10.14 to 10.17 Damage to HMS *Lion*. (*Royal Naval Museum*)

Fig. 10.14 *Lion* hit on Q turret. Destroyers taking up position to attack. (*Royal Naval Museum*)

Fig. 10.15 HMS *Lion*: the damage to Q turret.
(*Royal Naval Museum*)

Fig. 10.16 & 10.17 Damage to HMS *Lion*.
(*Royal Naval Museum*)

Fig. 10.17 Damage to HMS *Lion*. The destructive effect of the German armour-piercing shell is plainly shown. *(Royal Naval Museum)*

handing room below, to close the magazine doors and flood the magazines. So the ship was saved. Of all the brave deeds done that day, none had consequences so profound: had the ship and the men gone, and had the rest of the battlecruiser engagement followed its known course, the British squadron might well have faltered.

Disasters were to come. Although Beatty, aware that the range had closed to the advantage of the Germans, had turned away five points to S by E and another three to SW by S, the *Von der Tann* hit the *Indefatigable* aft at 1602, and later with two 11-inch (28-cm) shells abreast of 'A' turret. The damaged ship fell out of line, the forward magazine exploded, and the *Indefatigable* turned over and sank with the loss of all but two aboard her *(Fig 10.18; Map 6)*. At the time Chatfield thought of this disaster, symptomatic of all that was defective in British ships and gunnery, as 'just a disappointment'. The *Indefatigable* was, after all, 'a smaller and more weakly protected ship than those of the first division and was not a really serious tactical loss'. Twenty minutes later this estimate was proved disastrously wrong: the *Queen Mary*, under fire from the *Seydlitz* and *Derfflinger*, sustained hits on 'Q' turret and

Fig. 10.18 HMS *Indefatigable* sinks after magazine explosion. (*Imperial War Museum: Q 64302*)

forward, and at 1625 blew up *(Fig 10.19)*. Petty Officer Francis, one of the twenty survivors, whose action station was in 'X' turret, thought that a magazine explosion in 'B' turret sealed the ship's doom. 'Everything in the ship went as quiet as a church, and the guns were absolutely useless.' P.O. Francis got out of the turret, slid off the side of the ship into the sea and swam away: 'I . . . must have covered nearly 50 yards, when there was a big smash, and stopping and looking round the air seemed to be full of fragments and flying pieces.' The dauntless petty officer was pulled down by the suction of the sinking ship, but survived to be rescued and to return to Rosyth and eventually to Portsmouth and home.

Beatty, whose preferred station in battle was the open compass platform rather than the protected conning tower, had heard successively of the loss of the *Indefatigable*, the damage sustained by his own ship, the loss of the *Queen Mary* and the hits on the other ships of his squadrons including the next astern, the *Princess Royal*. So far as he could make out, the German ships were maintaining their line and stations and had not sustained serious injury, though hits on them had been observed. Turning to his Flag Captain, he remarked calmly: 'Chatfield, there seems to be something wrong with our bloody ships today.' Churchill's addition 'Turn two points to port' seems to be an invention, though the Navigating Officer of the *New Zealand* recalls that after the *Queen Mary* sank, the battlecruisers were in fact ordered to turn two points to port. Now reduced to four ships, three of which

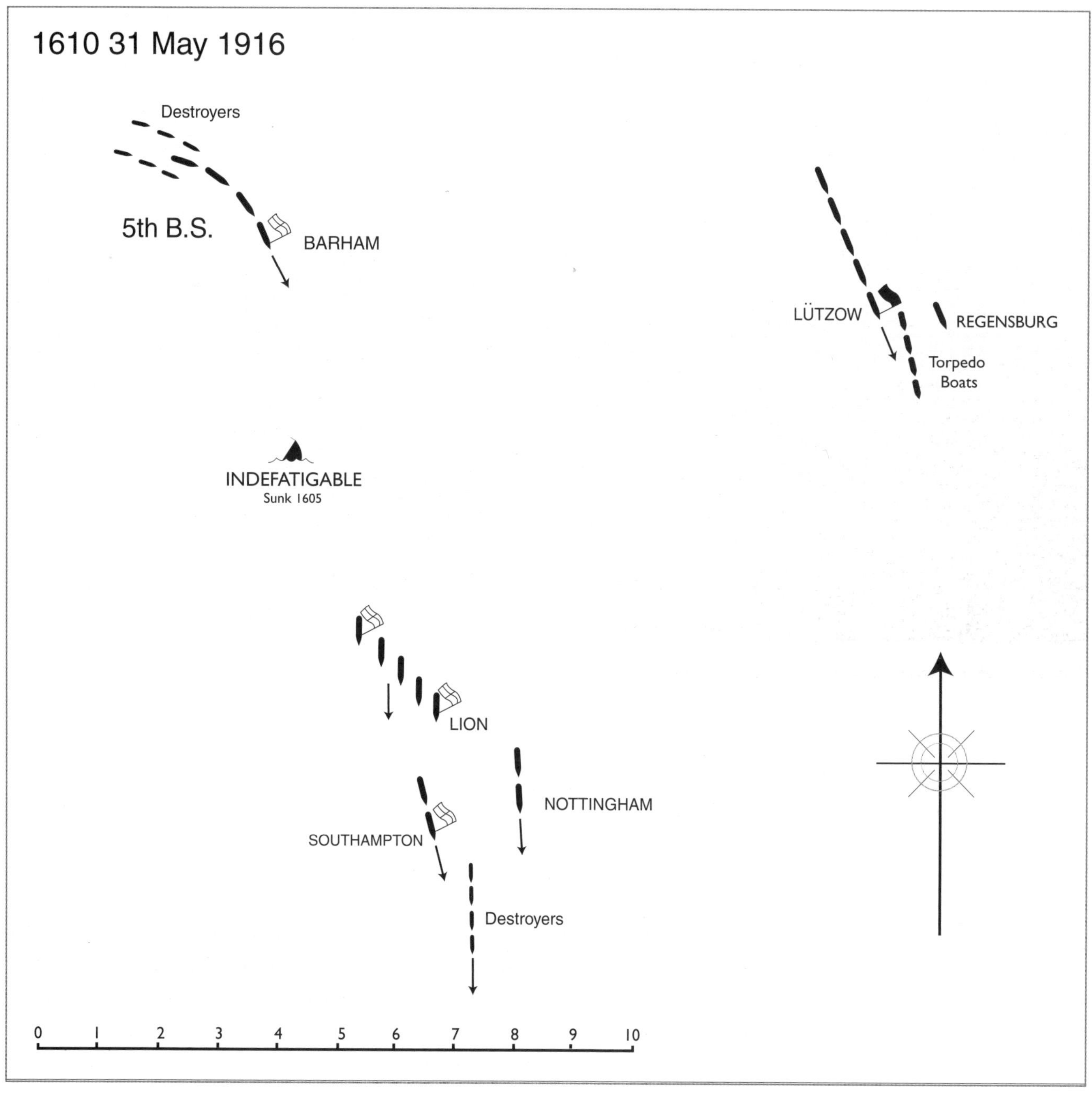

Map 6 The battlecruiser engagement. This was the situation soon after the sinking of the *Indefatigable*.

were damaged, the British battlecruiser squadron continued in action against five German ships. Not only were the Germans giving the British much more than they received, but the German armour-piercing shell was proving much more effective than the British. Also, the ships in action were approaching the High Sea Fleet at a closing speed of almost 40 knots, whereas Beatty's support, the Grand Fleet, was 50 miles to the north and slowly dropping further behind.

Two events now intervened to save the British battlecruisers. First, the Fifth Battle Squadron, steering E and later turning S, clashed at first with the German light cruisers, which prudently withdrew behind a smokescreen. Working up to full speed, the battleships sighted the *Moltke* and *Von der Tann* at a range of 20,000 yards

Fig. 10.19 HMS *Queen Mary* blows up after magazine explosion. (*Royal Naval Museum*)

At 1600 Beatty ordered his destroyers to attack

(18,300 metres), and opened fire (*Figs 10.20–10.21*). Soon the latter ship was hit aft by a 15-inch (38-cm) shell and severely damaged. Hipper, whose ships had been proceeding at only 21 knots, increased speed to 23 knots. Von Hase recorded that, 'We were now being subjected to heavy fire and so we steered a zig-zag course.' Secondly, at 1600 Beatty ordered his destroyers to attack with torpedoes to compel a turn away. At about the same time Hipper gave a similar order, and a savage combat between the light forces developed between the lines as the heavy ships bore away from each other. From a position ahead of the *Lion* twelve destroyers in three divisions charged the German Fleet. The Hon. Barry Bingham, commanding the *Nestor*, recorded that his ship and the following *Nicator* engaged the German torpedo-boats at a range of about 10,000 yards (9,100 metres) and fired on them with their 4-inch (10-cm) guns. Bingham claimed that two were sunk and the rest retired, while the British destroyers went on to attack the German battlecruisers. Torpedoes were fired: one may have hit the *Lützow*, and one certainly hit the *Seydlitz* but did not cause enough damage to slow the ship or reduce her fighting power. The *Nestor* was then hit and disabled, and came to a stop between the lines, subject to attacks from enemy torpedo-boats, a light cruiser and finally the

Fig. 10.20 HMS *Tiger* in action. She steamed through the débris of her next ahead, HMS *Queen Mary*. (*Royal Naval Museum*)

Fig. 10.21 HMS *Barham* leads the Fifth Battle Squadron into action. (*Royal Naval Museum*)

Fig. 10.22 HMS *Lion* and her three reamining consortssss in action during the 'run to the north'. (*From a painting by W.L. Wyllie. Royal Naval Museum*)

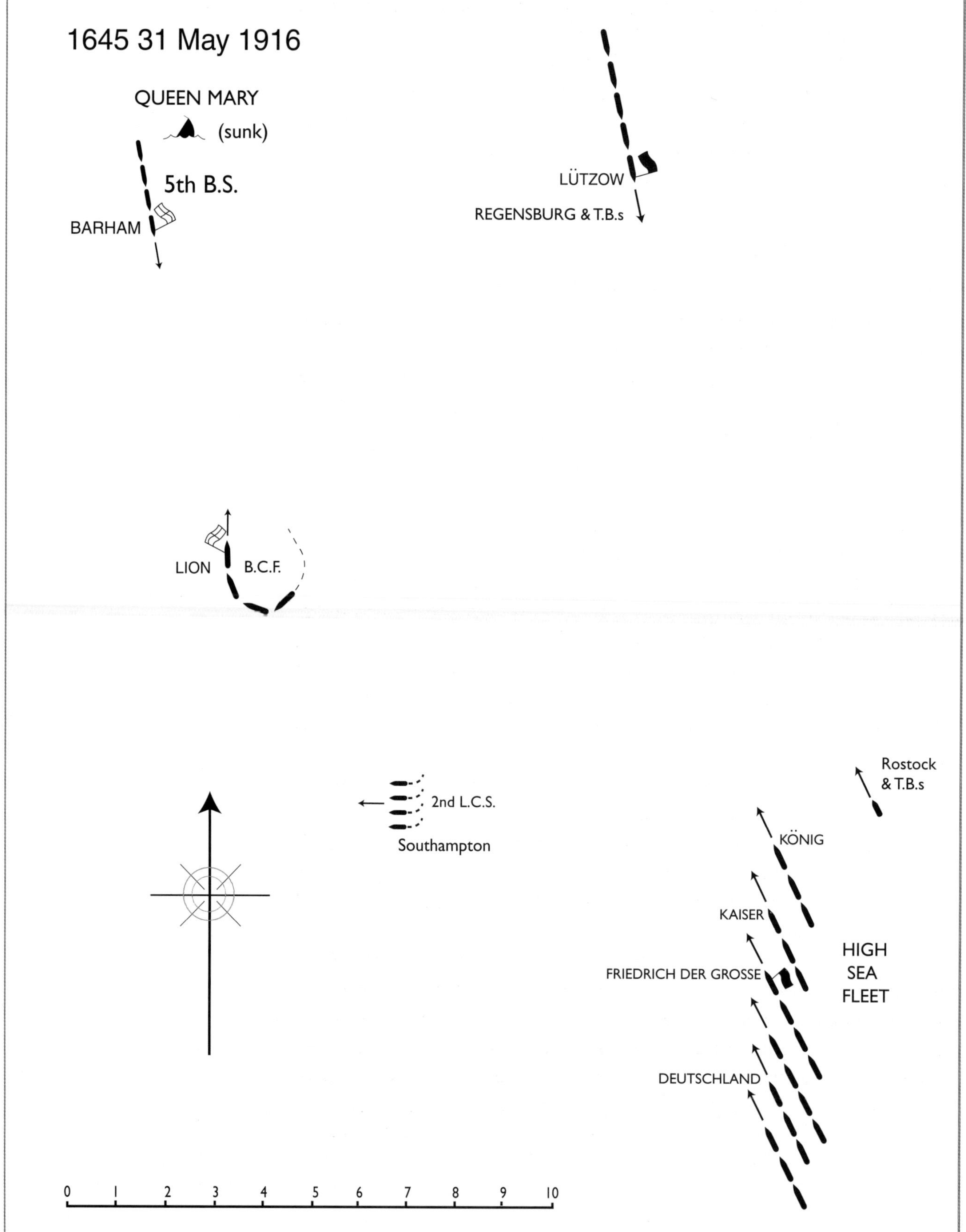

Map 7 British battlecruisers and Second Light Cruiser Squadron turn away on sighting the High Sea Fleet.

High Sea Fleet. As the *Nestor* began to sink, Bingham asked his First Lieutenant, M.J. Bethell 'Now, where shall we go?' Bethell, who was later mortally wounded, replied 'To heaven, I trust, Sir.' Bingham and a number of others were rescued from the sea by a German torpedo-boat, to spend the rest of the war as prisoners. Bingham was later awarded the Victoria Cross, but courage and leadership of this sort were no exception in the destroyers.

German battlefleet sighted

In the hour that the 'run to the south' lasted, the five German ships made thirty-two hits on the British battlecruisers and battleships, while the ten British ships made fourteen on the German ships. A decisive event now supervened: scouting ahead of the British squadrons had been left to Goodenough's four light cruisers. At 1630 the *Southampton* sighted a heavy pall of smoke to the south-east, and a little later was able to signal to Jellicoe and Beatty: 'Battleships in sight.' Some minutes later, having closed to about 6 miles, Goodenough was able to signal: 'Have sighted enemy battle fleet, bearing approximately south east, course of enemy north.' This was of course the signal for which the whole Navy, and the Grand Fleet in particular, had been waiting. At last the enemy had emerged from his lair and was in sight, the elusive enemy that they had scarcely hoped to see, huge and menacing. Once again the British had been caught at a tactical disadvantage: their battlecruiser screen had been depleted and damaged, the light cruiser screen had been dispersed, two squadrons of their heavy ships were rapidly closing an undamaged and greatly superior enemy, and a turn away would have to be executed while those ships were under fire. Amid the smoke and carnage and the thunder of the guns and of the hits, Beatty kept his head and made the correct decision. Permitting himself a sight of the advancing High Sea Fleet, he ordered at 1640 a 16-point alteration of course in succession to starboard – that is, a reversal of course by his leading ship, with the others following in succession. As the *Lion* turned she was hit again by the *Lützow*, and as the battlecruisers strove to regain the speed lost during their turns, they came under fire from the leading ships of the High Sea Fleet. The decision had been correct, but the order to turn in succession exposed each ship to heavy fire at the turning point *(Map 7)*. It would have been preferable to order a turn together, but it may be that the precise wording of the order was left to Seymour.

CHAPTER ELEVEN

THE RETREAT TO THE NORTH

As the battlecruisers began their retreat to the NW, the Fifth Battle Squadron was still steering SE, about 8 miles away on the *Lion*'s starboard bow, still shooting at Hipper's ships. It was urgently necessary that the Fifth Battle Squadron should soon turn to follow the battlecruisers; otherwise, these priceless ships and their crews might be overwhelmed by the gunfire of the High Sea Fleet. Beatty now took decisions which have been criticised. He signalled that the Fifth Battle Squadron should pass to port of his ships – that is, on the disengaged side – and later that the battleships should turn sixteen points to starboard in succession. Both squadrons turned a few points to starboard so that the ships could pass port to port. It is probable that the *Lion* and *Barham* passed each other on opposing courses and about 2 miles apart at 1651. About three minutes before this the *Lion* had made the signal to turn: it was flying when the ships passed. There is doubt about the time of hauling down the signal: in the event, it was not obeyed until 1654 *(Map 8)*. That lapse of time, and the combined speed of approach of the Fifth Battle Squadron and the High Sea Fleet, was enough to bring Evan-Thomas's ships within range of the German battleships. The direction to turn 'in succession' again exposed each ship to concentrated fire at her turning point. During this turn the *Barham* sustained damage in her fore part from a hit by a heavy shell (*Fig 11.1*). Eighteen men were killed outright, and fifty were wounded, some of whom died later from their injuries. Fleet Surgeon Penfold recorded that the larger of the two medical stations, 'on the middle deck, amidships', was wrecked and medical personnel were wounded. Although wounded, Penfold went to

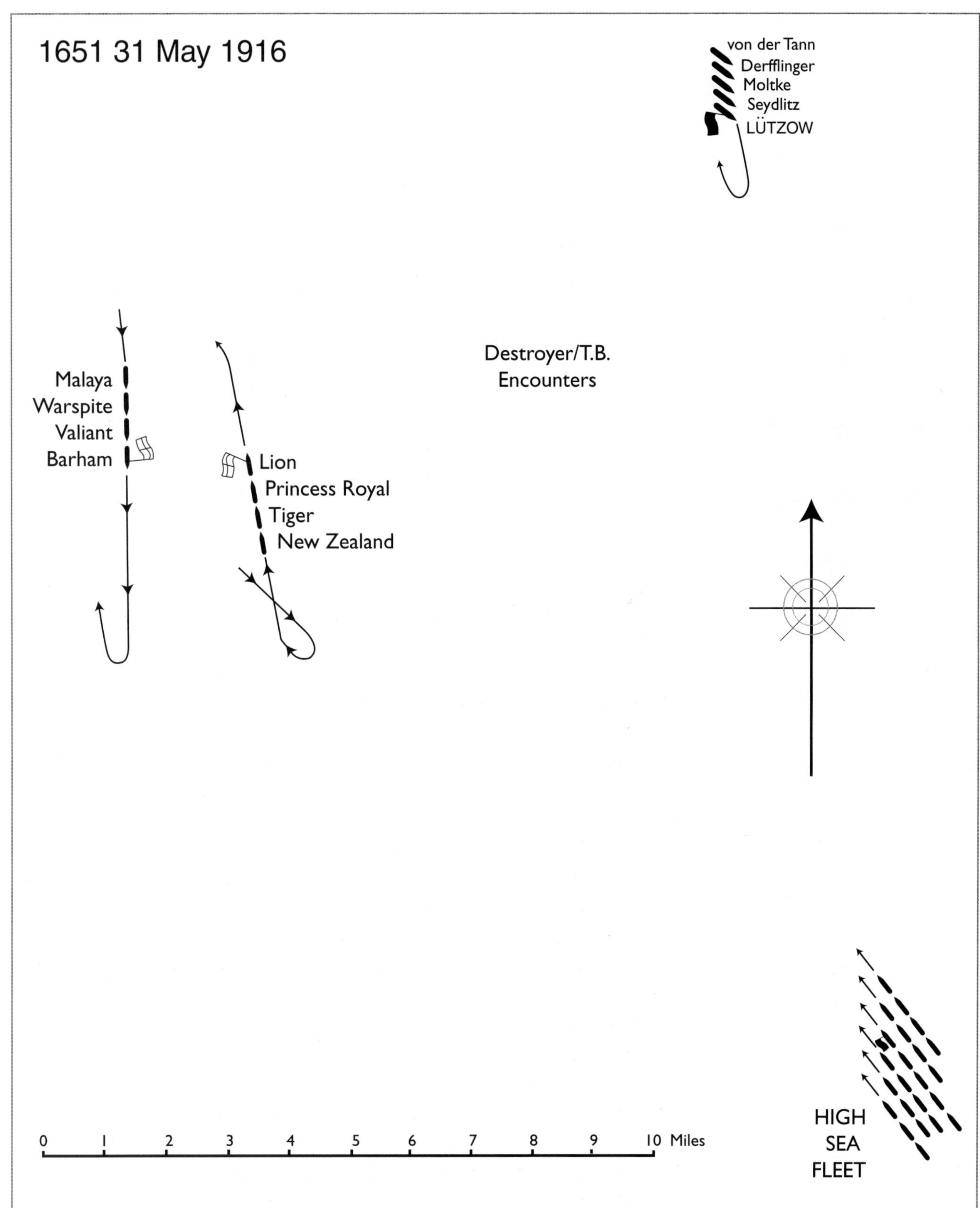

Map 8 5th Battle Squadron turns to follow the battlecruisers.

Fig. 11.1 Destroyers screening HMS *Barham*. *(Royal Naval Museum)*

work on the casualties, and so continued until on 2 June they were transferred to a hospital ship. These actions later gained for him the Distinguished Service Order.

During the turn the risk became so obvious that the captain of the *Malaya*, the last in the line, began the turn before the *Warspite*, the next in line, had finished hers.

As the Fifth Battle Squadron settled on a northerly course, the battlecruisers were about 3 miles ahead, again engaged with Hipper's squadron, which had turned at about 1650 to lead the High Sea Fleet. Though Evan-Thomas's ships worked up to their full speed, it was not enough to take them quickly out of the range of the German guns. The two rearmost ships, *Warspite* and *Malaya*, suffered particularly badly: the *Malaya* was hit by a heavy shell which wrecked the starboard 6-inch (15-cm) battery and caused many and terrible casualties, and later was hit below the waterline and suffered damage to her oil tanks. Her speed fell off, and, had not smart action been taken to limit damage and restore speed, she must have fallen astern and been destroyed *(Fig 11.2)*. The *Warspite* too suffered several hits from heavy shells, sustaining in particular damage in the steering compartment. Nevertheless, the two leading ships maintained a damaging fire on the German battlecruisers, and the two rear ships hit three of the leading German battleships. The *Seydlitz* suffered further damage which greatly reduced her fighting power, and the *Von der Tann* was in effect stripped of her main armament.

Fig. 11.2 Shell splashes over HMS *Malaya*. (*Royal Naval Museum*)

All around these central events there was activity. Goodenough's Second Light Cruiser Squadron, having dared the guns of the High Sea Fleet to see and report its position and course and strength, was dodging their fire by steering towards the shell splashes while running north behind the battlecruisers *(Fig 11.3)*. King-Hall, at his action station aft in the *Southampton*, underwent the uncomfortable sensation of being fired on from a distance at sea: '. . . we always seemed to look just as two or three of the great brutes flickered flames from their guns at us, and we knew that another salvo was on its way across. We knew that the time of

Fig. 11.3 Shell splashes near HMS *Birmingham* of Commodore Goodenough's squadron, under fire from the High Sea Fleet while steaming north to join the Grand Fleet. (*Imperial War Museum: SP 474*)

flight was twenty-three seconds, and the sub (sub-lieutenant) had a wrist watch with a prominent second hand . . . at the twenty-third second the sub would make a grimace, and as if in reply a series of splitting reports and lugubrious moans announced that the salvo had arrived.' King-Hall was able to notice that the German gunners were working a 'ladder' system of range-finding. Watching shell splashes creeping nearer is very damaging to morale. Alexander-Sinclair's and Napier's First and Third Squadrons were north of the action, running towards the advancing Grand Fleet. The Grand Fleet was steering SE in columns, working up to full speed. Jellicoe knew that the High Sea Fleet was at sea and engaged with the Fifth Battle Squadron, and that a fleet action was likely. He sent Rear-Admiral Hood's three Invincibles ahead with their light cruiser screen: their 25 knots allowed them to gain 5 miles in the hour on the Grand Fleet. All men in his fleet were at action stations.

Hipper's light cruisers were ahead of his battlecruisers, intermittently engaged with the British light cruisers. The High Sea

Fleet was in line ahead in pursuit of the Fifth Battle Squadron; Scheer, in the *Friedrich der Grosse*, the sixth in line, did not know that the Grand Fleet was at sea and rapidly approaching; rather, he thought that he and Hipper had brought off the *coup* that they had long planned – the trapping of an isolated British squadron.

At 1735 the *Falmouth*, the most northerly ship of Beatty's light cruiser screen, sighted to the north an armoured cruiser which turned out to be the *Black Prince*, one of the cruiser screen of the Grand Fleet. This information, passed to the *Lion*, indicated to Beatty that he was near the right wing of the Grand Fleet. Beatty now made an important decision, all the more remarkable because it was made in the stress of battle, after two hours of almost continuously close engagement, and yet was tactically correct. He brought the battlecruisers round to starboard to close Hipper's squadron and edge it off to the east. Hipper, seeing the British edging over ahead of his ships, thought that Beatty was trying to cross the 'T', and conformed to the easterly course. Thus, he was prevented from sighting the Grand Fleet in its advance. Von Hase, who was on the receiving end in the *Derfflinger*, gives this manoeuvre much praise: 'Admiral Beatty, by completely outflanking us in spite of our highest speed, accomplished an excellent manoeuvre, and his ships carried out an excellent feat of technique . . . brought us into such a position that we were completely enveloped by the English Battle Fleet and the English battlecruisers.' Gordon has some doubt about whether this was in fact Beatty's intention, but that is what happened, and even if it was partly due to luck it is hard to grudge Beatty a bit of that. After all, luck is often enough the determinant in battle: the particular quality that Napoleon demanded of his commanders was that they should be lucky.

Even if it was partly due to luck it is hard to grudge Beatty a bit of that. . . .

Deployment of the Grand Fleet

The *Iron Duke*'s wireless room had overheard the *Southampton*'s report that she had sighted the High Sea Fleet to her south-east and heading north, and that sighting had been confirmed by the *Lion*. Up to then, Jellicoe had been under the impression that Scheer's fleet was still in the Jade, but his composure was not affected. The Fleet was told at 1647 that the enemy's battlefleet was coming north, and three minutes later Jellicoe made to the Admiralty the signal 'Fleet action is imminent.' This was the signal for which all had for almost two years of war been waiting: for the first time since Trafalgar the Royal Navy was to be involved in a fleet engagement; although at the time no one could know this, it was also the last time.

Jellicoe, on the compass platform of the *Iron Duke*, knew that the High Sea Fleet was at sea somewhere to the south and east and that the battlecruisers and Fifth Battle Squadron were engaged with Hipper's battlecruisers in a fight running towards him. His fleet was still in columns abeam of one another, and had to be deployed into line ahead before it met the enemy. Such a deployment could most simply be done by the port or starboard wing column turning in that direction and the other columns following it in succession. The weather, initially clear, had become hazy. The deployment could not be started until the position and course of the High Sea Fleet was known: if it were started too early, the Grand Fleet might find itself in battle array in the wrong position or might even miss the enemy altogether; if it were begun too late, the Fleet might find itself involved in a complicated manoeuvre under fire. Beatty, on whom the responsibility for informing Jellicoe about the movements of the enemy was chiefly placed, had been silent between 1645 and 1800. Certainly, he had not been idle during that critical period, and the *Lion*'s wireless had been out of action.

Jellicoe . . . knew that the enemy fleet must be near, but he still did not know its exact position

Just before 1800 the *Marlborough (Fig 11.4)*, leading the starboard column of the Grand Fleet, saw gun flashes on her starboard bow and soon after that sighted the British battlecruisers in action on the same bearing. These sightings were signalled to Jellicoe, to whom they came as an unwelcome surprise. Positions had been calculated from dead reckoning, a method certain to be unreliable when ships were zig-zagging, and both the *Iron Duke*'s and *Lion*'s calculated positions were inaccurate. Jellicoe had expected to sight Beatty's force at 1800 about 12 miles away to the SE, but he found that in fact it was 6 miles distant on a bearing SSW. He knew that the enemy fleet must be near, but he still did not know its exact position. Beatty now steered eastwards about 2 miles ahead of and across the advancing columns of the Grand Fleet, and as he did so, Jellicoe signalled 'Where is the enemy's battlefleet?' Beatty, by then well ahead of and out of sight of the High Sea Fleet, could answer only 'Enemy battlecruisers bearing SE.' At 1810 Evan-Thomas in the *Barham* signalled 'Enemy battlefleet SSE'; at 1814, however, Beatty sighted the head of the German line and was able to signal by searchlight: 'Have sighted enemy's battlefleet bearing SSW.' No estimate of course or distance was given, but with the urgent necessity for action the information was enough for Jellicoe at 1815 to give the order to deploy on the port wing column – that is, to lead the Fleet to the south and east, between the High Sea Fleet and its bases *(Map 9)*. This tremendous decision, on which in truth hung the fate of the Fleet and the nation, was taken by Jellicoe in this period of extreme stress, on the basis of information necessarily incomplete, with incomparable coolness. 'Hoist equal-speed pendant south east' was his order to the Fleet Signal Officer. That was modified to 'Hoist equal-speed pendant south east by east' in response to Commander Woods' request, 'Would you make it a point to port, Sir, so that they will

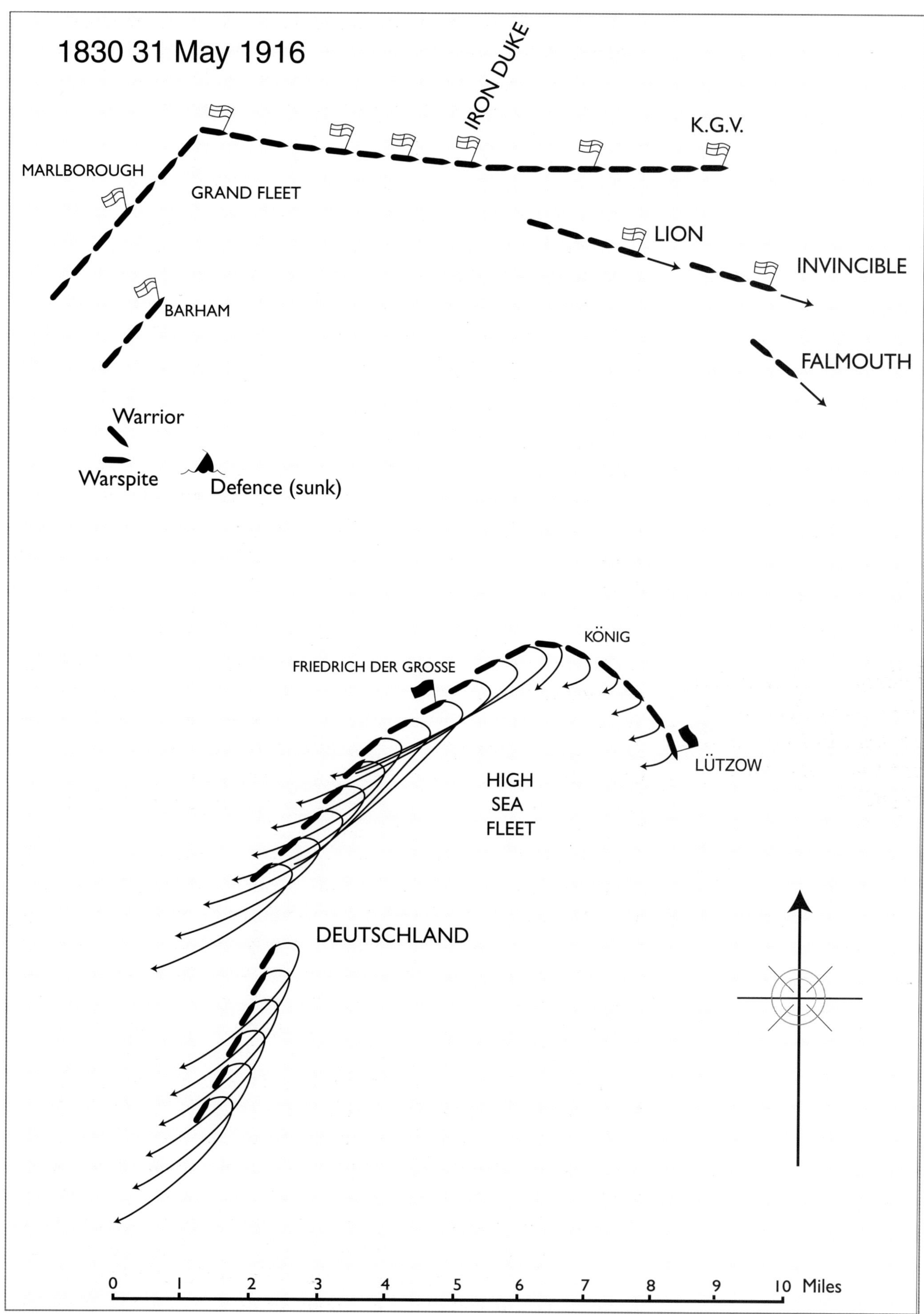

Map 9 The deployment of the Grand Fleet. The High Sea Fleet's Gefechtskehrtwendung is indicated.

Fig. 11.5 The Grand Fleet deploys. (*Royal Naval Museum*)

know it is on the port wing column?' The signal was hauled down at 1815, but before that the *Iron Duke* had begun the turn to port that was to bring the Grand Fleet across the head of the German line, between it and its bases, with most of its guns bearing on the enemy. The tactical advantage had passed decisively to the British *(Fig 11.5)*.

Meanwhile, Hood's Third Battlecruiser Squadron and its attendant light cruisers had pressed on ahead of the Grand Fleet. *Chester* and *Canterbury* of the light cruiser screen came into contact with Hipper's light cruiser screen and a sharp action ensued *(Fig 11.6)*. The decks of the British *Chester* were swept by high-explosive shell and many casualties were sustained. Among them was the sixteen-year-old Boy First Class J.T. Cornwell, sight-setter of the forecastle gun, who, though mortally wounded, remained at his post awaiting orders when the rest of the gun crew lay dead or wounded around him. His bravery was recognised by the posthumous award of the Victoria Cross. As the *Chester* turned and fled, Hood's battlecruisers, brought to the scene by the sound of the gunfire, opened fire on the German light cruisers with their 12-inch (30-cm) guns. The *Wiesbaden* in particular was badly damaged and was brought to a stop between the lines. Hood pressed on, and a little before 1800 sighted Hipper's battlecruisers, then steering E. They opened fire, and the German, under the impression that he had met the Grand Fleet,

Previous pages: Fig. 11.4 HMS *Marlborough*. Flagship of Vice-Admiral Burney, commanding the First Battle Squadron of the Grand Fleet. She opened fire on the High Sea Fleet in the first encounter, but later sustained a hit from a torpedo which reduced her speed to 17 knots. Here she is entering Grand Harbour, after the War. (*Royal Naval Museum*)

Fig. 11.6 HMS *Chester* in action with Hipper's light cruiser screen. She sustained damage and suffered many casualties from high-explosive shell. Among the casualties was Boy Cornwell, posthumously awarded the Victoria Cross. (*Drypoint by W.L. Wyllie, Royal Naval Museum*)

turned to SW to fall back on the High Sea Fleet and ordered his torpedo-boats to attack. They were met by a counter-attack by Hood's four destroyers. Once again the courage and resolution of the destroyer crews were displayed. Commander Loftus Jones led the assault in the *Shark*, a ship of 950 tons armed with three 4-inch (10-cm) guns and capable of 32 knots *(Figs. 11.7 & 11.8)*. She was hit and disabled early in the action, and Loftus Jones was wounded. Although subjected to heavy fire, the *Shark* continued firing until she sank with her colours flying. Her captain, mortally wounded, floated clear in a lifebelt but died soon afterwards. His bravery and resolution were recognised by the award of the Victoria Cross. Hipper, having sighted Scheer's fleet, turned back to a course NE.

Now occurred a singular and tragic episode. The *Defence*, flagship of Rear-Admiral Arbuthnot, a stern disciplinarian and physical fitness enthusiast (*Fig 8.3, page 103*), and *Warrior*, both of the Grand Fleet's armoured cruiser screen, steamed across the line of advance of Beatty's battlecruisers to attack Hipper's light cruisers and the crippled *Wiesbaden* in particular. No one can say what was in Arbuthnot's mind to cause him to order this rash move, but he

Fig. 11.7 HMTBD (Torpedo boat destroyer) *Shark* (Commander Loftus Jones VC), sunk on 31 May 1916, in action with Hipper's light forces. A 'K' class oil-fired boat of 950 tons, she was armed with three 4-inch guns and four 21-inch torpedo tubes, and could steam over 30 knots. (*Imperial War Museum: Q 21762*)

may have thought that he was correctly interpreting the admonition in the Battle Orders of the Grand Fleet to support its light cruisers. The eight-year-old cruisers advanced to shell the luckless *Wiesbaden*, causing the *Lion* to sheer away in order to avoid them. In the conditions of reduced visibility, Arbuthnot was unable to see the advance of the German battlecruisers, and his ships came under fire from them. The *Derfflinger* fired at the *Warrior*, and the *Lützow* at the *Defence*. The *Warrior*, badly damaged, turned away; the *Defence* blew up. Von Hase observed this from the *Derfflinger*: 'The English ship . . . broke in half with a tremendous explosion. Black smoke and debris shot into the air, a flame enveloped the whole ship, and then she sank before our eyes.' The *Warrior* would have followed her, had it not been for the involuntary intervention of the *Warspite*. The Fifth Battle Squadron, following Beatty's battlecruisers, was about to fall into line astern of the Grand Fleet, when the *Warspite*'s helm jammed and she described two complete circles round the *Warrior* under the fire of the High Sea Fleet, sustaining fifteen hits and diverting attention from the damaged cruiser *(Figs 11.9–11.10)*. The *Warrior* was later taken in tow by the *Engadine*, but failed to make harbour. Later, the *Warspite*, seriously damaged and intermittently out of control, was ordered home *(Fig 11.11)*. Thirty-two years later, after distinguished service in the Second World War and independent to the last, she met her end while under tow from Portsmouth to Faslane, going aground first in Prussia Cove and later in Mounts Bay and being broken up there.

It was not long before further disaster overtook the British: Hood's Third Battlecruiser Squadron, having crippled Hipper's light cruisers, came into action with his battlecruisers. The leading ship, *Invincible*, was shooting well and fast. Her Gunnery Officer, Commander (later Rear-Admiral) Dannreuther, a godson of Richard Wagner, was controlling the gunfire from the foretop, as he had done at the Falklands battle. This time he was confronting von Hase and the *Derfflinger* at a range of about 9,000 yards (8,200 metres). At 1831 'the *Derfflinger* fired her last salvo at this ship and then for the third time we saw the dreadful spectacle that we had already seen in the case of the *Queen Mary* and the *Defence* . . . there occurred a rapid succession of heavy explosions, masts collapsed, debris was hurled into the air, a gigantic column of black smoke rose towards the sky, and from the parting sections of the ship, coal dust spurted in all directions. . . .' A heavy shell had pierced the roof of 'Q' turret, burst inside it and ignited the chain leading to the magazine. The 'first of the battlecruisers' broke in half, and in that shallow sea the bow and stern projected, to mark the grave of an admiral and a thousand seamen and to signify the failure of British technology. Dannreuther simply stepped into the sea, and was later rescued together with five others of the company of that famous ship *(Figs 11.12 & 11.13)*.

Fig. 11.8 Commander Loftus Jones VC. In the *Shark* he led his division of four destroyers to attack the German torpedo boats. He was mortally wounded. His body was washed ashore on the Swedish coast, there to be buried in Viking fashion. *(Royal Naval Museum)*

Things were bad too for Hipper's squadron: the *Lützow*, having taken more than twenty hits by heavy shells, had tons of water on board and was almost unmanoeuvrable; she was later to be abandoned and sunk. The *Seydlitz*'s bows were under water and only one turret was capable of action, and all the *Von der Tann*'s big gun turrets were out of action *(Figs 11.14–11.16)*. While Hipper transferred his flag to a destroyer and sought a battlecruiser in a condition to act as flagship, Captain Hartog led the line in the *Derfflinger*. For Scheer in the *Friedrich der Grosse*, the effect of the British deployment was that an 'entire arc stretching from north to east was a sea of fire'. In fact, the reduced visibility and the presence of the *Warspite* and *Warrior* and *Wiesbaden* between the lines restricted the firing of the British battleships: the *Marlborough* opened fire at

Fig. 11.9 HMS *Warrior*. Armoured cruiser, completed in 1908, with an armament of 9.2 inch and 7.5 inch guns. She was seriously damaged by fire from the German battlecruisers, but was saved from destruction by the *Warspite*'s involuntary turn. However, she sank while under tow by HMS *Engadine*. (*Royal Naval Museum*)

Fig. 11.10 HMS *Warspite*'s involuntary turn around the stricken *Warrior*. (*Drypoint by W.L. Wyllie, in the author's possession*)

Fig. 11.11 Damage to HMS *Warspite*. (*Royal Naval Museum*)

1817 and was followed by the *Agincourt* (*Fig 11.17*). In the event, twelve at the most opened fire on the opposing German heavy ships. Among them was the *Marlborough*: William John Brewer, serving in that ship, recorded '6.17 pm. Opened fire. 7 salvoes were fired. The 5th and 7th salvoes clearly seen to hit . . . 6.21 ceased firing as enemy was hidden by cruiser [*Wiesbaden*] on fire . . . 6.25 opened fire 10,500 yards, 5 salvoes were fired [at the *Wiesbaden*].' Prince Albert, the future King George VI, serving as a sub-lieutenant in the *Collingwood*, was another to record his impressions of the action. All three royal princes saw service in the war (*Fig 15.4*, page 228).

The High Sea Fleet was running into the potentially deadly arc with the fire of many of its ships masked by the next ahead or unable to bear on the enemy. There was no question of turning under fire to a course parallel with that of the Grand Fleet and so continuing the fight. At 1833 Scheer gave the order for a *Gefechtskehrtwendung* – a sixteen-point turn away almost together. The rearmost ship began the turn, and the next ahead started her turn as soon as she saw the bow of the next astern beginning to move away. At the same time the light vessels made smoke to cover the manoeuvre and the torpedo-boats attacked. Of the leading ships only the *König* had suffered heavy punishment from the guns of the Grand Fleet, and none was seriously damaged. Only the *Warspite* of the British capital ships was damaged during the brief fleet action. Jellicoe was not at first aware that the Germans had retreated: he thought that they had simply been masked by the mist and smoke. Some of his ships did indeed see some German ships turn away, but these observations were not reported to the Commander in Chief.

Fig. 11.12 The destruction of HMS *Invincible*. The ship, hit on a turret amidships by heavy shell from *Derfflinger*, blows up and sinks. (*Royal Naval Museum*)

Fig. 11.13 The bow and stern of the *Invincible* project above the surface of the sea. The appearance is similar to that seen twenty-five years later, when the *Hood* succumbed to fire from the battleship *Bismarck*. (*Royal Naval Museum*)

Fig. 11.14 to 11.16 The unlucky *Seydlitz*
11.14 *Seydlitz* badly on fire aft and emitting clouds of smoke. (Probably at the Dogger Bank, 1915) (*Royal Naval Museum*)

Fig. 11.15 *Seydlitz* steaming home with her bows almost under. (*Royal Naval Museum*)

Fig. 11.16 Hits 21 and 22 on the *Seydlitz*, on the starboard side, abeam of the forward turret. Note the rolled-up torpedo net. (*Imperial War Museum: Q 20683*)

Fig. 11.17 HM Ships *Thunderer* and *Iron Duke* open fire. *Royal Oak* and *Superb* follow them. (*Royal Naval Museum*)

CHAPTER TWELVE

THE SECOND GERMAN ADVANCE

After some minutes Jellicoe realised that the enemy had turned away in retreat. It would have been inconceivably rash to turn and follow: visibility was decreasing, and the conditions were ideal for an attack by torpedo-boats. Division of the Grand Fleet into two columns to trap the Germans was equally or even more risky. The 'fast division' – the Fifth Battle Squadron – was in a bad way, with the *Warspite* effectively out of action and the *Malaya* seriously damaged. Jellicoe again made the sensible decision – namely, to place his fleet between the enemy and his bases. At 1844 he turned the fleet by divisions to a SE course, and ten minutes later to S. Only Goodenough's squadron of light cruisers attempted continued observation of the enemy. It was soon after the first alteration of course that the *Marlborough* was hit by a torpedo. She was, however, able to remain in the line of battle. Beatty's remaining battlecruisers were well ahead of the battlefleet. At about 1900 the *Lion*, *Princess Royal*, *Tiger* and *New Zealand*, followed by the *Inflexible* and *Indomitable*, made a 32-point turn to starboard – in fact, described a complete circle. The reasons for this turn remain obscure, and Beatty later tried to represent that his course had been plotted inaccurately. He averred that there were in fact two 16-point turns: the first to starboard and the second to port. The most likely explanation is, surely, that Beatty felt that his squadron was unsupported and that he was aiming to reduce the distance between it and the main fleet.

Scheer represents as follows his next actions. 'If the enemy followed us, our action in retaining the direction taken after turning would partake of the nature of a retreat: the ships in the rear might be damaged or have to be abandoned. So, I decided to force the enemy into a second battle by another determined advance. The manoeuvre was bound to surprise the enemy and upset his plans.' Scheer echoed the words of Nelson: '*Ich denke, es wird den Feind überraschen und in Bestürzung versetzen. Er wird nicht wissen, was der Zweck der Bewegung ist.*'* Most commentators have cast doubt on this explanation of what has been seen as a very rash move: at 1855, when about 10 miles to the west of the Grand Fleet, Scheer ordered a second Gefechtskehrtwendung, to starboard, to bring the fleet on to an easterly course. This course would bring his leading ships into contact with the rear divisions of the Grand Fleet, then steering S by E with some of its ships masking the broadside fire of others. Scheer's object may well have been to pass just astern of the Grand Fleet, doing what damage he could to the rearmost ships. At about 1910 the British sighted the German van, and a few minutes later they opened fire. Soon, Scheer found his fleet in much the same position that had obtained forty-five minutes previously. Hits were recorded on all the ships leading the German line, the light then being much more favourable to the British than to their enemy.

Scheer can hardly have hoped to pass behind the British array in his eastward course, but that explanation of his second change of course has generally been accepted by British commentators. The allegedly aggressive action did not in the event dismay Jellicoe nor upset his plans, though the reappearance of the High Sea Fleet certainly came as a surprise to him and to most of his commanders. Once again, Scheer was saved by superior German technology and good ship-handling: although his leading ships were hit repeatedly by heavy shells, none sustained fatal damage; none was disabled to fall prey to the concentrated fire from British guns. The *Colossus* was the only British battleship to be hit during this clash, but the *Seydlitz*, *von der Tann*, *Grosser Kurfürst* and four other German battleships were all hit by heavy shells. Yates notes that fifteen British battleships scored at least a hit each on an enemy ship. A third Gefechtskehrtwendung was ordered, and to cover it the remaining battlecruisers were ordered to charge the enemy, in what later became known as the 'death-ride': '. . . *ran an den Feind, voll einsetzen*'** *(Map 10)*. So they did, led by the *Derfflinger*, which suffered further damage. 'Hit after hit struck our ship . . . at 9.13 p.m. [2113] a serious catastrophe occurred. A 38 cm [15-inch] shell pierced the armour of "Caesar" turret and exploded inside . . . the blazing cartridge-cases emitted great tongues of flame which shot up out of the turrets as high as a house; but they only blazed, they did not explode . . .' A few minutes later a 15-inch shell pierced the roof of 'Dora' turret: again, the cartridges blazed but did not explode, and the ship drove on.

* I think it will surprise the enemy and dismay him. He will not know what the purpose of the manoeuvre is.

** Charge the enemy, give it all you have.

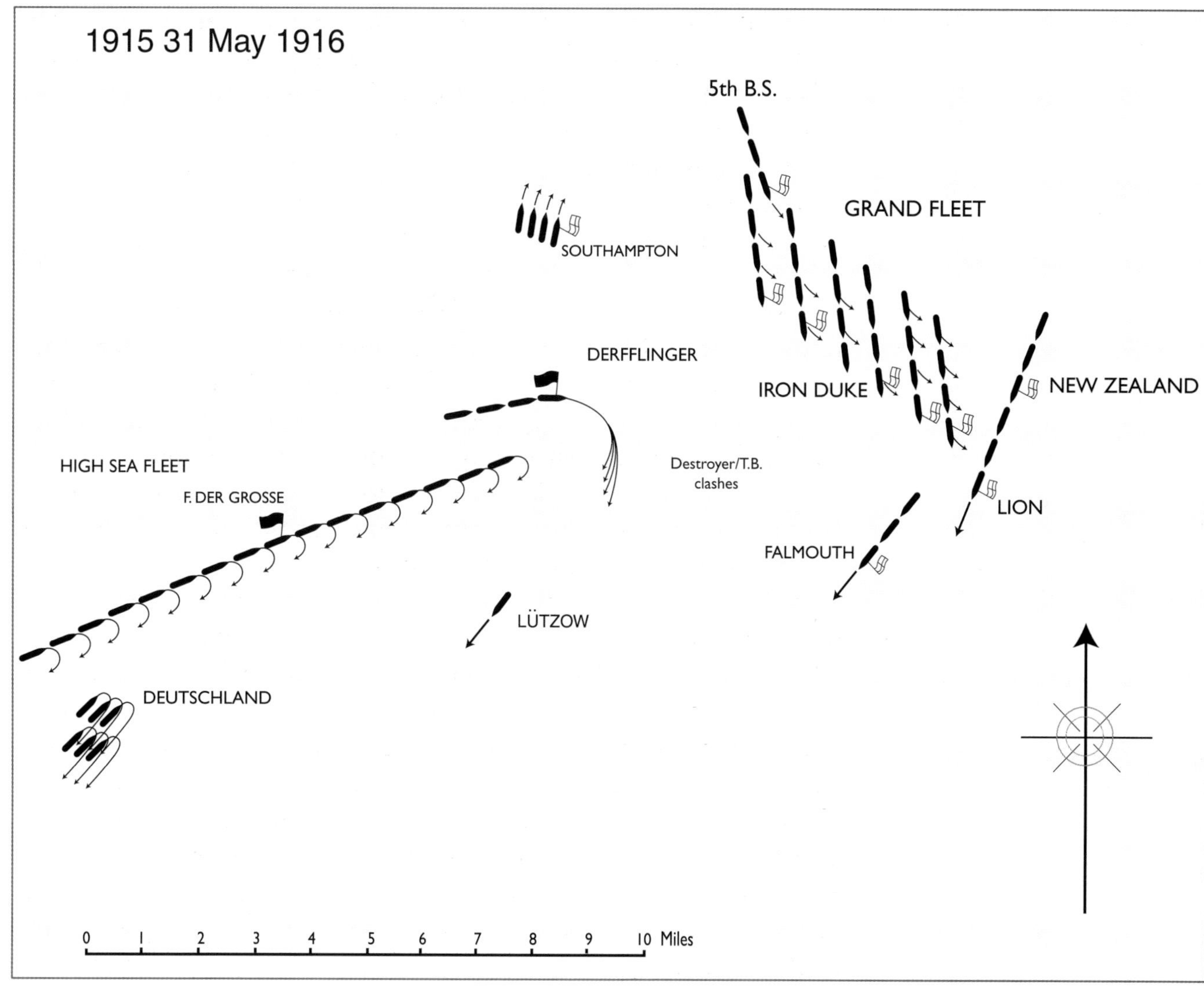

Map 10 The third Gefechtskehrtwendung and the 'death-ride' by Hipper's battlecruisers.

At the same time the German torpedo-boats attacked at ranges of about 7,000 yards (6,400 metres) and were met by concentrated fire from the secondary armament of the British battleships and by a counter-attack by the Fourth Light Cruiser Squadron and the Eleventh Destroyer Flotilla *(Fig 12.1)*. The attack was pressed home, and could have caused serious damage to the Grand Fleet had it not been for the vigilance of the lookouts and the alertness of the commanders. Jellicoe turned his ships away in two two-point turns, but eight of his ships had narrow escapes from the torpedo stream. Hipper's battlecruisers followed the battleships and the brief but savage action was over. Beatty's ships, ahead of the scene of action, continued on a course S by W. Twice the High Sea Fleet had run into the Grand Fleet; twice it had retreated, suffering on the second occasion far more damage than it inflicted

The Grand Fleet's turn away virtually ended contact between the two battlefleets and at the same time removed the possibility of decisive victory or defeat. Although Jellicoe had some time previously indicated to the Admiralty that a turn away would be his response to attack by torpedo-boats, he came in for much criticism

Fig. 12.1 German torpedo-boats during the battle. (*Royal Naval Museum*)

for the manoeuvre. It was indeed generally possible to see the tracks of German torpedoes and to take action to avoid the missiles: by pointing a ship directly towards or away from these tracks it was possible to 'comb' them and to present the smallest target possible. For this purpose, a turn towards was as effective as a turn away, but the latter course offered also the chance of outrunning the torpedo, whereas the former sharply increased the combined velocity of encounter. With so much to lose, and with knowledge of the British ships' vulnerability to underwater attack, Jellicoe took the safest course. He was uncertain about the efficacy of the methods for avoiding torpedo strike, and he could, after all, reckon that his fleet still stood between the High Sea Fleet and its bases. He may have thought that the action could be renewed the next day, 1 June, an anniversary still remembered in the Royal Navy for Howe's defeat of the French in 1794. Nevertheless, Scheer had, perhaps, after all, succeeded in his declared intention of 'surprising and confounding the enemy'.

Some criticism has been made of the Admiralty for retaining Commodore Tyrwhitt's Harwich Force in harbour until it was too late for it to arrive on the scene in time to affect the outcome. Indeed, the presence of this force of destroyers and light cruisers to the south and west of the High Sea Fleet could have been decisive in supplying Jellicoe with information at a critical time and in attacking the Germans with torpedoes. However, it has to be recalled that the defence of the eastern end of the Channel depended on the light forces at Dover, the Third Battle Squadron of pre-Dreadnought battleships (the seven remaining ships of the 'Wobbly Eight') and its attached Cruiser Squadron in the Swin, and the Harwich Force. Had the last left early on 31 May to join in the late stages of the battle, and had the Germans staged a raid on the eastern Channel with their pre-Dreadnought squadron, much damage might have been sustained. Knowledge of the event makes it possible to say that the Germans were credited with too much enterprise, and that the Harwich Force could have been spared for a role in the great battle. But then and there, by the time the full facts about German dispositions were known to the Admiralty, it was too late to order the Harwich Force to sea.

By the time the German dispositions were known to the Admiralty, it was too late to order the Harwich Force to sea

Now, at 1935, as the light began to fade, Jellicoe turned back towards the presumed position of the enemy, eventually steering SW in divisions. The battlecruisers were about 6 miles ahead of the leading battleships, and the German fleet was steering S by E. The ships' companies of both fleets, and in particular those of the ships that had been hotly engaged, were exhausted. The commanders too had suffered: Jellicoe had for the whole day borne the burden of having the fate of the British cause in his hand; Scheer had twice been repulsed after running head-on into a superior fleet. Hipper had for some time been in search of a flagship. Beatty seems to have come off best, in spite of having been in almost constant action since the first clash, having seen two ships of his squadron destroyed, and knowing that his flagship had suffered serious damage. At 1950 he made by wireless the following signal to the Commander in Chief: 'Submit van of battleships follow battlecruisers. We can then cut off the whole of the enemy's battle fleet.' To us, Beatty's intention is far from clear. It is almost certain that he could not then see any part of the German Fleet; all the information available to him indicated that it was already 'cut off', that the British Fleet stood between it and its bases. Perhaps once again Beatty found it difficult to convey his intention by signal. It seems likely that he had in mind an attack on the van of the German Fleet and that, recognising that his battlecruisers were in no condition for another fight with capital ships, he was asking for the support of the undamaged ships of the Grand Fleet. At the time there were perhaps seventy more minutes during which the light would suffice for action.

The inevitable delays and Jellicoe's uncertainty about Beatty's intention led to the former's response being delayed until 2000, by which time the main fleet's course was nearer W than SW. Jellicoe was, in fact, aiming at the enemy more sharply than was Beatty, but he ordered the Second Battle Squadron, leading the British line and commanded by Vice-Admiral Jerram, to follow the battlecruisers. Jerram could not, in fact, see them at the time, so he simply maintained a course a little south of west. Soon the *Falmouth*, the ship on the northern wing of Beatty's scouting cruisers, was in contact with Scheer's light cruisers, and at 2020 Beatty's ships saw and opened fire on the *Derfflinger* and *Seydlitz* advancing from the north-west. The battered German battlecruisers were saved by unlikely rescuers: the division of pre-Dreadnought battleships that would have been left in the Jade had Scheer used conventional wisdom. At a range of 5 miles their guns hit the *Lion*, *Princess Royal* and *Indomitable*; three of the old German ships were hit, and Mauve's squadron prudently retired. Beatty did not follow: visibility was poor, and he did not know how near Scheer's Dreadnoughts might be. At about 2045 Jerram, in the *King George V*, sighted some ships of the First Squadron of the High Sea Fleet (the Königs) at about 10,000 yards (9,100 metres), but, convinced that they were British battlecruisers, refrained from opening fire. In the *Orion*, the fifth in the line, Rear-Admiral Leveson's Flag Lieutenant urged him to turn towards the enemy and open fire: 'Sir, if you leave the line now and turn towards, your name will be as famous as Nelson's.' He was right, but was told that they must follow the next ahead. So ended the daylight action *(Map 11)*.

Beatty . . . did not know how near Scheer's Dreadnoughts might be

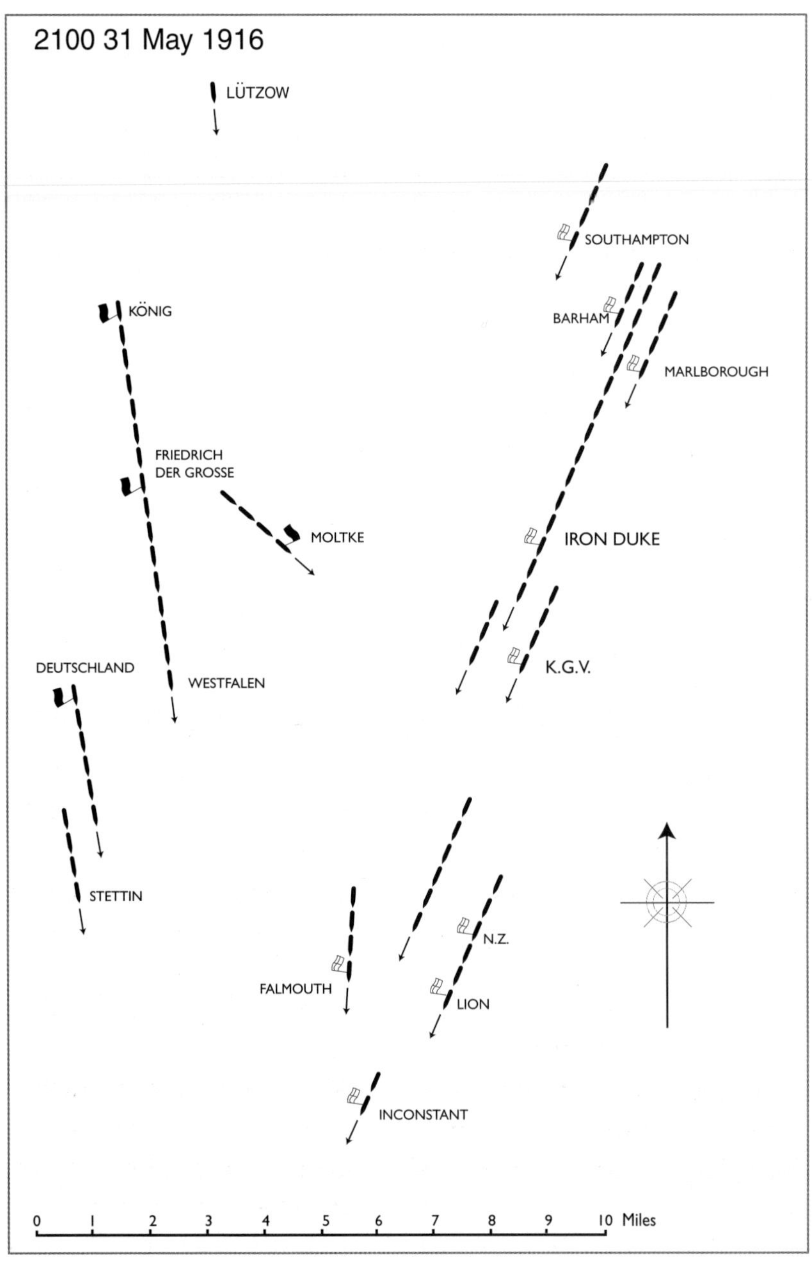

Map 11 Situation of the fleets at the end of the daylight action.

CHAPTER THIRTEEN

THE NIGHT ACTION

In arranging the disposition of his ships for the night, Jellicoe had to bear in mind the objective of renewing the action on 1 June by preventing the escape of the German Fleet southward or eastward. He dismissed the idea of a night action between the main fleets, knowing how little trained in this technique were his men and how primitive were the British searchlights. Indeed, an error made early on confirms Jellicoe's belief about his men's lack of training in night fighting: at 2130 the *Lion* signalled by lamp to the *Princess Royal*, the next astern: 'Please give me challenge and reply now in force as they have been lost.' The *Princess Royal* flashed back the 'secret' recognition signals. Part at least of this exchange was seen by the leading German light cruisers, and the vital knowledge was later used by them during the night. Jellicoe evidently thought, too, that protection against torpedo-craft during the night was best left to the secondary armament of the big ships, and that the best use of his destroyer flotillas was to dispose them astern of the battlefleet, to prolong the line and to attack German ships attempting to make for home that way. He may have thought, too, that in separating the battlefleet from the light forces he was avoiding the dangers of mistaken identification and damage to his own ships from the torpedoes of his destroyers. The main battlefleet was disposed in line ahead in divisions three abreast and a mile apart from each other. Following them were the remaining three ships of the Fifth Battle Squadron and the damaged *Marlborough*'s half-squadron of four ships. The battlecruisers were to the south-west; the light cruisers were disposed ahead and to the west. The course was S, the speed 17 knots *(Map 12)*.

Scheer's dispositions a few miles to the east were rather simpler. The battleships were in line ahead led by the *Westfalen*, with the *Derfflinger* and *Von der Tann* at the rear of the line and the *Moltke* and *Seydlitz* some 20,000 yards (18,300 metres) astern and separated from the main fleet. The light forces were to the east. The

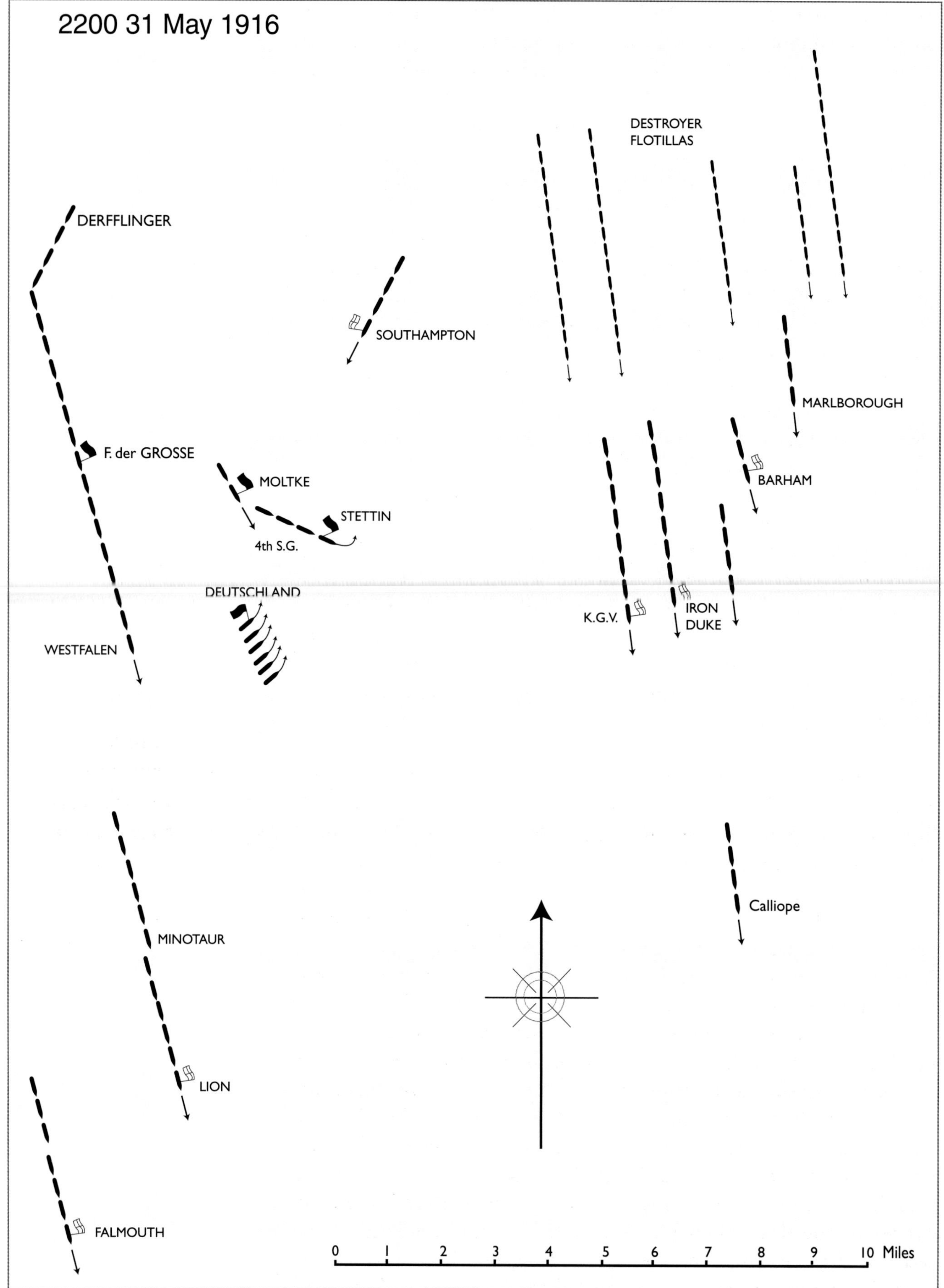

Map 12 Night stations of the opposing fleets.

course was SSE, the speed 16 knots. Scheer's first objective was to get his fleet home: he cannot have thought that if the engagement were renewed on 1 June his ships would inflict damage on the British sufficient to outweigh the damage that they themselves would suffer. The difficulty was that the Grand Fleet barred his road home. It was out of the question to go home by the long route via the Skagerrak and Kattegat into the Baltic; the direct route was partly barred by minefields laid in the Helgoland Bight by the British. Taking a more or less southerly course, Scheer could steer for the Frisian Islands off the coast of Friesland and Lower Saxony and pass to the Jade by the channel between them and the lower border of the minefield. The shortest routes were by the Horns Reef off Denmark and the Amrum Channel between the Amrum Bank and Amrum, an island off the coast of Schleswig-Holstein, and a more westerly one passing outside the Amrum Bank *(Map 13)*. To take one of these two routes would be the choice most likely to bring about a clash with the British Fleet.

Jellicoe, of course, knew all about Scheer's possible routes home. He seems to have thought that the passage by the Ems channel should particularly be borne in mind: he may have reckoned that if the more southerly route were chosen, there might be a chance for an engagement the next day, whereas with the Horns Reef/Amrum route sea room for a fleet action would be much restricted. In any case, his dispositions and actions were predicated on that assumption. The first signs of dawn would appear at about 0200, by which time the Grand Fleet would be centred on latitude of about 55 deg. 15'N, or just south of the latitude of Horns Reef. Meanwhile, Naval Intelligence at the Admiralty had intercepted wireless signals from Scheer and the commander of the German light forces, indicating strongly that the High Sea Fleet would return by the Horns Reef and Amrum passage. The signal was made to the *Iron Duke* at 2241: 'German fleet ordered home at 9.14 p.m. Battlecruisers in rear. Course S.S.E. 3/4 E. Speed 16 knots.' If that course were plotted from the accepted position of the High Sea Fleet at 2100, it would be shown to indicate the Horns Reef route. Jellicoe would have seen this signal at about 2330, but he did not alter the dispositions of his ships. For this he has been much criticised, on the grounds that he should have altered course in order to ensure a meeting of the fleets at dawn. By this time, however, the light forces in the rear of the battlefleet had become hotly engaged with heavy and light German ships, and the situation was particularly obscure and dangerous. Also, Jellicoe's faith in the intelligence reports from the Admiralty had suffered seriously earlier in the day, when not long after an assurance had been received that the High Sea Fleet was not at sea, it was sighted by Beatty's scouting cruisers. Although Jellicoe later affirmed that had other intelligence reports been sent him confirming the Germans'

Naval Intelligence at the Admiralty had intercepted wireless signals from Scheer

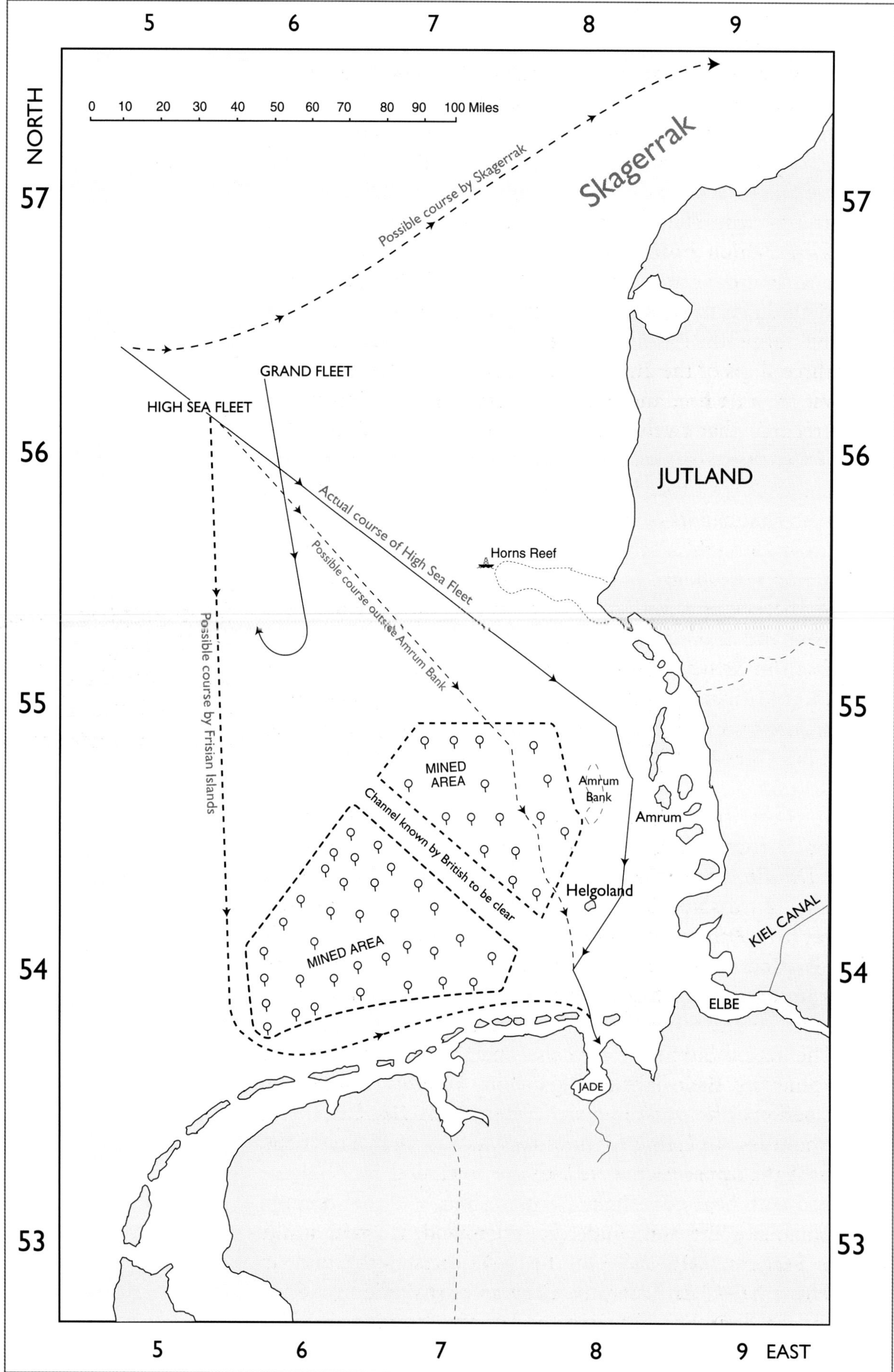

Map 13 The routes home available to the German Fleet.

route home, he would have altered course for the Horns Reef, one is bound to wonder whether he really believed in the possibility of a decisive encounter on 1 June in those narrow waters between the coast and the minefields, near to the German bases.

Scheer's tactic involved smashing through the ships in the rear of the British line on a course directed to Horns Reef. His signal '*Durchhalten*'* was repeated as the British light forces sought to obstruct the passage. There were a number of short and savage encounters, in which both sides suffered. In the first clashes destroyers and light cruisers were involved. At 2145, the light cruiser *Castor*, leading the 11th Destroyer Flotilla, having earlier in the day been engaged during the meeting of the main fleets, sighted and was sighted by three ships of the 2nd Scouting Group. The German ships were the first to open fire, and made hits. Staff Surgeon Holmes of the *Castor* records that twelve men were instantly killed and that there were in all forty-one casualties, chiefly from shell fragments. The opportunity for a mass attack with torpedoes was not taken, and the Flotilla resumed its course south.

At 2230 Goodenough's four light cruisers ran into the German Fourth Scouting Group under the command of Commodore von Reuter, and there was a fight at close range, during which the *Southampton* and *Dublin* suffered many casualties and were damaged. But the *Southampton* managed to discharge a torpedo, which hit the old light cruiser *Frauenlob* and instantly destroyed her. King-Hall, who experienced the horror of fighting at night at close range, describes the scenes on board the *Southampton*:

Southampton *managed to discharge a torpedo, which hit the old light cruiser* Frauenlob *and instantly destroyed her*

> We began to challenge: the Germans switched on coloured lights at their fore yardarms. A second later a solitary gun crashed forth from the *Dublin*, who was next astern of us. Simultaneously I saw the shell hit a ship just above the water-line and about 800 yards away . . . At that moment the Germans switched on their searchlights, and we switched on ours. Before I was blinded by the lights in my eyes I caught sight of a line of light grey ships. Then the gun behind which I was standing answered my shout of "Fire!" The action lasted 3½ minutes. The four leading German ships concentrated their lights and guns on the *Southampton*; the fifth and perhaps the fourth as well fired at the *Dublin* . . . In those 3½ minutes we had 89 casualties, and 75 per cent of the personnel on the upper deck were killed or wounded.

Of those manning the guns under his command, King-Hall and his Marine Sergeant-Major were the only ones not killed or wounded *(Figs 13.1–13.2)*. Later, the German First Battle Squadron and its attendant destroyers ran into the Fourth Destroyer Flotilla:

* Keep on.

Fig. 13.1 to 13.2 Damage to HMS *Southampton*. (*Royal Naval Museum*)

four British destroyers were sunk and four badly damaged, and two German light cruisers were disabled and one destroyer sunk. The *Tipperary* and *Spitfire*, leading the flotilla, initially ran into three German light cruisers, and the *Tipperary* was smothered in fire and destroyed. In this ferocious fighting humanity was not always predominant: a survivor from the *Tipperary* recalled that men on her Carley float hailed, in the hope of rescue, German survivors passing in two pulling boats. they were heard and seen, but were left to their fate. The remaining ships came under fire from the *Westfalen*, *Nassau* and *Rheinland* of Scheer's First Battle Squadron, and the *Spitfire* and *Nassau* collided. Remarkably, the little ship survived and managed to return to port. The *Broke*, attacking a battleship, was hit by heavy shells and suffered many casualties. Her wheel and telegraphs were destroyed and she collided with the *Sparrowhawk*, but finally made it home to the Tyne. The *Sparrowhawk* was not so lucky, sinking while under tow on the way home. The *Broke*'s 'pusser', Assistant Paymaster C.W. Johns RNR, had a narrow escape: shortly after he left the sick bay, where he had been talking with his friend, the surgeon, the ship was hit and the surgeon killed.

Fig. 13.2. (*Royal Naval Museum*)

The armoured cruiser *Black Prince*, one of Arbuthnot's fated squadron, ran into the German Dreadnoughts and was instantly smothered with fire and destroyed. In the very early dawn the Twelfth Destroyer Flotilla, under the command of Captain Stirling, came upon the Second Battle Squadron (the pre-Dreadnoughts) and torpedoed and sank the *Pommern*. There were, in addition, sightings of German ships by British capital ships: the *Malaya* saw the German battleship *Westfalen* and her Gunnery Officer trained his guns on her and asked Captain Boyle for permission to open fire. He was told that he must wait for the flagship to give the order to fire: the order was never given. The very severely damaged *Seydlitz* was seen from the *Marlborough* and later from the *Revenge* and *Agincourt*, but the order to fire was not given. The damaged *Moltke* was seen from four ships of the Second Battle Squadron but was not reported nor attacked. No one felt able to give the order to open fire. Nor were these sightings reported, and not many reports were made by the light forces engaged. The last is not too surprising: these ships and men were at the time very busy fighting for their lives. The big ships did not report their sightings, through fear of revealing themselves to the enemy by the use of

Fig. 13.3 HMS *Abdiel*, sent by Jellicoe to lay mines across the High Sea Fleet's course by the Amrum route. She was a flotilla leader, converted for mine-laying, capable of high speeds and so able to come and go swiftly and secretly. However, on 1 June 1916, her 'zeal none seconded, as out of season judged, or singular and rash' [*Paradise Lost*]. (*Imperial War Museum: SP 105*)

wireless or light. Both the German battlecruisers could almost certainly have been sunk had the action by the British matched that by the *Thüringen* in sinking the *Black Prince*.

All this activity and uproar was of course perceived in the *Iron Duke*, but Jellicoe remained unmoved – as indeed did Scheer in forcing passage for his fleet through the British rear squadrons. Jellicoe made no move to alter course; the utmost concession to the Horns Reef view of the enemy's course was to send the *Abdiel* to lay mines there *(Fig 13.3)*. One of these was to be hit by the *Ostfriesland* as she returned to port on 1 June. A commander of Jellicoe's experience must surely have known what was happening – namely, that Scheer was steering for home through the light forces of his enemy, brushing aside the opposition. He must surely have reasoned that the course that seems obvious to us – to turn the battlefleet towards the Horns Reef – would have led to confusion and probably to mistaken identification, and would the next day have put his fleet in narrow waters that were near enemy bases and unsuitable for a major action. The most that could have been expected was to pick off badly wounded German ships, and he judged that an insufficient advantage to weigh against the risks to his fleet. Meanwhile, Scheer got his fleet home. The battleship *Ostfriesland* struck one of the *Abdiel*'s mines, but was saved by her torpedo bulkhead. The *Seydlitz* went aground near the Horns Reef, because of her immensely increased draught, and was with some difficulty refloated and brought home. When dawn broke on 1 June

Fig. 13.4 to 13.7 HM Hospital Ship *Plassy* and casualties being transferred.

Fig. 13.4 *Plassy*, built in 1900 for the P&O Steam Navigation Company, 7,400 tons, twin-screw. Her main pre-war function was as a troopship. (*Imperial War Museum: RP 2559*)

the men of the British Fleet looked on waters where no enemy ship was to be seen. They had lost more than 6,000 men and 112,000 tons of warships; the Germans had lost nearly 3,000 men and 62,000 tons of ships. Turning his fleet and re-forming it into cruising order, Jellicoe swept the battle area, found only the wreckage of men and ships and at 1100 signalled the return to harbour. On this melancholy voyage the dead, many frightfully mutilated, were committed to the sea. The *Lion* had a hundred dead and more than fifty wounded.

In his report on the battle, Scheer claimed that he made for home because 'there was no certain prospect of defeating the enemy'. That was certainly an understatement: his fleet was in no shape to renew action against a Grand Fleet whose main body had not sustained serious damage. Hipper's battlecruiser squadron had been wrecked, and the light forces had been dispersed and damaged.

In October 1916 the *Journal of the Royal Naval Medical Service* published an account of the experiences in the battle of Fleet Surgeon Alexander MacLean DSO and Surgeon H.E.R. Stephens of the *Lion*. Their account was evidently scanned for any breaches of security, but it is nevertheless revealing. Nearly all the casualties occurred within the first half hour of the action; during the lulls the medical officers emerged from their stations to make tours of inspection and to have the wounded removed to the mess-deck, the main reception area, for primary treatment. Large (2/3 grain; 40 mg) doses of morphine, repeated if necessary, were given by injection to all the wounded, ten of whom died during the night of 31 May/1 June. Early in the morning of 1 June the wounded were moved into Beatty's and Chatfield's cabins, which had been cleared and rigged as operating theatres. There the medical officers and sickberth staff, much depleted by casualties, proceeded to operate on fifty-one cases, working continuously till 0015 on 2 June, and doing what they could for those seriously wounded. MacLean and Stephens commented on the fact that almost 50 per cent of the wounded suffered from burns of the face and hands alone. These were caused by the flash of high explosive so momentary, they thought, that 'clothing completely protected the rest of the body'. General burns, caused by cordite fires, were, however, 'very severe and fatal'. The doctors' comment that 'masks and gauntlets of non-inflammable material would probably save a very high percentage of casualties among repair parties on the lower deck' was to contribute to the introduction of protective clothing. On *Lion*'s arrival at the base on 2 June most of the wounded were transferred to the hospital

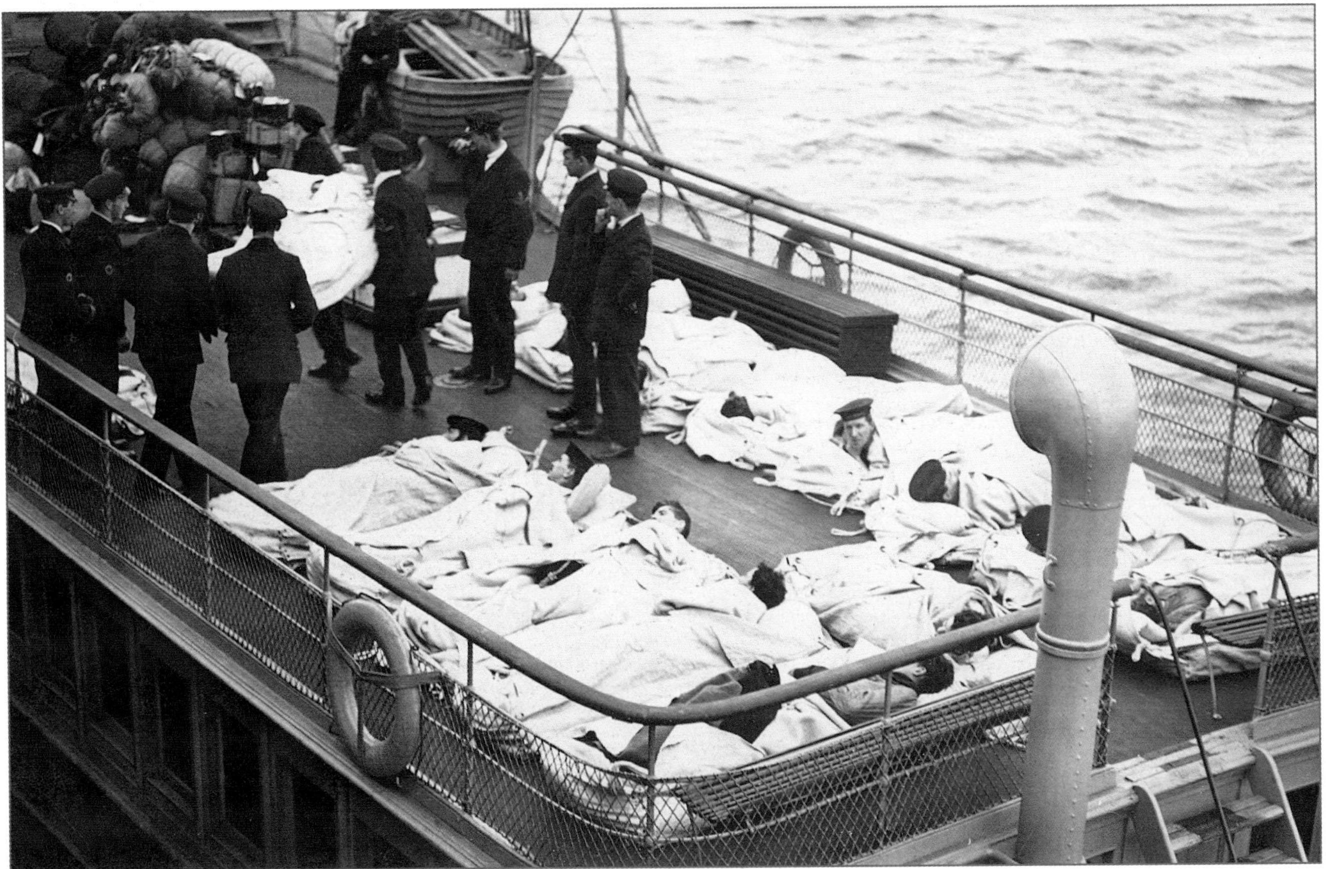

Fig. 13.5 Transfer of stretcher cases. (*Royal Naval Museum*)

Fig. 13.6 Casualties, mostly from flash-burn of the face, on board *Plassy*. (*Royal Naval Museum*)

Fig. 13.7 More survivors. (*Royal Naval Museum*)

ship *Plassy*, a 7,000-ton ship formerly of the P&O Line *(Figs 13.4–13.7, preceding pages)*. The lessons of these and other experiences were not lost on the naval medical department.

It is remarkable how few men seem to have broken under the strain of battle and the dreadful sights of seriously wounded and burned shipmates. Fleet Surgeon Penfold reports one case of 'insanity' in the *Barham* after her ordeal at 'Windy Corner': the man had seen a boy standing next to him killed. Penfold mentions the occasional incidence of 'neurasthenia' in men returning to the ship after recovery from their wounds. 'Neurasthenia' was the term used for what later became 'shell-shock', and, later still, 'battle exhaustion'. Today it has a more scientific-sounding name, Post-Traumatic Stress Disorder, but it still produces an equally ignorant reaction at the War Office. The credit for this resilience goes to the men and their leaders, but long afterwards we have seen that the terrible experiences were rarely forgotten and nearly always left their mark. They still do.

CHAPTER FOURTEEN

THE AFTERMATH

The news of Jutland

The Admiralty announcement about the battle was made public on 3 June and caused deep gloom in Britain:

> On the afternoon of Wednesday, 31st May, a naval engagement took place off the coast of Jutland. The British ships on which the brunt of the fighting fell were the battlecruiser fleet and some cruisers and light cruisers, supported by four fast battleships. Among these the losses were heavy. The German battlefleet, aided by poor visibility, avoided prolonged action with our main forces, and soon after these appeared on the scene the enemy returned to port, though not before receiving severe damage from our battleships. The battlecruisers *Queen Mary*, *Indefatigable*, *Invincible*, and the cruisers *Defence* and *Black Prince* were sunk. The *Warrior* was disabled, and after being towed for some time had to be abandoned by her crew. It is also known that the destroyers *Tipperary*, *Turbulent*, *Fortune*, *Sparrowhawk* and *Ardent* were lost, and six others are not yet accounted for. No British battleships or light cruisers were sunk. The enemy's losses were serious. At least one battlecruiser was sunk and one severely damaged; one battleship is reported sunk by our destroyers . . .

This communiqué was, it seems, largely the work of Balfour, who held the belief, unfashionable then and now, that in the field of public relations the best policy is to tell the public the truth. In order to assuage public anxiety the communiqué was later modified by the addition of claims that modern German battleships had been sunk. These claims were, of course, mistaken *(Fig 14.1)*.

The shock caused by the announcement was profound: I well recall my mother, who was in 1916 twenty years old, telling me of its effect

'The German High Seas Fleet came out and gave ours a whacking'

on public morale, and comparing it with the horror felt four years previously, when the news of the sinking of the *Titanic* broke. Charles Ingram Knowles, later to gain renown as one of the principal architects of the Youth Hostel movement, was then aged fifteen. He wrote in his diary for 5 June: 'On Friday night June 2nd came the news of a great British defeat off Helgoland. We had lost about 15 or 16 ships while the Germans had lost 2 or 3. The German High Seas [sic] Fleet came out and gave ours a whacking so it seemed and so the German reports let the neutrals know. But to-day (June 5th) the facts have come out: at least we are not absolutely sure but they are fairly accurate.' Knowles went on to record the battlecruiser action and the subsequent clash between the Grand and High Sea Fleets, and to record the figures for ships lost given in the later British communiqué. These included the claim that two German Dreadnought battleships and two battlecruisers had been lost.

The British had for years seen the Royal Navy go from victory to victory; they had, with the Navy, been preparing since the beginning of the war for the day when 'The Huns', the name derived from the Kaiser's ill-considered remark, would be thrashed at sea in another Trafalgar. Now they learned that three of their most famous Dreadnoughts had gone and that no more than a small price had been exacted in return. Even the later modification of the British statement, erroneously claiming the destruction of two German battleships and of one, probably two or even three battlecruisers, failed to bring conviction or to assuage grief and gloom *(Figs 14.2 & 14.3)*. In 'The Verdicts', Kipling well reflected the uncertainty of the time and acknowledged the nation's debt to the men who had fought, endured and died.

Not in the thick of the fight,
Not in the press of the odds,
Do the heroes come to their height,
Or we know the demi-gods . . .
(Rudyard Kipling: 'The Verdicts')

Jellicoe was deeply depressed

Jellicoe was deeply depressed by the outcome: it may indeed have precipitated the crisis of depression that later led to his removal from the Admiralty. An added factor may well have been the sinking by a mine on 4 June of the cruiser *Hampshire* as she passed the Orkneys carrying Lord Kitchener to Russia. Beatty was depressed and angry, feeling or affecting to feel that he had been 'let down' by his chief, to whom he had delivered the High Sea Fleet and who had let it go. Chalmers records that in the afternoon of 1 June Beatty came into the *Lion*'s charthouse, sat down and repeated the words 'There is something wrong with our ships', adding 'And something wrong with our system.' It was indeed unfortunate that the loss of three great ships and their crews should

Fig. 14.1 Wishful thinking? *Punch* (14 June 1916) does its best to encourage the idea of heavy German losses in the Battle of Jutland. (Courtesy of *Punch*, Ltd)

have been necessary to bring about this realisation. However, many senior officers recognised Jellicoe's achievement in twice ambushing the German Fleet and in remaining at sea when the enemy had retired from the field. The depleted but nevertheless still superior Grand Fleet was indeed reported ready for sea at four hours' notice on the evening of 2 June.

On the other side of the North Sea the German nation and the Kaiser celebrated the High Sea Fleet's victory and honoured the victors. Hipper was created a Baron, and so gained the coveted privilege of adding the prefix 'von' to his name. Scheer, however, disdained such ribands. The High Sea Fleet had indeed been extracted skilfully from the two difficult situations in which it had found itself, had in the process seriously damaged an important part of the Royal Navy, had crashed through the screen designed to keep it to the

Fig. 14.2 The chapel in HMS *Malaya* with, above, the plaque commemorating those of her company who lost their lives at Jutland. (*Royal Naval Museum*)

"Toll for the Brave, the Brave that are No More"

THE GREAT NAVAL BATTLE FROM THE PERSONAL POINT OF VIEW

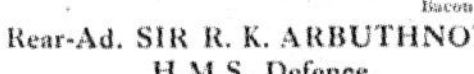

Bacon
Rear-Ad. SIR R. K. ARBUTHNOT
H.M.S. Defence.

CAPTAIN CECIL I. PROWSE
H.M.S. Queen Mary.

Swaine
COM. HARRY L. PENNELL
H.M.S. Queen Mary.

Maull and Fox
COM. SIR CHARLES R. BLANE
H.M.S. Queen Mary.

Lafayette
COM. LOFTUS W. JONES
H.M.S. Shark.

Russell
Com. R. H. D. TOWNSEND
H.M.S. Invincible.

Swaine
LIEUT. W. G. HALLILEY
H.M.S. Nomad.

REV. C. W. LYDALL
Drowned on eve of his wedding

MID. R. ROXBURGH
H.M.S. Indefatigable.

Speaight
Mid. the Hon. B. M. BAILEY
H.M.S. Defence.

Lafayette
LT. T. F. S. FLEMMING
H.M.S. Invincible.

THE KING'S TRIBUTE

I am deeply touched by the message which you [Admiral Jellicoe, on the occasion of his Majesty's birthday] have sent me on behalf of the Grand Fleet. It reaches me on the morrow of a battle which has once more displayed the splendid gallantry of the officers and men under your command. I mourn the loss of brave men, many of them personal friends of my own, who have fallen in their country's cause. Yet even more do I regret that the German High Seas Fleet, in spite of its

ADMIRAL THE HON. HORACE L. A. HOOD
Second in Command of the Battle-Cruiser Squadron.

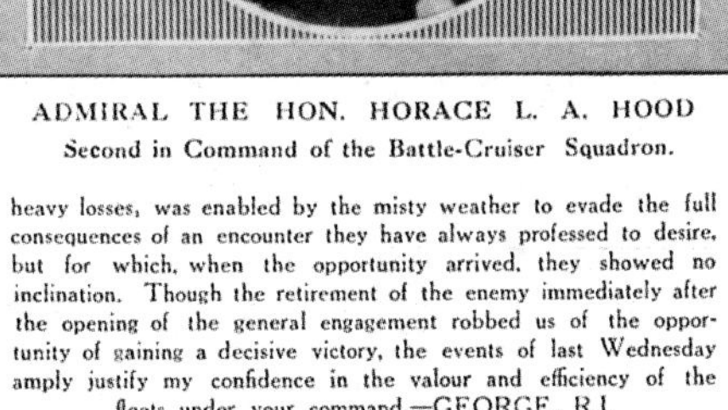

heavy losses, was enabled by the misty weather to evade the full consequences of an encounter they have always professed to desire, but for which, when the opportunity arrived, they showed no inclination. Though the retirement of the enemy immediately after the opening of the general engagement robbed us of the opportunity of gaining a decisive victory, the events of last Wednesday amply justify my confidence in the valour and efficiency of the fleets under your command.—GEORGE, R.I.

Maull and Fox
Capt. CHAS. J. WINTOUR
H.M.S Tipperary.

Swaine
LIEUT. E. T. DONNELL
H.M.S. Shark.

Lafayette
LIEUT. W. J. FLETCHER
H.M.S. Black Prince.

Russell
Rev. W. H. LE PATOUREL
H.M.S. Defence.

CLERK G. F. MIÉVILLE
H.M.S. Queen Mary.

MID. J. SCOTT (Defence)
Sir Percy Scott's elder son.

Fig. 14.3 Display, with tribute from HM King George V, commemorating officers who lost their lives in the battle. (*Royal Naval Museum*)

Overleaf: Fig. 14.4 *Seydlitz*, heavily damaged, in Wilhelmshaven after the battle. (*Royal Naval Museum*)

westward of the Grand Fleet, and had got back to port with the loss of only one modern capital ship. With the exception of the *Seydlitz (Figs 14.4 & 14.5)* and *Derfflinger* it was ready for sea by the middle of August, and at that time was joined by the new and impressive battleship *Bayern*, armed with 15-inch (38-cm) guns. It seems clear, though, that Scheer sustained the impression that the High Sea Fleet would never be able to inflict on the Grand Fleet sufficient damage materially to influence the outcome of the war in general or the war at sea in particular. From this feeling stemmed his recommendation of unrestricted submarine warfare. We may think now that Scheer underestimated the technical superiority of the German fleet and the tactical skill of its commanders.

Later German sorties

The statement that the High Sea Fleet never again emerged after Jutland was often made in Britain as some sort of excuse for the perceived failure of the Royal Navy. In fact, the German Fleet came out again on 18 August: Scheer planned a raid on Sunderland, and, as in May, put submarines on watch outside the English east coast ports. The Grand Fleet and the Harwich Force were ordered to sea, but the expected encounter never took place, because an erroneous report led Scheer to think that the Harwich Force, coming up from the south, was the Grand Fleet. He turned for home. In these operations the cruisers *Nottingham* and *Falmouth* were lost to torpedoes fired by submarines, and the

Fig. 14.5 *Seydlitz* being towed to dry dock. (*Imperial War Museum: Q 20683*)

The High Sea Fleet's last sortie . . . was an abortive affair

battleship *Westfalen* was torpedoed and damaged. The High Sea Fleet's last sortie of 1916 was in October: it was an abortive affair, in which the light cruiser *München* was torpedoed but not sunk. Marder records that this further evidence of the strength of the German ships and the inefficiency of British torpedoes greatly depressed Jellicoe. There was to be only one more sortie: in April 1918, Scheer took the High Sea Fleet to sea to intercept a convoy from Norway and to trap a part of the Grand Fleet. Postponement of departure because of fog, and later damage to the *Moltke* frustrated his intentions; returning, the *Moltke* took a torpedo from a British submarine but got back to harbour. Von Hipper's attempt in October 1918 to take the fleet to sea in a desperate attempt to damage the Grand Fleet was prevented by mutiny in some of his ships: by that time Allied successes in the land fighting had made it clear to the crews that the German cause was lost. The next time the High Sea Fleet went to sea was on 21 November 1918, when selected units steamed, escorted by the Grand Fleet, into the Firth of Forth to be interned. By then Beatty was in command of the Grand Fleet, flying his flag in the *Queen Elizabeth (Figs 14.6–14.10)*. Later, the German Fleet was moved to Scapa Flow, where on 21 June 1919 its ships were scuttled on the orders of the commander, Rear-Admiral von Reuter, before the delighted gaze of a party of schoolchildren out for a trip round the Flow. Twenty-eight years later the *Derfflinger* was still to be seen, bottom-up, being broken up at Faslane on the Gareloch.

Although it fell to Beatty to receive the 'surrender' of the German Fleet, neither he nor his officers and ships' companies was or were wholeheartedly convinced by their victory. They felt that their due prize – the defeat of the Germans in a fleet action – had been denied them, and that this surrender was somehow a tame ending to the years of vigilance and endeavour. They had hoped for an ending with a bang, not with a whimper. In fact, of course, the surrender of the pride of the German nation was a tremendous strategic triumph for the Royal Navy and the Allied cause, and the avoidance of further loss of life on both sides represented a gain for the world. It was the steady pressure exerted on Germany by the British blockade, dependent on the control of the seas by the Royal Navy, that so severely damaged German morale and led eventually to the defection of the formerly steadfast men of the High Sea Fleet.

So long as the High Sea Fleet existed, it could not be ignored, but increasingly after Jutland the German effort at sea went into the submarine war against shipping. The central North Sea became in effect a deadly No Man's Land, where the peril from mine and torpedo effectively discouraged naval operations. Beatty, succeeding Jellicoe in December 1916 in command of the Grand Fleet, was actually less adventurous than his predecessor in the

Figs. 14.6 to 14.9 The surrender of the German Fleet on 21 November 1918.

Fig. 14.6 Admiral Beatty on the compass platform of the *Queen Elizabeth*, with Chatfield. (*Royal Naval Museum*)

Fig. 14.7 *Hindenburg*, the newest German battlecruiser, on the way to 'internment'. (*Royal Naval Museum*)

Fig. 14.8 The battleships of the High Sea Fleet on their way to surrender, seen from an escort vessel. (*Royal Naval Museum*)

matter of aggressive action. Knowing at last the fatal weaknesses of British ships and British shells, he could hardly have been otherwise. An action in November 1917 against German minelayers and light forces in the Helgoland Bight involved the battlecruisers, including the very fast *Glorious*, *Courageous* and *Repulse*, supported by a squadron of battleships. The intention was foiled by defective planning and by the Germans' skilful use of smoke and torpedoes. Perhaps fortunately, the retirement of the British forces was covered by fog. During 1917 the dreadful toll of losses to submarines almost brought Britain to defeat: it was mainly the recognition, belated indeed, that convoy was the truly aggressive response to the submarine threat, that enabled the country to survive. Even that recognition might not have been enough had it not been for the accession in April 1917 of the United States, with its unlimited reserves of industrial power and materials, to the Allied cause.

Jellicoe went from the Grand Fleet to the Admiralty as First Sea Lord, but he was evidently at the time insufficiently strong to force on a reluctant Board the true solution to the submarine problem. He lasted there for less than a year before being retired. In January

1918 Jellicoe was raised to the peerage as a viscount. For his territorial title he chose Scapa. It was an appropriate choice, although initially it gave rise to some comment among the Germans, who thought it risible that the victorious commander should choose for his title the place where for most of the war his fleet had been at anchor. Jellicoe was right, and von Hase recognised that: '. . . by those four years at anchor the English fleet exerted that decisive pressure which ended in our whole fighting fleet being led to this same Scapa Flow where it lies on the sea bottom'. In 1919 Jellicoe was promoted Admiral of the Fleet, and in the same year undertook a cruise including visits to India, Canada, Australia and New Zealand in connection with imperial

Fig. 14.9 The surrender of the German Fleet, 21 November 1918. On the left, the *Derfflinger* leads the German line, followed by the *Von der Tann*. On the right, the *Resolution*. *(Painting by D. Macpherson, present at the event, in the possession of the author)*

QUEEN'S HALL

Sole Lessees – CHAPPELL & Co. Ltd.

Under the Direction of J. & N. TAIT

MATINEES
at 3 o'clock
on
FRIDAY
JANUARY 3rd
and
TUESDAY 7th
WEDNESDAY 8th
THURSDAY 9th
FRIDAY 10th
JANUARY

EVENINGS
at 8 o'clock
on
FRIDAY 3rd
SATURDAY 4th
MONDAY 6th
TUESDAY 7th
WEDNESDAY 8th
THURSDAY 9th
FRIDAY 10th
SATURDAY 11th
JANUARY

The German Battle Cruisers approaching the Rendezvous

"Deeds that Won the War" Films

SERIES I.

Surrender of the German Fleet

"The German Flag is to be hauled down at 15.57 (3.57 p.m.) (Sunset) to-day, Thursday, and is not to be hoisted again without permission."

Admiral Sir David Beatty's signal to the German Admiral, Nov. 21st, 1918.

The only complete Picturisation of this absorbing Historic Event

CONSISTING OF

4,000 feet of Film

ALSO

The American Fleet Meeting President Wilson

400 MILES OUT AT SEA

PRICES: Reserved, **5**/- and **3**/- Unreserved, **2**/- and **1**/- Tax extra.

Tickets obtainable at all Box Offices, including Keith, Prowse, Cecil Roy, and at the QUEEN'S HALL, LANGHAM PLACE, W.

Fig. 14.10 The event commemorated on film. The vignette shows the battleships of the High Sea Fleet. *(Author's collection)* defence. For four years from 1920 he held the post of Governor General of New Zealand, and at the end of that time was at last given an earldom. He died at his home in 1935.

Beatty went from the Grand Fleet to the Admiralty as First Sea Lord, and was later promoted Admiral of the Fleet. In 1919 he was raised to the peerage as an earl. As First Sea Lord he did good work for the Navy in very difficult times, but he was outmanoeuvred by Trenchard in the struggle for the control of the developing Fleet Air Arm. Beatty left the Admiralty in 1927 and retired to private life. Little by way of open criticism of the other came from either Beatty or Jellicoe, and it is moving to recall that in November 1935 Beatty, though at the time seriously ill, insisted on walking as a pall-bearer at Jellicoe's funeral. He died in March the following year.

Scheer and von Hipper both survived the war. The former went in 1918 from the High Sea Fleet to become Chief of Naval Staff, and witnessed the collapse of German power. He survived to preside in 1927 at the opening of the impressive memorial to the German navies at Laboe, at the seaward end of Kieler Förde. Scheer died in 1928. After leaving the Navy, von Hipper stayed near the sea, retiring to the Othmarschen district of Hamburg, west of Altona. There in 1932 he died. For Commodore von Reuter, who commanded the Fourth Scouting Group at Jutland and the German light forces in the action of November 1917, a more dismal fate was reserved: it fell to him as a rear-admiral to command the German ships that sailed to meet the Allied Fleet in November 1918 and were later interned at Scapa. Von Reuter later suffered the indignity of being publicly upbraided by Vice-Admiral Fremantle, commanding the British guard squadron, on the quarterdeck of the *Revenge*, after the German ships were scuttled on his order on 21 June 1919. Von Reuter survived until 1943.

CHAPTER FIFTEEN

THE DEBATE AND THE LESSON

The grievous disappointment felt by the public and indeed by the Navy at the failure to cripple the German fleet was soon manifest in a search for scapegoats. Almost at once began the 'feud' between the supporters of Beatty and those of Jellicoe, the former claiming that only Jellicoe's caution had stood between the Grand Fleet and a glorious victory, and the latter claiming that it was only because of Beatty's rashness that three great ships and their splendid crews had been lost. Churchill, doubtless glad to have the opportunity of drawing the attention of the public away from his contribution to the defects so harshly revealed in battle, did what he could to fuel this dispute. In particular, he criticised the decision to place the battlecruisers so far ahead of the battlefleet, the manner of Jellicoe's initial deployment, his 'failure' to use the fast Fifth Battle Squadron to envelop the head of the enemy line, his turn away in response to Scheer's second retirement and torpedo attack, and his failure to respond to the evidence during the night that the Germans were engaged with his light forces. He also criticised Evan-Thomas for his 'failure' to follow Beatty in his early move towards the German battlecruisers and for his tardy reaction to the meeting with the High Sea Fleet. Neither of the two last criticisms was at all fair; Evan-Thomas was rightly obeying orders, and the faults lay with the *Lion*'s signals department.

The criticisms of Jellicoe's proceedings were hardly justified, even with the benefit of hindsight. The battlecruisers were stationed far ahead of the battlefleet because previous experience had shown the justifiable reluctance of the Germans to become engaged with a superior force, and it was important to conceal from them for as long as possible the knowledge that such a force was at sea.

Jellicoe's deployment put the British battlefleet between the enemy and his home ports, and drew it out in line across the head of Scheer's array. No commander could hope to do better than that. By the time the Fifth Battle Squadron reached Jellicoe, it had lost one of its four units (the *Warspite*), another (the *Barham*) had been damaged, and a third (the *Malaya*) had sustained serious damage. Its speed had in any case been shown to be little if at all higher than that of the leading German ships. It was in no condition to act as a 'fast wing'. In turning away from the German torpedo stream, Jellicoe was reacting as he had long planned to a threat as yet unquantified and of a gravity as yet unmeasured. His refusal to become engaged in a night action was amply justified by the Navy's inexperience in such fighting. Lastly, Jellicoe was almost certainly right in rejecting the idea of a fleet action on 1 June in the narrow waters off the coast of Schleswig: the southern part of the North Sea was not in effect big enough to permit an action of this type to be fought to a finish.

Jellicoe was almost certainly right . . .

Lord Fisher's reaction

It is not easy to penetrate Fisher's reaction to the news of the battle and its result. A tremendous explosion of rage at the failure to destroy the High Sea Fleet might well have been expected. There were indeed verbal explosions, but the written rebukes were short and the letters to Jellicoe and Beatty were on the whole complimentary. Marder tells us that on the morning after the battle Sir Joseph Thomson, Fisher's colleague on the Board of Invention, got to the office to find him 'pacing up and down the room more dejected than any man I have ever seen. He kept saying time after time, "They've failed me, they've failed me! I have spent thirty years of my life preparing for this day, and they've failed me, they've failed me!" This was the only time I knew him to be doubtful about the issue of the war.' Jacob Epstein (1880–1959), who was at the time working on his bust of Fisher, recalled that 'One morning he came into my room . . ., filled with sardonic satisfaction. The Battle of Jutland had just been fought. Fisher read out to me "a message from Lord Nelson" on the event which he said he had received. It did not spare the Jacks-in-Office who, he alleged, had allowed the German Fleet to skedaddle back to harbour . . .' An agreeable and kindly light is shed here on the old Admiral by his letter of 27 June 1916 to Lord Derby, Director of Recruiting, asking for consideration to be given to excusing 'the first sculptor in the world' from military service. 'Lord Fisher is only sorry that he can't offer himself instead of Epstein, as he is doing nothing.'

The most important defect lay in the field of matériel

To Captain T. Crease RN, his former naval assistant, Fisher wrote, perhaps in part a little obscurely, '. . . I've declined to see *anyone at all* calling here about the [Jutland] disaster.

'After Cradock –0 von Spee'!
After Beatty – von Scheer'!
'After bad war direction – good war direction'!

'. . . .And Beatty not waiting for his supports. And how slow ships (no matter how heavily armoured) *are no use*! Had the whole of Jellicoe's battleships been speedier, *how different the situation*! the action begins at 2 p.m. He (Jellicoe) only gets up at 6 p.m.

The torpedoing of Marlborough *showed the vulnerability of this class of ship to underwater attack*

To Jellicoe and Beatty Fisher wrote in a generally congratulatory tone, but in a confidential letter to Lady Jellicoe he deplored 'the way that a base intrigue is booming Beatty as the sole hero'. On Jellicoe's comment on the 'inadequacy of the armour protection of our battlecruisers' he noted 'Never meant to get in enemy's range!' Much of Fisher's criticism was directed at the recall of Tyrwhitt's force and the failure to take the opportunity offered by the absence of the High Sea Fleet to mine extensively its return route through the Bight. Perhaps he may in the end have realised that the chief cause of the failure to destroy The High Sea Fleet resided in the defects of the weapon in whose construction he had played so decisive a part; that speed was not, after all, the best protection.

Sadly, Beatty did harm to his reputation by seeking to influence the content of the report on the battle prepared by a committee of officers led by Captain Harper. That report was completed in October 1919, and contained material which could be construed as being critical of the battlecruisers' gunnery. Beatty was appointed First Sea Lord in November 1919, and was consequently in a position from which he could exert considerable pressure, not only on Captain Harper but also on the Sea Lords and perhaps on the First Lord. Beatty persisted in attempts to alter the record so as to diminish the part played by the battleships and to excise any criticism, direct or implied, of the battlecruisers' performance. He was in particular concerned to remove the record of the 360 deg. turn: he must have thought that this evolution could be interpreted as indicating a less than aggressive intent. Jellicoe, though reluctant, was obliged to get involved in the controversy, and the whole affair festered for many years. In the upshot, the Harper Record was in effect suppressed: though a version was published in 1927, at the same time as Harper himself published his account *The Truth about Jutland*, it was not for many years that all the documents relating to the battle and to the controversy over the report were released to the public. Nowadays we are all too familiar with such proceedings. At the time and for many years afterwards, a nation in need of heroes was given the gallant Beatty: 'Beatty of the Battlecruisers', heroically taking on a superior German force and in the crisis of the battle ordering his ships to engage the enemy more closely; Beatty, the architect of victory, robbed of hard-earned triumph by Jellicoe's caution.

The standard of gunnery of the battlecruisers was hardly good enough

After eighty-five years the dispute still rumbles on, though it is now clear that even with the benefit of hindsight Jellicoe's proceedings cannot seriously be criticised, and that the most important defect of the British Fleet lay in the field of *matériel*. The German ships, battlecruisers in particular, were stronger and better sub-divided than the British; their guns were better and their gunnery more accurate; the German propellant charges were more safely housed than the British and their armour-piercing shells were much more effective; German training in night fighting and damage control was clearly better than the British. In one respect only was the British Fleet markedly superior to the German: that was in centralised fire control, and even then the extent of fitting was incomplete. The adequacy of the armour protection of the British battleships was never seriously put to the test, but the torpedoing of the *Marlborough* showed the vulnerability to underwater attack of this class of ship, completed in 1914. It is perhaps significant that the British battleships of this class had 12-inch (30-cm) armour belts, whereas their near contemporaries, the Kaisers, had 14-inch (35-cm) belts. Yet from time to time British industry showed that it could compete with the best from overseas: at the time of the completion of the *Queen Mary* Vickers produced for the Japanese the *Kongo*, a battlecruiser of 27,000 tons armed with eight 14-inch (35-cm) guns, heavily protected and capable of 27 knots. Later, of course, the Japanese constructed their own battleships and improved on British designs.

The event represented the climax of the careers of professional naval officers, for which all their experience should have prepared them

The officers and ships' companies of both nations displayed equally steadfast courage and resolution throughout the fearful ordeal of battle, but the British received special encouragement from their consciousness of the Royal Navy's long tradition of victory. That confidence was, alas, betrayed by those who sent them into the fight with defective weapons.

The proposal that Beatty should have maintained his distance from the German ships in order to have the advantage of the longer range of the 13.5-inch (34-cm) guns of his most modern ships does not really bear examination: the standard of gunnery of the battlecruisers was hardly good enough to allow them fully to exploit that advantage. Beatty's error lay principally in his lack of appreciation of the superiority of German ships and gunnery, which led to his failure to concentrate his forces before the battlecruiser action and to the consequent destruction of the *Indefatigable* and *Queen Mary*. Information about the relative strengths of the British and German battlecruisers was, after all, available to him at the time. Beatty had seen at the Dogger Bank the effects of German armour-piercing shells on his own flagship, and he knew how long it had taken Sturdee to sink German cruisers with British 12-inch (30-cm) shells. He should certainly have discussed with Evan-Thomas his plans for action in the event of a meeting with the

German battlecruisers. Those plans could have been made in the relative calm of the Firth of Forth instead of being improvised in the crash and chaos of battle. Finally, Beatty's misplaced loyalty to his Flag Lieutenant, about whose deficiencies he had had ample warning, could easily have led to the isolation and destruction of the *Malaya*, one of the most valuable ships in the Fleet. As it was, the ship was severely damaged and many men were horribly killed. In later years, indeed, Beatty recognised the part played by Seymour in the setbacks in the North Sea: 'He lost me three battles.' One such loss would, perhaps should, have been enough.

Defeat and destruction of the British Fleet would have meant defeat for Britain and . . . the Allied cause

Scheer has been criticised for his supposed ineptitude in twice running his fleet into the centre of a superior force. It is indeed plain that the first sighting of the Grand Fleet was almost but not entirely unexpected. However, the High Sea Fleet was well prepared for just such an eventuality: the well-practised Gefechtskehrtwendung not only extricated the German Fleet but also confused Jellicoe and his commanders. It was indeed an impressive feat to turn the line of ships under fire to a reciprocal course without damage to any of them, and at the same time to threaten the superior fleet with a stream of torpedoes. Few commentators accept Scheer's explanation for his second collision with the Grand Fleet, preferring to believe that his plan was in fact to pass astern of the British array. Certainly, it was more difficult the second time to extricate the German Fleet, and in the process Hipper's battlecruisers were badly damaged. On the other hand, the Grand Fleet too was damaged and pushed towards the east, and the aggressive action by the German torpedo-boats may have had some effect in inhibiting Jellicoe's desire to close the enemy before darkness fell.

What might have happened?

It is very hard to criticise decisions made by men under fire, with the crash and thunder of guns around them and facing the prospect of sudden death or mutilation, in the first great sea battle of modern times; it is harder still if the critic is a civilian or even a 'chocolate sailor'. Even so, the event represented the climax of the careers of professional naval officers, for which all their experience and training had or should have prepared them. There is no doubt that had Beatty's full force of six battlecruisers and four fast battleships, the latter armed with 15-inch (38-cm) guns, engaged Hipper's force of five battlecruisers from the start, there would have been every chance of crippling the German force before it could get away to the safety offered by Scheer's guns. From what we know of Hipper's temperament and his confidence in his ships and men it is reasonable to surmise that he would not on seeing the superior British force simply have run away. It would indeed have been difficult for him to escape. He and his squadron were on this occasion acting as the scouting force on which Scheer was depending to give him timely warning of the approach of the enemy, and it was up to him if possible to lead the British ships to the High Sea Fleet, damaging them as much as possible in the process.

Scheer may not have appreciated the full extent of the vulnerability of the British Fleet

Certainly too, bolder action by British commanders during the night action could have cost the Germans the crippled ships that in the event made port. It is, however, pushing imaginary conclusions too far to suggest that a prolonged gun duel between the main fleets would have resulted in the sinking of more than the German pre-Dreadnoughts: the German Dreadnoughts were too tough and the British armour-piercing shell was too ineffective. Earlier suspicions about these shells were confirmed by the test of battle, and later, perhaps, by information reaching the Admiralty through Chatfield. The latter relates that in August 1916, during a luncheon on board the *Lion*, he heard from a 'Swedish naval officer, who had been attached to the Swedish Legation in Berlin', that German naval officers considered the British shell 'laughable'. They had told him that it broke to pieces on the German armour. One is bound to wonder about the authenticity of this story: German naval officers were hardly likely to disclose this valuable information even to a friendly neutral. Chatfield should, perhaps, have told the story to the Marines. On the other hand, even limited success would have done much for the morale of the British public, though it would not materially have altered the course or duration of the war. All observers agree that defeat and destruction of the British Fleet would have meant defeat for Britain and, almost certainly, for the Allied cause. Jellicoe could not have allowed the High Sea Fleet to sail unchallenged through the North Sea or have permitted the Grand Fleet to be demolished, without very serious consequences for his country. At the very least, the effect on civilian and Service morale would have been catastrophic: people were used to the idea of the great ships guarding Britain's shores and seaways, and would have been deeply discouraged by the demolition of that image. In practical terms, the loss of the Grand Fleet would have been followed by the gradual assertion of German power over the oceans of the world, the resumption of German world trade and the ending of the blockade of Germany. In the United States, the loss of British sea power might well have encouraged thoughts about a dismemberment of the British Empire and a reckoning with Japan. It might at least have led to the abandonment of any idea of intervention on the side of the Allies. In the event, the dismemberment of the British Empire had to wait until 1945.

It has widely been assumed that a similar defeat of the German Fleet would not have brought the same penalty for the Central Powers. Correlli Barnett does not share this view: he points out that such a defeat would not only have been a devastating blow to German morale but would also have opened German home waters to the British Fleet and interfered profoundly with the submarine campaign. The danger of invasion would have disappeared, and additional ships and manpower would have become available for the struggle against the submarines. Perhaps too, the Baltic and the German Baltic coast would have been opened to the British Fleet; even to amphibious operations there as proposed by Fisher? It just might have been possible to avert the dreadful slaughters of the Somme, Champagne and Passchendaele offensives and the damage done by them to the Allied nations.

> Offer the Ram of Pride instead of him.
> But the old man would not so, but slew his son
> And half the seed of Europe, one by one.
> (Wilfred Owen: 'The Parable of the Old Man and the Young')

Who won?

In the campaign of 1794, of which the battle of the Glorious First of June was a part, the British Fleet decisively defeated the French Fleet but suffered a strategic setback because of the safe arrival in port of the convoy that was being protected by that fleet. So at Jutland, the tactical advantage went to the German Fleet; which, though inferior in numbers, destroyed important British capital ships and damaged others, while suffering casualties in men and ships much lighter than the British. The stark contrast is well shown in the exhibition at the German naval memorial at Laboe. The battle did not end the challenge by the German surface fleet, but the impression that it made on the fleet's commander was such as to persuade him that no action by his surface ships would materially alter the course of the war. In that sense, the battle was truly decisive. Scheer may not, however, have appreciated the full extent of the vulnerability of the British Fleet produced by the inefficiency of its armour-piercing shell, nor the length of time that would elapse before that defect was corrected. The British failure to inflict mortal damage on the High Sea Fleet led to the need to maintain the elaborate apparatus of the Grand Fleet until the end of the war, with all that that implied in demands on men and manufactures and on the light vessels that might otherwise have been used against the submarines.

The abiding lesson of Jutland is, surely, that the British public should never relax its vigilance

Conclusion

It has to be concluded that the efforts of Fisher and his acolytes were not by themselves sufficient to modernise the Royal Navy in time for the First World War. The tradition of obedience to orders and suppression of initiative was too strong and too deep-seated to yield to a few years of Fisher's leadership. The time available to Churchill before the outbreak of war was not enough to enable the

Fig. 15.1 & 15.2 Foreign fields. Graves of British and, below, German seamen in Jutland. (*Royal Naval Museum*)

Fig. 15.3 HMS *Courageous* as she was in the 1930s, after her conversion from 'large light cruiser' to aircraft carrier. She was to be torpedoed and sunk in the Western approaches in September 1939, with the loss of more than five hundred of her complement. (*Author's collection*)

Navy and its senior officers in particular to get used to new ideas. The particular technical failure concerned was, of course, the design of armour-piercing shell for the capital ships. Chatfield recalls being told by Dreyer, who went to the Admiralty as Director of Naval Ordnance in March 1917, that tests had shown that the existing shells had serious defects. They failed to penetrate when they hit armour at an oblique angle, and their lyddite burster was so sensitive that it exploded almost on impact. Even worse, a consignment of shells that had not been tested at all had been delivered to the Fleet in 1914. It remains a serious criticism of the Admiralty organisation that so grievous a defect had not been detected, or that if detected it had not been remedied. In effect, the Grand Fleet remained without an effective armour-piercing shell for most of the war. The reason is clear, and it is not flattering to those in charge of affairs: shells were tested against armour plate, the angle of impact being about 90 deg., on the assumption that action would be joined at ranges of about 10,000 yards (9,100 metres). In the event, the ranges at which firing began were around 15,000 yards (13,700 metres), and at that distance the trajectory of the shell was such that the angle of impact was oblique. That that was likely to be so could, one imagines, have been deduced from the fact that the big guns were designed to fire at ranges up to 20,000 yards (18,200 metres). The Germans had evidently anticipated this event: their armour-piercing shell pierced armour at long range only too well. It is not pressing conjecture too far to speculate that, at some time, someone in the Admiralty or in the firms supplying armaments must have had the idea that the systems for testing armour-piercing shells were defective and that he was told to keep quiet. In our own day we have seen the ugly fate of 'whistleblowers' and the tardy attempts at rehabilitation when the predictions proved true; we have seen, too, the deliberate misleading of the public over the accuracy – or rather, inaccuracy – of bombs dropped by high-flying aircraft of the Royal Air Force.

> I could not dig: I dared not rob:
> Therefore I lied to please the mob.
> Now all my lies are proved untrue
> And I must face the men I slew . . .
>
> (Rudyard Kipling: 'A Dead Statesman')

The roll of those to be faced is long and getting longer: to those who died in the *Indefatigable*, *Queen Mary* and *Invincible* are added those who died in the *Hood*, the *Prince of Wales*, the *Repulse*, and more recently off the Falklands in the *Sheffield* and the *Antelope* (*Figs 15.1 & 15.2*). The abiding lesson of Jutland is, surely, that the British public should never relax its vigilance and should never abate its questioning of the decisions of its 'leaders', and that the 'whistleblower' and the 'troublemaker' should be cherished and even from time to time rewarded. Few institutions or causes are regularly safe in the hands of politicians.

The enemy came to know that whenever he encountered the Royal Navy he would be attacked with skill, resolution and daring

The legacy of Jutland

In the event, what happened after Jutland was almost as decisive as any project imagined after victory at sea might have been, though the effects were not to be apparent for twenty-four years. There was little that Jellicoe could do about his ships' strength, apart from increasing the thickness of armour protecting their magazines and giving additional armour to ships then building, especially to the very fast battlecruisers *Renown* and *Repulse*. Fisher's latest and least conventional ships *Glorious*, *Furious* and *Courageous* had to be left more or less as they were, though in the end all finished as aircraft carriers *(Fig 15.3)*. Attention was focused on the production of new shells which would penetrate the heaviest armour before bursting, but it was not until April 1918 that these began to be supplied to the Fleet. Opposition at the Admiralty had to be overcome before this essential change could be made. The problem of flash fires spreading to magazines was tackled by the fitting of flash-tight doors to the magazines. The installation of director-controlled firing for the secondary armament of the capital ships and to cruisers was accelerated. Control of searchlights was improved and star shell was introduced. Rangefinding was improved by the introduction of longer rangefinders to improve accuracy at the great distances at which actions were likely to be fought. Systems of damage control were revised. The Intelligence Department of the Admiralty was re-organised so that the cryptographic section sent intelligence reports rather than simply sent deciphered signals to the Operations Division. Grand Fleet Battle Orders were revised to give more latitude to individual commanders, to modify the tactics of the light forces and to give some flexibility in manoeuvring to avoid torpedoes.

The effects of the reforms stemming from Jutland were never to be tested in a fleet action during the First World War or, for that matter, in the Second; but their effect and that of subsequent reforms on the Royal Navy were profound. The Royal Navy was between the wars underfunded and had its Air Arm almost crippled by control shared with the Royal Air Force; its technical development was hampered by the shortcomings of British manufacturing industry. Nevertheless, it was able to dominate the narrow seas and, eventually, the Atlantic, and to bring the German and Italian Navies to defeat. There were indeed grievous disasters, as when the *Hood* perished under the guns of the *Bismarck*, and the *Prince of Wales* and *Repulse*, sent by Churchill on a fatal and futile mission and commanded by an officer who fatally underestimated the effectiveness of aerial attack, were sunk by Japanese torpedo-bombers. But the evidence of new thinking and new policies in the Navy was amply shown by Harwood's cruiser squadron's crippling of the heavily armed small battleship *Graf Spee*, by Tovey and Dalrymple-Hamilton in the sinking of the *Bismarck*, by the successful attack on the Italian battleships in Taranto by aircraft of the Fleet Air Arm, by the actions fought by Burnett's cruisers and Sherbrooke's destroyers in the Barents Sea, by Cunningham's rout of the Italian Fleet and the sinking of three of its cruisers off Cape Matapan, by the combination of forces under Fraser's command that led to the sinking of the *Scharnhorst* by the *Duke of York*, by Admiral Ramsay's colossal feats of organisation in operations Dynamo, Torch and Overlord, and by the long, hard and bitter fight that led to the defeat of the submarine.

It is tempting to speculate on the results that might have obtained had the British been able to launch torpedo-carrying seaplanes

There were, too, many instances of individual gallantry and initiative: Fegen taking the armed merchant cruiser *Jervis Bay* into battle against the heavily armed small battleship *Admiral Scheer* and giving time for much of his convoy to disperse; Roope in the destroyer *Glowworm* ramming and severely damaging the heavy cruiser *Hipper*; the old *Renown* battling heavy seas to hit the new battlecruiser *Gneisenau* three times with 15-inch (38-cm) shells at a range of 9 miles. The enemy came to know that whenever he encountered the Royal Navy he would be attacked with skill, resolution and daring. This late but splendid flowering of the Royal Navy in the wake of Jutland enabled Britain to postpone until 1945 her inevitable decline and demise and more or less gracefully to yield to the United States the mastery of the seas. In effect, Jutland did for the Royal Navy what the Boer War did for the Army: it brought forcibly to official attention the facts that the

Navy had failed to keep up to date and that, if nothing were done about it, the country would go down before a more advanced organisation.

The great strategic lesson of the naval war in general and of the battle of Jutland in particular was not learnt at the time; indeed, it was not learnt for another twenty-five years. It was, that the day of the Dreadnought battleship was over, terminated by the power of underwater weapons and, only a little later, of airborne ones. The two great visionaries Fisher and Scott, and probably Scheer too, saw this at the time, and when the war was over began an assault on the policy of building Dreadnought battleships, claiming – rightly as it emerged much later – that the sea weapons of the future were the submarine and the aeroplane. The power and menace of the submarine and its torpedoes were indeed well known at the time, and it is clear that the operations of the High Sea Fleet could have been hindered as well – probably better – by a large fleet of submarines and by torpedo-carrying aircraft as they were by the Grand Fleet.

The potential of the torpedo-carrying aircraft had indeed been adumbrated by Captain, later Rear-Admiral Murray Sueter. In 1914 he and his colleague Hyde-Thomson registered their invention of a 'torpedo-carrying seaplane'. In the same year, a torpedo was dropped from a seaplane at Calshot, the problem of giving the craft sufficient power to lift a 1,000-pound additional load having been overcome. Later, in the Dardanelles campaign of 1915, Squadron-Commander Edmunds and Flight-Lieutenant Dacre sank with three seaplane-launched torpedoes three Turkish vessels: a merchant ship, an ammunition ship and a tug. Sueter was then Director of the Admiralty Air Department. He was moved to the post of Superintendent of Aircraft Construction, and finished the war in charge of units of the Royal Naval Air Service in Italy. A torpedo-carrying seaplane was developed, but, with Sueter's departure for Italy, was forgotten. The project was revived too late for the aircraft to play any part in the war. The success against the Turkish ships was, doubtless, achieved in the absence of any serious opposition, but in those days and for some time afterwards the defence even of battleships against aircraft was primitive. It is tempting, though vain, to speculate on the results that might have been obtained had the British been able on 1 June 1916 to launch torpedo-carrying seaplanes from the *Campania* against Scheer's retreating ships. In the event, the justification of Sueter's work was twenty-five years in coming: in November 1940 Fairey Swordfish torpedo-planes launched from the carrier *Illustrious* attacked the Italian Fleet in the harbour of Taranto and sank three battleships. This success was achieved by these obsolescent aircraft in the face of heavy fire.

Those who have dealt with large organisations will recognise the symptoms . . .

Predictably, no one with power to act took any notice of Fisher's or Scott's comments or even of Sueter's arguments based on actual results, though the last served as an MP from 1921 to 1945 and had another claim to fame as one of the originators of the tank. Perhaps those in charge of affairs were influenced by the power and majesty of the great ships, and ignored their vulnerability. The Royal Navy rather tardily continued the development of the aircraft carrier, but was hampered in the parallel development of carrier-borne aircraft by command shared with the Royal Air Force and by the defects of British aerial technology. The United States Navy did better, but it was the Imperial Japanese Navy that fully recognised the potential of the carrier-borne bomber and torpedo-aircraft and planned accordingly. These miscalculations by the British led to the grievous losses of the *Prince of Wales* and *Repulse*; the Americans' tardiness in recognising the extent of Japanese airborne power led to the disaster of Pearl Harbor. It was very fortunate for the Allied cause that the American carriers escaped that disaster; that the crippling of American battleship power did not disable the whole of their naval effort was testimony to the loss by the battleship of the chief role in naval warfare. At Midway, the battle that in 1942 virtually decided the course of the war in the Pacific, the opposing fleets were never within sight of each other. The United States Navy learned so well the lesson of the power of the submarine-launched torpedo that its submarines made even the vast Pacific dangerous for the Japanese battlefleet and merchant shipping.

It is of course a general principle that no one holding views opposed to those of the management should be appointed to any position of influence

Some general reflections

Most large organisations, and government departments in particular, suffer from inbuilt inertia and dislike of change. It is of course impossible to run a department of state or a business if every decision is questioned and every order ignored; it is very hard for a person who has made his or her way to the top to accept that a younger subordinate has surpassed him or her in ability and inventiveness. Yet those in charge should always be ready to listen to criticism and informed suggestions, and if necessary to change course. Almost 150 years ago Florence Nightingale and Sidney Herbert encountered mindless opposition when they attempted reform of the medical department of the Army. The power of the officials, led by Sir Benjamin Hawes, the Permanent Secretary, was almost too much for them: had it not been for Miss Nightingale's position in Society and her standing with the Queen, and Sidney Herbert's strong political position, the path to reform would have been blocked. 'The War Office', said Miss Nightingale, 'is a very slow office, an enormously expensive office, and one in which the Minister's intentions can be entirely negatived by all his sub-departments, and those of each of the sub-departments by every other.' Those who have dealt with large organisations and with government departments will recognise the symptoms and signs. It is very inconvenient for someone in charge to have a person of inferior

Fig. 15.4 Prince Albert, Lieutenant RN, third from left, with his brothers the Prince of Wales and Prince Henry and his cousin Louis Mountbatten, the second son of the former First Sea Lord, right. The occasion in 1920 is the departure of the Prince of Wales on a world tour. Prince Albert served at Jutland, as a sub-lieutenant in the *Collingwood*; Mountbatten later served as a midshipman in *Lion*. (*Hulton-Deutsch Collection/Corbis HU005436*)

position come forward with a plan for the better conduct of affairs. So it was in the case of the first effective antibiotic, penicillin, whose development was held back for twelve years because the principle underlying it conflicted with that held by the head of the department responsible and with the commercial interests of that department. It took the hammer of war to stimulate the work necessary for the production of one of the first drugs that actually cured and did not kill. Radar, the system that superseded optical techniques for detection and ranging, whose use underlay British successes at sea and in the air during the Second World War, was nearly strangled at birth. In this case, fortunately, opposition by Churchill's trusted chief scientific adviser was not in the end decisive.

Many devices are available for suppressing initiative and rendering restful the lives of those in charge of ministries, departments and other organisations. One of the best ways is to ensure that potentially troublesome people are not appointed to posts in which they can cause trouble. In one agency of the government it was for long common practice to appoint the second worst candidate to the post. To appoint the worst would have been too obvious and might have drawn the attention of the occasional independent observer to the proceedings of the appointing committee. In former days, the class system was useful: choice was limited to a close circle of persons high in Society. It was unlikely that any of these would care to step outside the circle by making trouble, because to do so would involve ostracism from the founts of hospitality, advantageous marriage and honour. As the nineteenth century drew to a close, the Royal Navy increasingly became one of the favoured fields of activity for the sons of the upper classes. In fact, the system of officer entry operated strongly against the lower middle and working classes. Thus, many men of talent and ability were excluded from command. The system of advancement of men with connections with the Court surely operated in the appointment that gave Sir Berkeley Milne command in the Mediterranean at the outbreak of war in 1914. The consequences were very serious for Britain and indeed for the Allied cause in general. Nowadays it is, of course, a general principle of public and corporate life that no one holding views opposed to those of the management should be appointed to any position of influence. Elaborate processes have been devised and consultants appointed to ensure such a result.

The men of the Prince of Wales *and* Repulse *had to pay the price*

If a person with original views and an independent outlook actually gets appointed to a position of responsibility, any number of processes can be used to silence or get rid of him or her. He or she can simply be ignored or have his or her views misrepresented to facilitate removal with or without compensation. Lord Cochrane, a 'difficult' man but an inspired leader of men and handler of ships and indeed of fleets, was removed by conviction for a crime of which he was almost certainly innocent. He was later to play a significant part in the liberation from colonial rule of Chile and Brazil. Sir Evelyn Baring, later Lord Cromer, successfully ignored General Gordon after that unlucky military genius had in error been appointed to the Governor-Generalship of the Sudan and had got himself and his largely Egyptian army trapped in Khartoum. In many cases the 'troublemaker' can be persuaded to silence by the threat of loss of promotion or the promise of advancement or the conferment of an 'honour'.

A great variety of expedients for dealing with cases resistant to these methods is of course available to politicians: the Royal Commission which may take years to produce a report which in turn can be left to gather dust; the 'independent' inquiry whose conclusions reflect the known views of the minister; the suppression of critical reports; the public vilification of the 'troublemaker'. We have in recent years seen this phenomenon widely manifested. There is the ongoing saga of the Chinook helicopter that crashed in the Hebrides, successive inquiries exonerating the pilots while the official version remains that the pilots were entirely at fault. No one apparently questions why the victims, twenty-five senior Northern Ireland security officers, had been allowed to board the same aircraft together. In the field of medicine there have been notorious examples, most notably the case in which two surgeons' disappointing results in a particular cardiac operation were apparently suppressed until a number of children had died. The anaesthetist who blew the whistle in this case found himself practising in Australia. In some cases, the irritating personality can be appointed to a post apparently of honour and responsibility whose tenure will remove him or her from the centre of trouble. Fisher dealt with Sturdee in this manner in 1914, and Churchill was to do the same with Admirals Phillips in 1941 and Cunningham in 1943. Unfortunately for Fisher, Sturdee returned from the Falklands a popular hero. Phillips went to his death, but Cunningham was tougher than all of them and survived.

Things were made more difficult for British Governments of the twentieth century by the progressive decay of the country's industrial base and the abrogation by the big capitalists of their responsibility for nurturing British technology and manufacturing skills. As German, American and Japanese technology raced ahead, British technology declined. At the same time British complacency increased and popular denigration of 'foreign' products was encouraged. The older among us remember being encouraged to believe that German tanks being prepared for the assault on France in 1940 were made of plywood and canvas. Those who a little later had to meet those tanks in battle had to pay the price for the deception. The men of the *Prince of Wales* and *Repulse* had to pay the price for the fatal underestimation of the power and efficiency of the Japanese air weapon. Neither the submarine nor the torpedo was developed in Britain: the submarine was an American development, and the torpedo was developed in the Adriatic for the Austro-Hungarian Navy. British industry was unable to produce for the Fleet Air Arm an effective torpedo-bomber; the atomic bomb had perforce to be developed in the United States. After the end of the Second World War the British invention of the angled flight deck for aircraft carriers was ignored by the Admiralty until its development by the American Navy showed how much it could reduce risk in flying-on and flying-off. It was fortunate for the Allied cause in the later war that in constructing their aircraft carriers the Japanese did not adopt and modify another British innovation – the armoured flight deck. In many other respects we are fortunate that the scales that obscured our leaders' vision blinded also that of the leaders of our country's enemies, but it will not do to continue to rely on such good fortune.

APPENDIX

The opposing fleets and principal commanders 31 May/1 June 1916

GRAND FLEET

BATTLE FLEET (van to rear)

Second Battle Squadron

1st Division

King George V (Capt Field; flag of V/A Sir M. Jerram)
Ajax (Capt Baird)
Centurion (Capt Culme-Seymour)
Erin (Capt Stanley)

2nd Division

Orion (Capt. Backhouse; flag of R/A A. Leveson)
Monarch (Capt Borrett)
Conqueror (Capt Tothill)
Thunderer (Capt Fergusson)

Fourth Battle Squadron

3rd Division

Iron Duke (Capt Dreyer; flag of Adm Sir J. Jellicoe)
Royal Oak (Capt Maclachlan)
Superb (Capt Hyde-Parker; flag of R/A A. Duff)
Canada (Capt Nicholson)

4th Division

Benbow (Capt Parker; flag of V/A Sir D. Sturdee)
Bellerophon (Capt Bruen)
Temeraire (Capt Underhill)
Vanguard (Capt Dick)

First Battle Squadron

5th Division

Colossus (Capt Pound; flag of R/A E. Gaunt)
Collingwood (Capt Ley)
Neptune (Capt Bernard)
St Vincent (Capt W.W. Fisher)

6th Division

Marlborough (Capt Ross; flag of V/A Sir C. Burney)
Revenge (Capt Kiddle)
Hercules (Capt Clinton-Baker)
Agincourt (Capt Doughty)

Third Battlecruiser Squadron (temporarily attached)
Invincible (Capt Cay; flag of R/A Hon H. Hood)
Inflexible (Capt Heaton-Ellis)
Indomitable (Capt Kennedy)
Armoured Cruiser Squadrons
1st Cruiser Squadron
Defence (Flag of R/A Sir R. Arbuthnot)
Warrior
Duke of Edinburgh
Black Prince
2nd Cruiser Squadron
Minotaur
Hampshire
Cochrane
Shannon
Light Cruisers
4th Light Cruiser Squadron
Calliope (Pendant of Cdre C. Le Mesurier)
Constance
Caroline
Royalist
Comus
Attached to Battle Fleet
Boadicea
Blanche
Bellona
Active
Attached to Third Battlecruiser Squadron
Chester
Canterbury
Destroyers
4th Flotilla (Capt Wintour (Captain (D IV)) 19 ships
11th Flotilla (Cdre Hawksley (Commodore (F)) in *Castor* (L.C.) 16 ships
12th Flotilla (Capt Stirling (Captain (D XII) 16 ships
Attached
Oak (destroyer)
Abdiel (flotilla leader converted for minelaying)

BATTLECRUISER FLEET (van to rear)
Fleet Flagship
Lion (Capt Chatfield; flag of V/A Sir D. Beatty)
First Battlecruiser Squadron
Princess Royal (Capt Cowan)
Queen Mary (Capt Prowse)
Tiger (Capt Pelly)
Second Battlecruiser Squadron
New Zealand (Capt Green; flag of R/A W. Pakenham)
Indefatigable (Capt Sowerby)
Fifth Battle Squadron (temporarily attached)
Barham (Capt Craig; flag of R/A Evan-Thomas)
Valiant (Capt Woollcombe)

Warspite (Capt Phillpotts)
Malaya (Capt Boyle)

Light Cruisers

1st Light Cruiser Squadron
Galatea (Pendant of Cdre Alexander-Sinclair)
Phaeton
Inconstant
Cordelia

2nd Light Cruiser Squadron
Southampton (Pendant of Cdre Goodenough)
Birmingham
Nottingham
Dublin

3rd Light Cruiser Squadron
Falmouth (Flag of R/A Napier)
Yarmouth
Birkenhead
Gloucester

Destroyers
1st Flotilla (Capt Roper (Captain (D I)) in *Fearless* (L.C.) 9 ships
9th and 10th half-Flotillas: 8 ships
13th Flotilla (Capt Farie (Captain (D XIII)) in *Champion* (L.C.) 11 ships

Engadine (seaplane carrier)

HIGH SEA FLEET

BATTLE FLEET (van to rear)

3rd Battle Squadron

5th Division
König (Capt Brüninghaus; flag of R/A Behncke)
Grosser Kurfürst (Capt Goette)
Kronprinz (Capt Feldt)
Markgraf (Capt Seiferling)

6th Division
Kaiser (Capt v. Keyserlingk; flag of R/A Nordmann)
Kaiserin (Capt Sievers)
Prinzregent Luitpold (Capt Heuser)
Friedrich der Grosse (Capt Fuchs: flag of V/A R. Scheer)

1st Battle Squadron

1st Division
Ostfriesland (Capt v. Natzmer; flag of V/A Schmidt)
Thüringen (Capt Küsel)
Helgoland (Capt v. Kameke)
Oldenburg (Capt Höpfner)

2nd Division
Posen (Capt Lange: flag of R/A Engelhardt)
Rheinland (Capt Rohardt)
Nassau (Capt Klappenbach)
Westfalen (Capt Redlich)

2nd Battle Squadron (pre-Dreadnoughts)

3rd Division
Deutschland (Capt Meurer; flag of R/A Mauve)

Hessen (Capt Bartels)
Pommern (Capt Bölken)
4th Division
Hannover (Capt Heine; flag of R/A v. Dalwigk z. Lichtenfels)
Schlesien (Capt F. Behncke)
Schleswig-Holstein (Capt Barrentrapp)
Fourth Scouting Group
Stettin (Pendant of Cdre v. Reuter)
München
Hamburg
Frauenlob
Stuttgart
Torpedo-Boats
Regensburg (L.C.; pendant of Cdre Michelsen)
1st (half) Flotilla: 4 boats
3rd Flotilla: 7 boats
5th Flotilla: 11 boats
7th Flotilla: 8 boats

SCOUTING FORCES
First Scouting Group (Battlecruisers)
Lützow (Capt v. Trotha; flag of V/A Hipper)
Derfflinger (Capt Hartog)
Seydlitz (Capt v. Egidy)
Moltke (Capt v. Karpf)
Von der Tann (Capt Zenker)
Second Scouting Group (Light cruisers)
Frankfurt (Flag of R/A v. Trotha)
Wiesbaden
Pillau
Elbing
Torpedo-Boat Flotillas
Regensburg (L.C.; pendant of Cdre Heinrich)
2nd Flotilla: 10 boats
6th Flotilla: 9 boats
9th Flotilla: 10 boats

BIBLIOGRAPHY

Bacon, Admiral Sir Reginald. *The Jutland Scandal*. London, Hutchinson & Co., 1925.

Barnett, Correlli. *The Swordbearers*. London, Eyre & Spottiswoode, 1963.

Beaverbrook, Rt. Hon. Lord. *Politicians and the War 1914–1916*. London, Oldbourne Book co., 1960.

Belloc, Hilaire. *The Cruise of the Nona*. London, Constable & Co., 1925.

Bennett, Geoffrey. *The Battle of Jutland*. London, B.T. Batsford Ltd, 1964.

——. *Naval Battles of the First World War*. London, Batsford, 1968.

Brown, D.K. *The Grand Fleet: Warship design and development, 1906–1922*. London, Chatham Publishing, 1999.

Campbell, John. *Jutland. An Analysis of the Fighting*. London, Conway Maritime Press, 1986.

Chalmers, Rear-Admiral W.S. *The Life and Letters of David, Earl Beatty*. London, Hodder & Stoughton, 1951.

Chatfield, Lord. *The Navy and Defence*. London, William Heinemann, 1942.

Childers, Erskine. *The Riddle of the Sands*. London, Smith, Elder & Co., 1903.

Churchill, W.S. *My Early Life*. London, Macmillan & Co., 1930.

——. *The World Crisis* (six volumes). London, Thornton Butterworth Ltd, 1923–31.

——. *Marlborough: his Life and Times* (four volumes). London, George G. Harrap & Co. Ltd, 1933–8.

——. *The World Crisis*. Abridged and revised edition. London, Macmillan & Co., 1941.

Corbett, Julian S. *Naval Operations (History of the Great War)* Volumes I–III. London, Longmans, Green and Co., 1920–3.

Crankshaw, Edward. *The Fall of the House of Habsburg*. London, Longmans, Green and Co., Ltd, 1963

Davis, Norman. *Europe: a History*. Oxford, Oxford University Press, 1996.

'Etienne' (Stephen King-Hall). *A Naval Lieutenant 1914–1918*. London, Methuen & Co. Ltd, 1919.

Fawcett, H.W. and Hooper, G.W.W. (eds). *The Fighting at Jutland*. Third Edition 1921, printed by Maclure, Macdonald & Co., Glasgow.

Fisher, Admiral of the Fleet, Lord *Memories*. London, Hodder & Stoughton, 1919.

Fisher, H.A.L. *A History of Europe*. London, Edward Arnold & Co., 1936.

Gordon, Andrew. *The Rules of the Game*. London, John Murray, 1996.

Grey, Edward (Viscount Grey of Fallodon). *Twenty-Five Years* (two volumes). London, Hodder & Stoughton, 1925.

Gröner, Erich. *Die deutschen Kriegsschiffe 1815–1945*. Band 1. München, J.F. Lehmanns Verlag, 1966.

Groos, Otto. *Der Krieg zur See 1914–1918*. Nordsee (Band 5). Herausgegeben vom Marine-Archiv. Berlin, Mittler & Sohn, 1925.

Haldane, R.B. (Viscount Haldane). *Richard Burdon Haldane*. London, Hodder & Stoughton, 1929.

Harper, J.E.P. *The Record of the Battle of Jutland*. London, HMSO (Cmd 2870), 1927.

Harvey, Robert. *Liberators*. London, John Murray, 2000.

Hase, Georg von. (tr Arthur Chambers and F.A. Holt). *Kiel & Jutland*. London, Skeffington & Son Ltd.

Hickey, D., Smith, G. *Seven Days to Disaster. The Sinking of the* Lusitania. Collins, London, 1981.

Holmes, J. McA. 'Treatment and disposal of wounded in a light cruiser during the Battle of Jutland', *Journal of the Royal Naval Medical Service II*: 426–36.

Home, John and Kramer, Alan. *German Atrocities in 1914; A History of Denial*. Yale, 2001.

Hough, Richard. *The Hunting of Force Z*. London, 1963.

——. *Dreadnought*. London, Michael Joseph, 1965.
——. *First Sea Lord*. London, George Allen & Unwin Ltd, 1969.
Jane, Fred T. *All the World's Fighting Ships 1898*. London, Sampson Low, Marston & Co.
—— (ed.). *Fighting Ships 1914, 1915, 1916*. London, Sampson Low, Marston & Co.
Jellicoe, Admiral Viscount, of Scapa. *The Grand Fleet 1914–16*. London, Cassell & Co. Ltd, 1919.
Kemp, Peter (ed). *The Oxford Companion to Ships and the Sea*. London, Oxford University Press, 1976.
Kennedy, Paul M. *The Rise and Fall of British Naval Mastery*. London, Allen Lane, 1976.
Kipling, Rudyard. *Rudyard Kipling's Verse*. (Definitive Edition) London, Hodder & Stoughton, 1954.
——. 'Their Lawful Occasions'. In: *Traffics and Discoveries*. Macmillan & Co., 1903.
London, Charles. *Jutland 1916*. Osprey Publishing Ltd, 2000.
Lowis, Geoffrey. *Fabulous Admirals*. London, Putnam, 1957.
Ludwig, E. *Bismarck*. London, George Allen & Unwin Ltd, 1927.
——. *Kaiser Wilhelm II*. London, G.P. Putnam's Sons Ltd, 1926.
Macdonell, A.G. *England, their England*. London, Macmillan & Co. Ltd, 1946.
Macintyre, Captain Donald. *Jutland*. London, Evans Brothers Ltd, 1957.
MacLean, A. and Stephens, H. 'Surgical Experiences in the Battle of Jutland', *Journal of the Royal Naval Medical Service II*: 421–5. 1916.
Madge, Tim. *Long Voyage Home*. London, Simon & Schuster, 1993.
Mahan, A.H. *The Influence of Sea Power on History*. London, Sampson Low, Marston & Co., 1892.
Manchester, W. *The Last Lion*. London, Michael Joseph, 1983.
Marder, A.J. *From the Dreadnought to Scapa Flow*. Volumes I–V. London, Oxford University Press, 1961–70.
—— (ed.). *Fear God and Dread Nought. The correspondence of Admiral of the Fleet Lord Fisher* Volumes I, II & III. London, Jonathan Cape, 1952, 1956, 1959.
Massie, Robert K. *Dreadnought*. London, Jonathan Cape, 1992.
—— *Castles of Steel*. London, Jonathan Cape, 2003
Newbolt, Henry. *Naval Operations (History of the Great War)*. Volumes IV & V. London, Longmans Green and Co., 1928, 1931.
Niemann August. *Der Weltkrieg: Deutsche Träume*. Berlin–Leipzig, W. Vobach, 1904.
Owen, Wilfred. *The Collected Poems*. London, Chatto & Windus, 1963.
Pakenham, T. *The Scramble for Africa*. London, Weidenfeld & Nicolson, 1991.
Pakula, Hanna *An Uncommon Woman*. London, Weidenfeld & Nicolson, 1996.
Palmer, Alan. *The Kaiser*. London, Weidenfeld & Nicolson, 1978.
Penfold E.A. 'A Battleship in Action', *Journal of the Royal Naval Medical Service III*: 44–56, 1917.
Roskill, Stephen. *The War at Sea*. Volumes I–III. London, HMSO, 1954–61.
——. *H.M.S. Warspite*. London, Collins, 1957.
——. *Churchill & the Admirals*. London, Collins, 1977.
——. *Admiral of the Fleet Earl Beatty*. London, Collins, 1980.
Scheer, Reinhard. *Germany's High Sea Fleet in the World War*. London, Cassell & Co. Ltd, 1920.
Sitwell, Sir Osbert. *Laughter in the next room*. (Fourth volume of *Left Hand, Right Hand!*). London, Macmillan & Co. Ltd, 1949.
Sueter, Murray F. *Airmen or Noahs? Fair play for our Airmen*. London, Sir Isaac Pitman & Sons Ltd, 1928.
Tarrant, V.E. *Jutland. The German Perspective*. Brockhampton Press, 1999.
Tennyson-d'Eyncourt, Sir Eustace. *A Shipbuilder's Yarn*. London, Hutchinson & Co., 1948.
Van der Kiste, John. *Dearest Vicky, Darling Fritz*. Stroud, Sutton Publishing, 2001.
Van der Vat, Dan. *The Ship that Changed the World*. London, Hodder & Stoughton, 1985.
——. *The Grand Scuttle*. Leith, Edinburgh, Waterfront Communications Ltd, 1986.
Waldeyer-Hartz, Hugo von. *Admiral von Hipper* (tr F. Appleby Holt). London, Rich & Cowan, 1933.
Warner, Oliver. *The Sea and the Sword*. London, Jonathan Cape, 1965.
Wedgwood, C.V. *The Thirty Years' War*. London, Jonathan Cape, 1938.
Yates, Keith. *Flawed Victory*. London, Chatham Publishing, 2000.
Young, Filson. *With the Battlecruisers*. London, Cassell & Co. Ltd, 1921.
Battle of Jutland, Official Despatches. London, HMSO.
Der Krieg zur See 1914–1918. Nordsee (Band 5). Herausgegeben vom Marine-Archiv, Berlin, Mittler & Sohn.

INDEX

Note: British warships are filed under HMS and German warships are filed under SMS. Page numbers in **bold** type indicate illustrations or diagrams.